Khrushchev

Khrushchev

Mark Frankland

Introduction by Harry Schwartz

STEIN AND DAY/*Publishers*/New York

First published in the United States of America by
Stein and Day/*Publishers,* 1967

Library of Congress Catalog Card No. 67-16690

Printed in the United States of America

Stein and Day/*Publishers*/7 East 48 Street, New York, N.Y. 10017

Contents

Khrushchev

Introduction: Russia Since Khrushchev
by Harry Schwartz

This essay is being written at the end of a week in which three major events occurred: The United States and the Soviet Union reached an historic agreement on a major international issue. The Premier of the Soviet Union completed an extremely cordial visit to France. A member of the Kremlin ruling circle delivered a bitter public denunciation of Communist China and its leader, Mao Tse-tung. It might have been a typical week in the Khrushchev-ruled Russia of 1964, but actually it was a week in December 1966, 26 months after his downfall.

The more things change the more they remain the same! This must be the dominant conclusion of the analyst who surveys the first years of the post-Khrushchev leadership. It is the perception the Chinese express in their bitter accusations that the Brezhnev-Kosygin group represents "Khrushchevism without Khrushchev." Khrushchev, the man, lives in obscurity and disgrace, but the policies he followed flourish almost without exception as though he were still at the helm. In this book Mr. Frankland defines the essence of Khrushchev's line as the attempt to assure peace abroad and prosperity at home. It is the heart of his successors' line too.

But of course peace and prosperity do not mean quite the same thing to a Soviet leader as they do to a Western politician. Brezhnev and Kosygin today, like Khrushchev yesterday, are Marxist-Leninists who see history moving inevitably toward world Communism. As Mr. Frankland writes in this perceptive aand well informed volume: "The belief that the world was changing in the direction prophesied by Marx was absolutely central to Khrushchev's way of thinking. . . . For Western leaders to complain of this process was as pointless in his eyes as would, for a medieval Christian, have been the protests of unbelievers when they found themselves condemned to hell." But in Khrushchev's mind—as in Brezhnev's and Kosygin's—this "inevitability" of historical development relieved the Soviet Union from taking overly dangerous risks toward speeding up the process. Khrushchev miscalculated when he sent missiles to Cuba, as Mr. Frankland properly points out, but he retreated quickly. His basic strategic concept was that the Soviet Union could best help the cause of world Communism by becoming richer than the United States, an example that Marxism really worked.

It is because Brezhnev and Kosygin share this view that the war in Vietnam has not had more serious consequences to date. That could change, of course, but at this writing the United States has been bombing a Socialist country, North Vietnam, for over a year and a half. It has sent almost 400,000 American soldiers to prevent the victory of the "national liberation struggle" in South Vietnam. Yet to this time nothing fundamental has changed, just as nothing fundamental was altered by the 1960 U-2 crisis or the even more dangerous 1962 Cuban missile confrontation.

One wonders if all this was foreseen by the victorious band of conspirators who took over in mid-October 1964. It is true that their original public criticism of Khrushchev centered more on his methods than his aims. Even while they attacked "subjectivism," "hare-brained scheming," and one-man decision making, they still pledged their fidelity to peaceful coexistence and to the effort to raise Soviet living standards. But certainly they thought the break with China could be repaired once Khrushchev's clumsy hand was lifted from Soviet foreign policy. At least some among them thought that Khrushchev had pandered to consumers at the expense of the military's dreams of missiles and anti-missiles. And, we now know, there were neo-Stalinists in the new ruling group, men who felt it imperative that the old tyrant be largely rehabilitated in order to repair the grievous damage Khrushchev's de-Stalinization had caused at home and abroad.

The months since October 1964 have taught the new Soviet rulers that life is more complicated than they thought, that Khrushchev's failures were not caused only by his impulsiveness or his lack of good staff work. The new rulers have come up against hard realities that no amount of good bureaucratic preparation has been able to surmount. They have learned that in many situations the range of alternatives is very limited. Consider these lessons of the 1964–66 period:

1. China has turned out to be all the things Khrushchev said it was. It has proved impossible to buy Mao off by improving Soviet manners and ending public polemics, by offering to resume economic aid, or even by asking for a truce to permit unified help for the Vietnamese Communists. Perhaps worst of all, the men who removed Khrushchev now have to ask themselves whether they did not encourage Peking's obstinacy by purging their master. Khrushchev's ouster, after all, was Mao's greatest political victory since he conquered China.

2. Brezhnev and Kosygin have found the United States just as unpredictable and just as indispensable as Khrushchev did. The new rulers applauded Lyndon B. Johnson's victory over Barry Goldwater and then watched in horror as the President adopted much of the Goldwater prescription in Vietnam. In the face of American military superiority they have had to accept repeated American bombing of North Vietnam, confining themselves to sending Hanoi military and economic aid. Finally, as Khrushchev did in the summer of 1963, they have had to try to improve relations with the United States—the treaty on space law, the direct Moscow-New York air connection, etc.—in order to offset the growing Chinese threat. And all this while American planes rained bombs daily over Vietnam.

3. Brezhnev has found Soviet agriculture just as provoking as Khrushchev did. In March 1965 Brezhnev announced a vast new and very expensive agricultural program. The huge investments he promised were precisely along the lines Khrushchev had tried, and been unable, to provide. The price increases Brezhnev offered were greater than those Khrushchev had given. Result: The 1965 grain harvest was well below the 1964 Khrushchev harvest and once again Russia had to spend hundreds of millions of dollars for

grain from Canada and Australia. The weather had been more powerful than Brezhnev, just as so often it had been more powerful than Khrushchev. And if the 1966 harvest was a record, the thought could not be entirely avoided that Khrushchev had had his record years too—when the weather was favorable, of course.

4. Khrushchev could find no satisfactory formula to handle Soviet intellectuals and he blew hot and cold in the effort to find one. The same thing has been true of his successors. They began by bidding for the support of the intellectuals, implying that no more of the crudities of Khrushchev's late 1962-early 1963 policy would be tolerated. But then they put Andre Sinyavsky and Yuli Daniel on trial for, in effect, treason, and found themselves faced by an organized resistance among the intelligentsia. Even worse, the intellectuals dared to speak up and force withdrawal of the plans to rehabilitate Stalin at least partially at the 23rd Communist party Congress.

5. Any indictment of Khrushchev by his Kremlin colleagues must have included a paragraph about the slim results of his political and economic efforts in the underdeveloped world. Brezhnev and Kosygin have had no better luck. They have had to sit passively by and watch such leading "progressives" as Algeria's Ben Bella and Ghana's Nkrumah swept from power. In Indonesia they have had to swallow a worse pill. They have been forced to accept the bloody extermination of the Indonesian Communist party's cadres and the reduction of Sukarno to a near puppet. And, adding insult to injury, they have had to tell the new rightist Indonesian rulers that the Soviet Union would not press for immediate repayment of Indonesia's large debt, but would grant a moratorium similar to that of the highly pleased capitalist nations.

This list could be extended but the point is plain enough: The colorless bureaucratic "collective leadership" of today has no more been able to find magic answers to its problems than the verbose Khrushchev could. It has changed the style more than the substance of Soviet policy.

The emphasis above on the major stream of continuity in

the strategy and tactics of the Soviet regime since Khrushchev is not, of course, intended to deny that there has been change as well. Premier Kosygin's success at the Tashkent Conference in early 1966 in getting India and Pakistan to end their fighting was a major new step. The economic reforms introduced in September 1965—with their emphasis on sales and profits rather than production alone—began what may be an historic new stage of Soviet economics. And the decision to suspend Soviet manned space flights from Leonov's "walk in space" in early 1965 to the end of 1966 was a deliberate decision to give up a propaganda weapon Khrushchev had valued highly. Moreover Moscow these days rarely makes any boasts about soon defeating the United States economically or any claims that by 1980 the Soviet Union will be "on the threshold of Communism."

No doubt there will be further changes as time goes on and as new problems and new possibilities arise. But it still remains noteworthy that the core of Soviet policy at the end of 1966 is so similar to what it was the day before Khrushchev was pushed into oblivion.

Now, as then, the Kremlin seeks to avoid involvement in distant wars. In the effort to pursue Soviet national interest, the new leaders, like Khrushchev, have worked closely with the United States on a series of major problems. They have honored the limited nuclear test ban treaty, concluded a space law treaty, and now granted that the United States is serious about seeking to end the proliferation of nuclear weapons. They worked closely with Washington to keep U Thant at the United Nations. And all this has been done while Soviet military and economic aid streams to Vietnam and Peking cries unceasingly about Soviet-American "peace conspiracies."

Domestically the improvement of the Soviet standard of living is still the highest priority aim. Khrushchev's grandiose dreams of Communism tomorrow have been repudiated; instead, the Soviet people have been told the automobile age is finally about to begin for them. And major contracts have been made with Italy's Fiat and France's Renault to assure that this promise will be fulfilled.

The importance of all this is even clearer if we go further back than the Khrushchev period. What we have called here the Khrushchev line was really first the Malenkov line. It was Malenkov in August 1953 who first sounded the clarion call for a dramatic rise in Soviet living standards. It was Malenkov in early 1954 who first said publicly that a war involving modern weapons would be mutual suicide for all concerned. Khrushchev defeated Malenkov and then took over his line. Brezhnev and Kosygin did the same to Khrushchev. The names, the faces, the styles of public elocution change; the underlying reality remains unchanged.

The Soviet people had enough of war and its sacrifices in World War II to satisfy them for generations. Even Stalin did not dare to try to take them into the Korean War. Brezhnev and Kosygin have similarly preferred to stay on the sidelines in the Vietnam War. The new generation of Soviet people that has come to maturity since World War II takes past Soviet accomplishments for granted. Its members want the fruits of the affluent society. They know their contemporaries live better even in Eastern Europe, let alone in Western Europe and the United States. It is the pressure of this generation which makes the Malenkovs, Khrushchevs, Brezhnevs and Kosygins behave as they do. There is no sign that that pressure will lessen in the foreseeable future.

Preface

A biography of a living, if not actually still ruling, statesman must necessarily be a tentative affair. But when the biography is of a living Soviet figure, then it must be very tentative indeed. This is mainly because most of the material that biographies are usually based on is simply unavailable. In Khrushchev's case, a biographer has no access to private letters or diaries. If Khrushchev, who is now a sick man living in political isolation, were to write his autobiography, it is unlikely that it would ever be published in Moscow. Worse still, it is not yet possible to check on such simple matters as Khrushchev's promotion up the Party hierarchy as a young man by referring to Soviet records. The bulk of information used in this book has therefore been taken from published Soviet sources, primarily newspapers. Luckily Khrushchev was by nature garrulous, and after achieving power, often spoke about his past. Although hardly disinterested, these asides are a very useful additional source of information. Since this is a book for non-specialists, there are no references to sources for this or that fact. But I would like to assure readers that there are no statements of fact about Khrushchev's life that available material suggests at least to be very likely true.

This is therefore an essay in biography, rather than a full-scale biography. But I hope that, by showing Khrushchev's life as a whole, it will help people to understand better what one important Soviet politician was like, and thereby make the whole Soviet system itself more approachable than it often seems.

I should like to thank David Shapiro of Essex University, who read the book in manuscript and made many helpful comments, and also the Editor of the *Observer*, who made it possible for me to find time to produce the book.

Prologue

On Sunday 26 February 1956, sensational rumours about what had happened at the end of the 20th Party Congress began circulating in Moscow. It had been announced on the Friday morning that the final session of the Congress that afternoon would be closed to all but Soviet communists. The closed session turned out to be a long one, and the Congress did not finish its work until 2 p.m. on the Saturday. It was clear to foreign communists who met their Soviet comrades afterwards that something had happened to make them, as an Italian communist journalist put it, 'terribly upset'. And well they might have been. For the delegates to the Party Congress had been present at no less than the posthumous murder of the reputation of Joseph Stalin. The murder weapon itself was simple – facts: facts already known or guessed in the Western world, but for years vigorously denied in the Soviet Union as slander. The murderer was in the circumstances far more unusual – an apparently typical proletarian communist who had himself risen to power under Stalin's patronage and been implicated in some of Stalin's crimes. Nikita Khrushchev, now first secretary of the Soviet Communist Party, had in his day praised Stalin as fervently as anyone else. His political life, as much as the life of any Soviet communist who had survived into the 1950s, seemed to be founded on a faith in Stalin as the infallible leader who had translated into cement and steel the magnificent plans of Soviet Russia's founder, Vladimir Lenin. Khrushchev, like the average Soviet man, had acknowledged Stalin as the military genius of the great war against Hitler – a feat which had given Stalin a genuine popularity for the first time among the many people who still thought of themselves as Russians rather than communists. In short, Stalin was connected with everything that Khrushchev, as a communist and a Russian, had reason to be proud of. Or so it seemed until the afternoon of 24 February 1956.

The informed observer would, however, already have noticed a very remarkable difference in style between Khrushchev and

Stalin. It was not just that Khrushchev and his colleagues had by 1956 abandoned many of the worst practices of Stalinism, important though that was. Khrushchev, for all his long history as a Stalinist, was obviously a completely different man from his old master. Stalin had been secretive, calculating, distant. He had ruled the country with terrible genius from the fastness of the Kremlin or the privacy of his well-guarded dacha. Khrushchev liked talking to people, was impulsive. He could be a bully but he lacked Stalin's cold cruelty. He liked to see things for himself and was already by 1956 notorious for his junkets through the country, where no detail was too small for his attention. Stalin had been an intellectual. Khrushchev was above all a practical man, who understood results better than ideas. Stalin had achieved the dignity appropriate to a demi-god by cleverly concealing his small stature. Khrushchev, with a thick, short body and the nose of a Russian peasant boy, radiated energy and could at times, in spite of his physique, achieve an almost leonine dignity, but he constantly threw it away by a gesture or movement that belonged more to the life and soul of a peasant wedding party than to a grave leader of the Soviet Union.

But nothing had prepared even the shrewdest observer for the speech which Khrushchev made that Friday afternoon. In three hours Khrushchev turned Stalin from the benevolent leader of genius, in whom every Soviet child was brought up to believe, into a sinister despot, proper heir to the Tsars who had terrified and tormented Russia in her dark past. Khrushchev's revelations fell into three main categories. The first described Stalin as the murderer of innocent communists. Lenin, Khrushchev reminded the Congress, had before his death warned against Stalin's excessive rudeness and capriciousness, and even suggested that Stalin should yield his post as General Secretary of the Party to a more tolerant, more loyal and compassionate person. Lenin's advice had been ignored with terrible consequences. Starting in December 1934 with the mysterious murder of Sergei Kirov, one of the most popular Soviet leaders of the day, Stalin, Khrushchev said, had begun to pursue a policy of mass repression against loyal Party members. When Khrushchev recited how this had reached a peak with the arrest and execution of 98 of the 139-strong Central Committee elected at the 17th Party Congress in 1934, his audience murmured in indignation. Out of the 1,966 delegates attending that Congress, well over half had been arrested 'on charges of anti-revolutionary crimes'. There had been no basis whatsoever, Khrushchev said, for Stalin's mass terror, and Stalin had succeeded only by falsification and torture on a gigantic scale. He described in detail the elaborate process by which innocent communists had been forced to confess to ludicrous crimes, thought up by the interrogators of the secret police. And Stalin had personally supervised all this, working through his police chiefs. He had been ready to destroy anyone who to his sick mind suddenly seemed suspicious. No one had really known what he had been up to, and no one had been able to stop him. Even after the war Stalin had continued to kill all whom he distrusted. The notorious Leningrad Affair of 1948, in which one of the most brilliant Soviet economic administrators, Voznesensky, disappeared, had been Stalin's work. And only his death had prevented him from developing the so-called Doctors' Plot into another wave of terror. Stalin had personally supervised this last case, ordering the investigators to 'beat, beat and once again beat', and threatening the Minister of State Security that he would be 'shortened by a head' if he did not extract the necessary confessions. Khrushchev finally described how Stalin, when he informed the other Soviet leaders of the plot, had told them: 'You are blind like young kittens; what will happen without me? The country will perish because you do not know how to recognize enemies.'

Khrushchev's attack on Stalin's reputation as a war leader was possibly even more appalling to his audience. Khrushchev said that Stalin had wilfully ignored all the warnings he had received of Hitler's plan to attack the Soviet Union, and that when the attack did come he had panicked and been unable to take any decisions until his colleagues had successfully urged action on him. Stalin had already damaged the Soviet Army by his unjustified annihilation of many of its best commanders, and as soon as the war began to go better for the Soviet Union, had appeared jealous of any fame won by their successors. The films and books that Stalin had produced to glorify himself as a commander of genius, Khrushchev said, 'make us feel sick'.

Khrushchev spent the last part of his speech elaborating on the ways in which Stalin stage-managed his own glorification. There was his 'Short Biography' – 'an expression of the most dissolute flattery, an example of making a man into a godhead, of transforming him into an infallible sage'. But Stalin had not been content to let others write these works of praise for him: whenever he judged it necessary, he had added his own embellishments, here to point up his skill as a military strategist, there to underline his claim to be the true heir of Lenin.

Khrushchev tried to turn Stalin from a demi-god into a devil and to transfer onto him all the guilt about the Soviet past which he and his listeners dared not acknowledge in themselves. In this way the Soviet Union might be able to make a fresh start, free of the intolerable memories of the last twenty years. Khrushchev knew quite well that anything more than this ritual denunciation would threaten the whole Soviet political system, and in particular the authority of the Communist Party that lay at its core. Yet he could not be sure that he would be able to contain the discussion of the past within these narrow limits, and he knew that if it did break out of them, he would very likely be the first to suffer. The speech therefore told a great deal about the man who was ready to make it under such circumstances. He was clearly gifted with remarkable daring and optimism. He was also ready to be dishonest on a huge scale to protect the system he believed in, apparently without realizing that this very dishonesty might in turn damage it. In this, and in his belief that he could safely limit the repercussions of his speech both in the Soviet Union and among communists throughout the world, he demonstrated an extraordinary lack of imagination. Here was a man who apparently did not bother to think out the consequences of what he was doing if the immediate gain seemed great enough, who indulged in pragmatism to an immense degree. These qualities were not easily recognized by the outside world at the time. Little was known about Khrushchev's life before the death of Stalin, and it was in just those years before 1953 that he formed the prejudices, convictions and habits which he later brought to the leadership of the post-Stalinist Soviet Union. While Khrushchev in his speech to the 20th Party Congress seemed to be breaking with his country's past, his own political attitudes were firmly rooted there. In the end he was as much a prisoner of that past as those Soviet communists who refused to give up their belief in Stalin even after the revelations of that day in February.

Chapter 1
Kalinovka and the Donbas

Nikita Sergeyevich Khrushchev was born on 17 April 1894 in Kalinovka, a small village in the province of Kursk that lies just on the Russian side of the border with the Ukraine. Sergei Nikanorovich, his father, was a poor peasant who each winter left his family to earn money in the coalfields of the Donets Basin three hundred miles to the south-west.* There were many peasants like Sergei Khrushchev in Kursk province. Although it was in the Black Earth zone, long famous for its rich soil, Kursk and other Black Earth provinces were cursed by terrible rural overpopulation, and each year thousands of families abandoned their villages to settle in the new industrial towns or travel thousands of miles to the vast Siberian plains. Those who stayed behind endured a life of hardship and squalor that bore no relation to the sentimental image of Russian peasant life. Diseases like diphtheria, typhus and syphilis were rife. No one expected the Russian peasant to eat much meat, but in the Black Earth villages he had little even of cabbage and cucumber which, pickled or fresh, traditionally supplied the vitamins in a peasant's diet. It was common for the grain supply of poor families to be exhausted by Christmas. No wonder that a Russian doctor who studied the life of two villages in Voronezh province, which lies next to Kursk, discovered that even the usually ubiquitous Russian bug shunned most of the peasant huts because they were too poor a source of food. This poverty was to dominate

* There is a story, apparently deriving from a Russian émigré, that Khrushchev's father was the descendant of a Tsarist government official who had an estate near Kalinovka which he lost, together with his rank, because of his support for reformist political views. This story may be connected with Sergei Nikolayevich Khrushchev, an official in the Ministry of Internal Affairs at the end of the nineteenth century. There is, however, no proper evidence to contradict the Soviet version of Khrushchev's origins. Khrushchev himself often referred, apparently spontaneously, to his peasant background. In America in 1959 he said that his grandfather had been 'an illiterate peasant serf. He was the landlord's property and could be sold or even, as was often the case, traded for a dog.'

Khrushchev's memories of peasant life: in later years he used the *lapti*, rough boots made of bast that the Kalinovka peasants wore because they could not afford leather ones, as the most vibrant symbol he could command of all that was bad and backward in old Russia.

Like all the village boys Khrushchev began work early, guarding the village's animals and acting as a watchman. Later he worked as a herdsboy for the local big landowner, a woman called Shaufusova, who farmed 5,000 hectares in a style far in advance of the primitive methods of the Kalinovka peasants. At some time between the age of seven and twelve he went to the village school. The schoolmistress, Lidiya Mikhailovna Shevchenko, a young woman who had been shattered by Kalinovka's poverty when she first arrived, taught the children scripture, elementary arithmetic and reading and writing. Khrushchev was at the school for perhaps only two years; but in the world of general illiteracy that he inhabited, even this rough education was an important advantage.*

The year 1905, in which Khrushchev was eleven, saw the first substantial revolt of the Russian urban intelligentsia and proletariat against Tsarist autocracy. It was preceded, and then accompanied, by peasant violence which swept the country like the wind across the steppes. Behind the violence lay the same land-hunger and poverty that afflicted Kalinovka, and not surprisingly it was in the area round Khrushchev's village, in Kursk province, that the violence of 1905 began. The peasants burnt the farm buildings and woods of the landowners and seized their grain and cattle. As the year went by and the violence spread, the landlords themselves were attacked. At the sight of the Russian people – for the peasants, to all intents and purposes, were the Russian people in those days – in collective and bloody revolt, the autocracy lost its nerve and combined its crushing of the revolution with concessions. To cajole the peasants, the re-

* It has often been said that Khrushchev was illiterate until after the Revolution, but again there is no evidence of this. His Kalinovka teacher certainly existed. She was at a Kremlin New Year's Eve Party in 1960 and was publicly toasted by her old pupil. Khrushchev remembered his lessons in the Bible well enough to use biblical quotations in his later political speeches and on one occasion quoted a poem he had learnt at school to point an agricultural moral.

demption payments on land acquired by them at their liberation from serfdom in 1861 were abolished. These payments had certainly been a heavy burden, but their removal was not enough to help poor peasants like Sergei Khrushchev. In spite of his annual journey to the Donbas coal mines, he was never able to save up enough money to buy a horse, and without a horse to work his land no peasant could hope to become prosperous. In 1908 he took what must have seemed the only course open to him and moved his wife and son and daughter to the Donbas. They settled at the Uspenovsky mine, a couple of miles south of the industrial centre of Yuzovka, where Sergei had done his seasonal work. The family had two rooms in a one-storey house; although in winter one of the rooms had to be given over to seasonal workmen.

In 1908 the Donbas was the most important industrial region in the Russian empire. It mined coal, which fed the furnaces of its iron and steel mills, which in turn fed the factories producing heavy engineering equipment. Financially the Donbas was dominated by West European capital. The young Khrushchev only had to go to Yuzovka to see this expressed in the simplest terms. The town had been built and was still owned by the British New Russian Metallurgical Company. Its name commemorated the Welshman, John Hughes, who headed the company when the town was founded in 1869, and its centre, where the well-to-do lived, was appropriately called the 'English Colony'. And when in 1909, aged fifteen, Khrushchev became an apprentice fitter, after a year as a herdsboy on a local estate, it was at the German-owned Bosse engineering works.

The living and working conditions in the Donbas were as bad as the most lurid political agitator could have depicted them, and Khrushchev's experience gave him an emotional charge that seems genuinely to have lasted all his life. There is no doubt that he thought he had seen the true face of capitalism – and foreign capitalism, at that – in the Donbas. In Yuzovka itself the workers lived in shanty settlements round the town centre. The mining villages, like Uspenovsky, were little more than a collection of huts set on drab steppe-land. Wages were pitiful and as often as not paid irregularly. Many of the miners and workers were in debt to the company store which, like company stores the world over, was cursed for the bad quality of its goods. Trade unions were banned, and the local police readily provided force to back up the employers. A propaganda sheet put out by the Yuzovka Bolsheviks in 1913 described the miners' lot in somewhat biblical but not far-fetched language:

> When we descend into the dark underground of the shafts to earn for ourselves and our families pitiful farthings, under the eternal fear of death [the accident rate was far higher than that of British mines at this period], at the same time the debauch of feasting capitalist-robbers is heard ... drinking our blood, not giving thought how to improve our penal life of woe, nor how to secure safety of work in that hell where, because of their greed, hundreds of workers perish....

At the same time the primitive level of life hampered the work of the political parties. A Social-Democrat* cell had been set up in Yuzovka in 1903, but its organization was practically non-existent by 1908. Apart from the repressions that followed the 1905 revolution, all the parties suffered from the lack of a local intelligentsia. A Donbas Social-Democrat paper also complained about the difficulty of working with miners of low intelligence and no education, 'two-thirds of whose time is spent underground, and the rest, in most cases, devoted to Bacchus'. This traditional outlet for Russian troubles was well catered for in Yuzovka, which had over two dozen state liquor shops and pubs for a population of 50,000. The fact, too, that so many of the workers and miners were still part-time peasants, returning each harvest-time to their villages, made recruitment by the political parties all the more difficult. By contrast the young Khrushchev, as an apprentice fitter, was well on the way to entering the labour aristocracy as a skilled worker. The Bosse factory, one of the main suppliers of mining equipment in the Donbas, was a good training ground and a far more desirable place to work than the mine that employed Khrushchev's father. According to a Soviet biographer, Khrushchev had a talent for the job (which is perfectly plausible), and even managed after a while to make his own motor cycle out of old parts.

His work for Bosse was suddenly ended by an event which shook the whole of Russia. In April 1912 a strike at a British-

* The official name of the Bolshevik Party until 1919 was the Russian Social Democratic Labour Party, or Social Democrat for short.

owned goldfield on the Lena River in Siberia was terminated by military action which killed two hundred workers, and strikes broke out all over Russia in response. Although Khrushchev was now eighteen, his role in the strike at the Bosse works was a humble one. He acted as no more than a messenger for the strike committee. But even this was enough to bring him to the notice of the local police, and together with others involved in the strike he was dismissed from the factory. Khrushchev's training apparently stood him in good stead because he found work without too much difficulty as a mechanic at Mine 31 in Rutchenkovo. Once again Khrushchev was working for foreign capital, because the Rutchenkovo mines then belonged to a French company.* His work included supervision of the mine's lifting gear and gave him the privilege of his own room provided by the mine, although for a time he went on living with his parents at Uspenovsky.

Then, in the summer of 1914, came the war. So fateful in its consequences for Russia, it brought little immediate change in Khrushchev's life. He avoided conscription into the army, presumably because he was a skilled worker, and at the end of the year moved to the Rutchenkovo mechanical workshops which served ten of the surrounding mines. It was also around this time that Khrushchev married: nothing is known about his wife except that she gave him a son in 1916 and a daughter two years later. Khrushchev's political activities, as far as they are known, did not go beyond the decent minimum, considering his later career. He helped organize strikes by the Rutchenkovo miners in 1915 and 1916, but this work never seems to have gone beyond his own immediate working world. Indeed the problem of just what his political feelings were at this time becomes acute as one looks at his actions in 1917, the year of Revolution.

On 15 March 1917 Tsar Nicholas II abdicated after spontan-

* Khrushchev said later that he also worked at a Belgian-owned chemical plant. This is repeated in some of the official biographies but not in the most detailed Soviet account of his Donbas days, *The Story of an Honorary Miner*. In later years Khrushchev liked to stress episodes in his life to suit the audience of the moment. He told businessmen at the British Trade Fair in Moscow in 1961 that he played left-half in a football team 'when I worked for one of your great engineering firms, Hughes.' In fact there is no record of him ever working for a British firm although he may well have played soccer.

eous and undirected revolution had erupted in St Petersburg. It had taken the war, so heavy in loss of life and prestige, to destroy an autocracy whose obstinacy had been matched only by its short-sightedness. The news of the revolution came to Rutchenkovo in the shape of a telegram from the capital to the local railwaymen. Khrushchev read the message in the Rutchenkovo workshops. In an article written for a local paper five years later he described how the 'Tsar of the mine' – the local police chief – and his assistant were still walking round in swords and spurs, but that now 'no one feared them, rather it was they who were frightened and did not know what to do.' But it seems that Khrushchev, although he was now twenty-three, was not absolutely clear what he should do either. The big unanswered question is why he did not become a Bolshevik, if not before 1917, then at least in the Revolution year itself. In the first place he was certainly old enough. The Jewish leather-worker Lazar Kaganovich, who headed the Yuzovka Bolsheviks at the time of the March Revolution and who was to become in turn Khrushchev's patron, colleague and enemy, was only one year older, but he had been a Bolshevik since 1911. Of Khrushchev's nine colleagues in the Party Presidium after Stalin's death only three joined the Party after him, and then with good reason because they were considerably younger.* Nor can it be said that he had had no chance to join the Party. Although there was no Bolshevik organization in Rutchenkovo in March 1917 or before, the settlement was only a walking distance from Yuzovka, where there was an organization, and on his own admission Khrushchev often went to Yuzovka before 1917 to collect newspapers and illegal political literature. The Yuzovka Bolshevik organization was certainly small at the start of 1917, but by October of that year it had some two thousand members, an increase which reflected the general growth of Bolshevik strength throughout the Donbas. There seems to be no reason, therefore, why Khrushchev should not have joined the Party at least in 1917 had he wanted to do so.

* The nine, in English alphabetical order, and with birth and Party joining dates, are: Beria, 1899, 1917; Bulganin, 1895, 1917; Kaganovich, 1893, 1911; Malenkov, 1902, 1920; Mikoyan, 1895, 1915; Molotov, 1890, 1906; Pervukhin, 1904, 1919; Saburov, 1900, 1920; Voroshilov, 1881, 1903.

Against this it should be remembered that the situation in the Donbas in 1917, as throughout the whole of Russia, was one of extreme confusion. The defence of the Revolution was associated exclusively with the Bolsheviks as yet only in the mind of the Bolshevik master strategist, Lenin. In the Donbas the Bolsheviks were still overshadowed by two other revolutionary parties, the Socialist Revolutionaries (usually called the S.R.s for short) and the Mensheviks. The S.R.s, exponents of terrorism, demanded the socialization of land – a programme naturally popular with the peasants and the many Donbas miners and workers of peasant origin. The Mensheviks were the product of an informal split in the Social-Democratic party in 1903 which had also produced the Bolsheviks. They did not become a properly organized party until 1917, but even before then they had stood for a more moderate sort of Marxism than the Bolsheviks. It was the S.R.s and the Mensheviks who controlled the local soviets (councils) set up in the Donbas in March 1917 on the model of St Petersburg, including those of both Yuzovka and Rutchenkovo.

The purges of the 1930s were later to draw in blood a line to divide the Bolsheviks as the one true revolutionary party from all the unfortunate rest, and it has since been impossible to suggest that any Soviet leader with a pre-revolutionary history ever deviated from Bolshevism since the first moment of his political consciousness. But, perhaps, for Khrushchev the differences between the parties were not so very important as long as they were all busy trying to defend the Revolution. For one thing, Khrushchev did not come to Bolshevism by the intellectual path followed by so many of its old adherents. No Soviet source gives any evidence that Khrushchev was seriously acquainted with the theory of Bolshevism in 1917. The best that the most detailed biography of his Donbas days can do is to suggest that he first heard Marx's *Communist Manifesto* read about 1912 in the hut of a miner friend, Pantelei Makhinya. Makhinya, described later by Khrushchev as 'a very close friend of my youth', was self-educated and read a good deal – so as to 'live better and to understand his role in society', according to Khrushchev – and was also an amateur poet, but no claim is made for his ever having been a Bolshevik either. He would seem rather to have been the sort of worker of intelligence who felt stifled under Tsarism and passionately welcomed the Revolution, though from no one definite political angle.* And this may well have been true for Khrushchev, too.

With no chance of an intellectual training (and, if his later career is any guide, with no inclination for the intellectual approach anyway) Khrushchev must be supposed to have become a revolutionary from the compelling experiences of his own life. In Kalinovka he had felt the hopelessness of the land-hungry peasant, and in the Donbas the growing anger of a proletariat condemned to all the squalor of an industrial revolution in a society that politically had remained to all intents and purposes feudal. And once the Revolution had started, Khrushchev was himself actively involved – albeit at a humble level – in practical measures for its defence. He was elected a member of the Rutchenkovo soviet, one of whose first acts was to disband the local police.† The Donbas soviets became the focal point for the undeclared war that now started between the mine-owners and the miners. The former closed many pits, although not in Rutchenkovo, and real wages fell disastrously. In return, the soviets demanded an eight-hour day and other basic improvements. As the weeks went by the need for actual physical defence of the Revolution became more and more pressing. In St Petersburg, the Provisional Government set up after the Tsar's abdication hovered uneasily between bourgeois liberalism and moderate

* Khruschev read a poem by Makhinya to a Soviet Writers' Congress in 1959. He prefaced it by saying: 'In my friend's poem are expressed the thoughts of an intelligent, thinking worker of that time [i.e. before the Revolution] about the purpose of man's life.' The poem began

I love with a truthful book
To light the fires of emotions,
In order in our bustling life
To burn and burn and never burn out.

† The mystery of Khrushchev's political loyalties at this time is increased by a recent history of the Ukrainian Communist Party (*Narisi Istorii Komunistichny Partii Ukraini*, Kiev, 1961) which describes Khrushchev as chairman of the Rutchenkovo soviet. If this is true, it suggests that Khrushchev was acceptable to the S.R.s and Mensheviks who dominated the soviet, and so could scarcely have been a dogmatic supporter of the Bolshevik line. *The Story of an Honorary Miner* implies that Khrushchev only chaired occasional sessions of the soviet, which is quite another matter.

socialism, and tried to continue the hugely unpopular war with Germany. A Ukrainian nationalist government, set up in Kiev after the Tsar's fall, might have threatened the miners had its authority stretched to the Donbas. Then in August counter-revolution appeared in the forbidding shape of General Kornilov, the Russian Commander-in-Chief, who attempted to march on the capital and end the rule of the soviets.

The main beneficiaries of Kornilov's defeat were the Bolsheviks, who only a little earlier had been suspected of planning their own coup. The so-called Military-Revolutionary Committees (Revkoms) that now sprang up all over the country to thwart another counter-revolution were often controlled by them. Khrushchev was a member of the Rutchenkovo Revkom, which like many others at once set about organizing a workers' militia, known as the Red Guards. If anything convinced Khrushchev that the Bolsheviks were right it must surely have been their practical revolutionary skill as it was displayed in these months. In Lenin the Bolsheviks had a genius whose grasp of the revolutionary process was many times surer than that of any of his opponents and almost all his colleagues. The ideological controversies that lay at the bottom of left-wing opposition to Lenin and alienated many from him meant nothing to Khrushchev. Indeed, if he had ever heard of them, they almost certainly did not interest him. We can only infer from what we know of the later Khrushchev that in 1917, as afterwards, he was mainly moved by practical considerations. Fully supporting the idea of Revolution (but with little definite idea about what its content should be), he was the sort of man who would support the political party which seemed best able to establish the Revolution and put it into practice, and the Bolsheviks now answered that description best.

It is certainly hard to imagine that Khrushchev regretted Lenin's overthrow of the Provisional Government on 7 November. Apart from its unpopular policies on the key issues of the war and land, the Provisional Government had since September come close to taking the side of the Donbas mine-owners in their conflict with the miners. It had dispatched a commissar to the Donbas, supported by Cossack troops and empowered to use force. True, the Donbas soviets, controlled by the Mensheviks and S.R.s, refused to recognize Lenin's coup, but the tide was now running against them. The country was dividing up for civil war, and in the Donbas the political quarrels of the capital must soon have become lost in the rush to look to the revolutionary defences. Rutchenkovo increased its Red Guard to four hundred men in November and in early December it came together with the other militias under the control of a coordinating central staff of Donbas Red Guards. The same month, Khrushchev and the Rutchenkovo Red Guard saw their first action when the Cossack General Kaledin led his cavalry in a series of punitive raids against the mining towns. The Cossacks, who had an ugly reputation as the Tsar's strong-arm men, naturally caused chaos among the more or less untrained miners. Khrushchev and the Rutchenkovo Red Guard were helping defend Yuzovka against a Cossack attack, when support arrived in the shape of slightly more experienced forces from St Petersburg and Moscow, under the hero of the storming of the Winter Palace, Antonov-Ovseyenko.

One can imagine a better introduction to war. Refusal to obey orders and flight in the face of fire were common on both sides. The fighting, too, was ruthless even at this early stage of the war, with the taking, as opposed to the killing, of prisoners already an exception. But thanks to the reinforcements the Bolshevik forces were now the stronger, and they were able to push the Whites out of the Donbas. Khrushchev, as a member of the Rutchenkovo Red Guard which was now incorporated in the 1st Donbas Red Guard Regiment, apparently stayed with Antonov's forces until Kaledin was defeated and then in the spring of 1918 returned to Rutchenkovo. He seems to have arrived there only shortly before the German army, which had entered the Ukraine officially as the ally of the anti-Bolshevik Ukrainian nationalist government, but in fact as its master. The Germans were of course no friends of the Bolsheviks and their supporters, and the position of men like Khrushchev in territory occupied by them was perilous. One Soviet source has it that Khrushchev was denounced to the Germans as a Red and went into hiding, finally to escape into the open steppe through a mine shaft.

Chapter 2
Civil War and After

With the whole of the Ukraine in hostile hands, Khrushchev's first thought must surely have been to make for Kalinovka. It was natural for a Russian to return to his native village in time of trouble, but he may have had another reason as well. Many miners and their families had left the Donbas at the time of the first Kaledin raids and made for their villages in Russia proper, and it is quite possible that Khrushchev's father and mother did the same, taking with them his wife and young son. How Khrushchev got to Kalinovka, and how long it took him, we do not know, but given the confusion of the times the three-hundred-mile journey was probably not too dangerous. Once in Kalinovka he appears to have taken part in the division of the local landowners' estates among the peasants. The anxiety to claim land which they believed to be theirs by right helped draw Donbas miners, like Khrushchev's father, back to their villages in the first place, and it may well have affected Khrushchev too. The future was, after all, obscure, and the possession of land, to those born peasants, must have seemed the only possible security.

Very little else is known about Khrushchev's stay at Kalinovka except that he worked for a time in the local Revkom. Of the most important step he took at this time – joining the Bolshevik Party – all that can be said is that it almost certainly took place between April and the autumn of 1918.* Perhaps he would have joined a little earlier had he not been fighting or travelling since the previous December, but by the time he reached Kalinovka the Bolshevik claim to complete support must have been overwhelming in the eyes of a working man who wanted to help the Revolution. True, since November 1917 Lenin's daring and ruthless policies had alienated many who might otherwise have supported him. Bolshevism's dictatorial methods made enemies

* An article in the Polish paper *Polityka*, 11 July 1959, implied that Khrushchev joined the Bolshevik Party after his twenty-fourth birthday in April 1918. He was presumably already a Party member when he joined the 9th Army as a commissar in the autumn.

of the other left-wing parties. The peace of Brest-Litovsk in March 1918, which signed away the Ukraine and much else to Germany, horrified old-school patriots. And the well-to-do peasants were driven into opposition by the Bolshevik encouragement of class war in the village as part of the emergency plan to extract food for the towns. But what did this matter to a young man like Khrushchev? He was not a politician or a soldier. On the contrary, he belonged by birth to that vast army of Russian have-nots who now had their first chance to escape the exploitation of centuries.

The whole Civil War was in essence a vast and bloody settling of accounts between classes that had lost contact with each other. It was waged with cruelty by both sides and, most important of all, it gave a fierce justification to the ruthless methods of rule, including the terrorization of dissident political parties, that the Bolsheviks employed. By the summer of 1918 White forces were rallying ominously in Siberia and in South Russia. At the same time the Western allies, angered by Bolshevik Russia's withdrawal from the war and her repudiation of Tsarist debts, were preparing to intervene. They suspected the Bolsheviks at first as German stooges, but soon came to see them simply as a revolutionary threat to the bourgeois world. Trotsky's Red Army, the brilliant creation of an intellectual with no military experience, was still only embryonic. It was a situation which called for bold decisions and harsh commands. Who better than Lenin to take and give them, and who better to carry them out at the lowest level than a man like Khrushchev? For it was at the lowest level of the Party that Khrushchev went back to the Civil War in the autumn of 1918. He was sent to work in the political department of the 9th Army, which was fighting against the anti-Bolshevik general Denikin in the north of the Donbas. Denikin's army, which presented by far the greatest military danger to the Bolsheviks, was then threatening Tsaritsyn, the Volga city which blocked the south-eastern route to Moscow. A mighty row was going on in Tsaritsyn between its military leaders – Voroshilov, a one-time Donbas worker, and Budyonny, an ex-NCO of the Tsarist cavalry, on the one hand, and Trotsky on the other. The point at issue – Trotsky's policy of appointing ex-Tsarist officers to the Red Army – was not so important as the participation of

Stalin, who had arrived in Tsaritsyn in the summer and supported Voroshilov and Budyonny. To a Bolshevik of any standing this quarrel between the two important Party leaders must have seemed ominous, for it was one of the first public signs of what Isaac Deutscher has called 'the greatest and most violent feud in Russian history'. Its importance in Khrushchev's story is paradoxically that he almost certainly knew nothing of it. Like many others who became loyal executants of Stalin's policies, he was for long to remain unaware of their roots in Stalin's dark nature.

While Stalin was manoeuvring against Trotsky, Khrushchev was engaged in the humble but important work of forming Party cells in the front line units of the 9th Army. He was, in other words, the most junior sort of military commissar, the Party's representative at the army's grass roots. But even at Khrushchev's lowly level the commissars were something of a secret weapon, because they were able to give the illiterate Red soldiers a sense of purpose that was vital in such a bewildering and savage war. The White Armies had nothing to match them, and indeed as the war went on and the policy of the Whites veered more to the right, it would have been impossible to reach the White troops in this way. Trotsky's rather grand statement that in the commissars 'we obtained a new communist order of samurai who – without caste privileges – are able to die and to teach others to die for the cause of the working class' is a necessary reminder of the heroic side of the Civil War (for heroic it was, although certainly not romantic). But much of Khrushchev's work must have been basic to the point of crudeness. For example, one of the commissar's most important jobs was simply to keep the troops under his care fighting, because desertion was as chronic in the Red Army as in the White (two and a half million Red Army soldiers had deserted by the end of 1920, although many returned to the ranks later).

The Western Allies promoted their plan to intervene in the Civil War by dividing Russia into areas of influence. General Denikin fell to the lot of the French and British (Britain awarded him the Order of the Bath); but although the supplies of equipment, and notably tanks, certainly helped, the Allied contribution was never great. In fact intervention was half-hearted from the start but to Khrushchev and the Red soldiers who had to face Denikin's army in the grim days of 1918 and 1919, the contribution of the Allies did not look so inconsiderable. It was intervention which helped create the belief that Soviet Russia was the one pure citadel in a wicked and aggressive world that was constantly intent on its destruction. This belief – which was not unrelated even to Tsarist Russia's attitude to the West – was elevated into dogma by Stalin and was still to colour the attitude of Khrushchev to the outside world after Stalin's death.

Denikin's threat was at its greatest in 1919, the year that Red Russia was also invaded from Siberia by an army under the White Admiral Kolchak, and an army under General Yudenich in the west reached the suburbs of Petrograd. In retrospect, the Reds' position was not as bad as it then appeared, although it must have seemed desperate to Khrushchev and the men of the Red armies at the southern front who were pushed back by October to Oryol, only 250 miles from Moscow. But the tide turned at Oryol. Numerically superior Red armies counter-attacked, and soon Khrushchev was involved in one of the most famous episodes of the war, Budyonny's raid of December 1919 into the Donbas. The Bolsheviks had originally opposed the idea of cavalry, partly because the Cossacks who had formed the core of the Tsarist cavalry were usually hostile to Bolshevism. But eventually Trotsky, as Commissar for War, gave the order 'Proletarians to horse', and Budyonny's 1st Cavalry Army was born. The originality of the Donbas raid lay in its rapid movement of infantry who, Khrushchev's unit among them, were pulled on sledges behind the cavalry.

By the spring of 1920 Denikin's army had been forced back down the Black Sea coast to Novorossisk, where part of it managed to escape with the help of the French and British navies. Units of the 9th Army, including Khrushchev's, chased another part of the White forces as far down the coast as the Georgian seaport of Sochi, and with their surrender there Khrushchev's first military career came to an end. It had been in no way particularly remarkable, although one Soviet source claims that by the war's end Khrushchev was working in the political department of the 9th Army, which implies promotion. Men like Khrushchev were the NCOs of the Bolshevik armies – a group essential to victory, but also destined to anonymity in the history books. Again, Khrushchev's part in the war, compared with that of the men who later were his colleagues at the top of the Soviet hierarchy, was worthy but quite undistinguished. He still lived in a totally different world from the Bolshevik leaders. His understanding of the Revolution and its direction was still very naïve. Many years later, on his epic visit to the United States in 1959, he gave a unique portrait of himself that tells more about what he was like at this time than all the other known facts about his Civil War days. Speaking at the 20th Century–Fox studios in Hollywood – he had been provoked for various reasons into an emotional survey of his own career – he described how, towards the end of the Civil War, he was

> quartered in the house of an educated family. The landlady was a graduate of the St Petersburg Institute of Young Maids of Gentle Birth [the most famous of the aristocratic girls' schools of old Russia]. As for me, I suppose I still smelled of coal.... There were other educated people in that house – a lawyer, an engineer, a teacher and musician. We Red Army men mixed with them. When they saw me, a Communist, they saw that, far from eating human flesh, I was starving.... Sometimes I had no bread but I never tried to take any away from them, or, indeed, ask for anything. They came to respect me.... We were still unpolished, uneducated workers at that time, but we wanted to receive an education, to learn to govern the state.... I remember the landlady asking me, 'Tell me, what do you know about the ballet? You're a simple miner, aren't you?' To tell the truth, I didn't really know anything about ballet at that time, because I hadn't seen any then. I had never seen a ballerina. But I said to her, 'just wait, we're going to have everything, and ballet too.' Frankly speaking, if I had been asked at that time just what we were going to have, I might not quite have known what to say, but I was certain there was a better life ahead.

This is the picture of a man for whom the Revolution was made, not of a man who in any real sense made it. But the Bolshevik leadership, on the other hand, had for years been thinking and arguing about revolution, and had no shortage of ideas. Equally important, it operated with a military discipline that never left its NCOs like Khrushchev without orders. This was never more necessary than at the end of the Civil War which, although it confirmed the Bolsheviks in power, left the country exhausted and ravaged. The system of 'war communism', the dictatorship of the

the centre over all aspects of life that had been introduced to wage the Civil War, was now applied to the equally urgent task of restoring a destroyed economy.

In the Donbas alone one third of all industrial enterprises were ruined, and Khrushchev along with other mineworkers was released from the army to be drafted as an industrial soldier to restore them. Men who avoided work in the mines were punished as deserters, and even the mine administration at Rutchenkovo, where Khrushchev was sent, was divided along military lines into two 'divisions' each consisting of twelve 'mine regiments'. Khrushchev came back to find that his old mine, No. 31, was producing so little coal that it could not feed its own electric power plant, and the whole Donbas produced in 1921 only a fifth of its 1913 tonnage. The Rutchenkovo mine administration had been put under Yegor Abakumov, a Bolshevik who later worked with Khrushchev on the building of the Moscow subway and after that became deputy head of the Soviet coal industry. Khrushchev was appointed his deputy in charge of political matters – a sort of mine commissar.

Years later Khrushchev said that 'it was much easier to have talks with Red Army men during the Civil War than to explain the new tasks when I returned from the war and worked in the mines.' One problem was to explain the appalling conditions of life that the miners now had to endure, even worse than before 1917. To the general devastation was added a chronic food shortage, which in 1921 turned into famine. Parties of armed miners had to be sent into the surrounding countryside to force food out of the reluctant peasants, and there was always a chance that they would be attacked by the bands of peasant anarchists, Ukrainian nationalists, or plain brigands that still roamed unchecked over much of the Ukraine. This time of troubles brought its private tragedies for Khrushchev, too. His close friend Pantelei Makhinya was killed in a skirmish with Ukrainian nationalists. And during the famine his young wife died, possibly from one of the epidemic diseases which ravaged the hungry country, leaving him with a son of five and a daughter of three.

Khrushchev's job in Rutchenkovo was in theory a political one and it doubtless involved a good deal of propaganda which, knowing the later Khrushchev, must have compensated in forcefulness for what it lacked in subtlety. It was his job to explain to the miners the first great change in the post-war Party line brought about by the introduction of the New Economic Policy (NEP). This was a tactical retreat by Lenin after the rigours of war communism had become almost unbearable, and it involved relaxation of some controls together with permission for a measure of private enterprise. NEP soon helped the economic situation, but it was regarded by many idealistic communists as a terrible betrayal of principle, and some in their despair even committed suicide. We do not know how Khrushchev reacted, but we have his own word for it that NEP caused confusion in Rutchenkovo too. One local Bolshevik who had fought well in the Civil War tore up his Party card and hired a mill. 'He thought', Khrushchev recalled, 'if there's NEP, it means the communists are retreating, are opening the way to private capital, and one must adapt so as not to be late.' But it is easy to see how in the Donbas, under both war communism and NEP, it must have been the practical problem of restoring coal production as quickly as possible that dominated Khrushchev's work as much as anyone else's. In this way a pattern was set for the rest of Khrushchev's life: a pattern of political work closely involved with the bricks and mortar of the economic construction that has been at the core of Soviet history since the Revolution.

In 1922 Khrushchev was lucky enough to get the chance to remedy his almost total lack of formal education. That year he was sent to the Workers' Faculty (Rabfak) of the Don Technical College at Yuzovka, one of eight rabfaks set up in the Ukraine to provide men like him with a crash course in basic subjects before they went on to specialist studies. This was a definite sign of the Party's approval, because there were then only some 1,500 places in the Ukrainian rabfaks. The students were chosen largely for their loyalty to the régime and proletarian background, with the aim of producing as soon as possible a new class of Soviet specialists to replace those who were trained before the Revolution, and whose dubious allegiance to the new régime was to worry the Bolsheviks for years. Khrushchev received an additional accolade in his appointment as Party secretary for the whole technical college, an important job, on its own scale, which must have carried the approval of the Yuzovka Party leadership. (It is not altogether clear if Khrushchev got the job as soon as he joined the rabfak or if he held it for all his three years of study.)

Conditions at the technical college were primitive. The teaching was done in the old Yuzovka school of commerce and in the Cossack barracks, which the students themselves had to rebuild from ruins. A good deal of self-help went into acquiring rudimentary equipment for the laboratories and workshops, and the textbooks on mining (the college's speciality) had to be printed by the students. Lectures on historical materialism, one of the basic Marxist studies introduced by the Bolsheviks, were given by a student because no teacher was qualified to give them. Khrushchev's own studies must often have been interrupted by his responsibility for the college's political health (he had to remove the pro-rector for declaring a holiday to celebrate a religious festival, and another teacher for being a Monarchist), and by the general organizational work that would be demanded of a Party secretary in such chaotic times.

But whatever else he learnt there, the rabfak did give him his first proper introduction to Marxism. This was a very important event, because, on his own admission, Marx's writings struck him almost as a revelation. 'When I listened to lectures on political economy', he told a French journalist in 1958, 'and the lecturer spoke about the wage system under capitalism, about the exploitation of the workers, it seemed to me that Karl Marx had been at the mine where my father and I worked.' The ideas of Marxism excited Khrushchev because they seemed to have been proved true by his own experience. Marx provided Khrushchev with an explanation of all that he and his family had endured before the Revolution and must have seemed to him to have transformed his personal experience of the Donbas mines and their owners into scientific laws about the development of human society.* Khrushchev was undoubtedly a very able man, but his gifts did not include a speculative mind, and his intellectual grasp

* Zola's *Germinal*, which is about French miners, had a similar effect on Khrushchev. In an interview in 1960 he said: 'When I read [Zola's] book about miners, I felt I saw my own life, my own mine and my own daily round described in it. The more so that I used to work at some mines that used to be French-owned.'

of Marxism always remained rudimentary. In the event, of course, it was lucky for him that his Marxism did not extend far beyond a collection of basic maxims. A more intellectual approach, in the years ahead, was to prove all too often a fatal liability.

In 1924, the year before he left the technical college, Khrushchev married again. His wife, Nina, was a Yuzovka school teacher. It appears to have been a happy marriage and it gave Khrushchev three more children, two girls and one boy. This fruitful private side of Khrushchev's life remains largely hidden through the difficult years ahead, but it would be unwise to ignore it or underestimate its influence on him.

After graduation from the technical college, Khrushchev was appointed in April 1925 to be Secretary of the Petrovo-Marinsky district Party Committee close by Stalino, as Yuzovka had been renamed in keeping with the spirit of the coming age. This put Khrushchev at the lowest command post in the Party's territorial hierarchy and not a moment too soon, because he was now thirty-one, which was certainly not young in revolutionary Russia. Khrushchev's reminiscences of Petrovo-Marinsky capture something of the epic nature of Party field-work in Soviet Russia's first years: a horse the only means of transport to villages where Bolsheviks had been shot at by angry peasants; drunken chairmen of village soviets who were controlled by anti-Bolshevik kulaks (rich peasants) and had to be removed; above all, work with miners whose living conditions, and liking for alcohol, remained as deplorable as ever. This work seems to have convinced Khrushchev that a Party official had himself to have first-hand knowledge of the activities under his supervision. His successor at Petrovo-Marinsky got into difficulties because, although far better educated than Khrushchev, he knew little about mining. The miners complained, Khrushchev recalled later, that 'if a secretary does not know the mine, what sort of a leader is he?' This question sums up the demands which Krushchev was to make on himself, on other Party workers, and later still on the whole Party; and which were to form the core of his ideas on how the Party should operate.

In the same month that Khrushchev went to Petrovo-Marinsky, Lazar Kaganovich – the man who briefly headed the Yuzovka Bolsheviks in 1917 – became head of the Ukrainian Party. And it is from this time on that Stalin can truly be said to dominate Khrushchev's career, a domination that was to persist even after the dictator's death. Lenin himself had died in January 1924, and Stalin, who had already alarmed Lenin by his abuse of the great power he had acquired as the Party's General Secretary, was now able to begin the elimination of his rivals. To this end it was essential to secure solid support in the great regional Party organizations, and the appointment to the Ukraine of Kaganovich, already known as a Stalin man, was part of this plan. With typical efficiency Kaganovich managed to replace almost the entire Ukrainian Central Committee in the short space of two years.

Khrushchev was exactly the sort of man that Kaganovich was seeking to promote in the Ukrainian hierarchy. He and men like him were malleable precisely because their approach to Bolshevism was not intellectual, because they knew nothing of the pre-revolutionary world of Bolshevism. Stalin's gradual destruction of all open opposition meant little to such men. They had never known the free though fierce discussion of the early Bolshevik intellectuals. Also unlike many Russian intellectuals, they were confined in their experience to Russia, and the idea that opposition could be contained within a political system was quite foreign to them. Indeed, they probably shared the primitive Russian suspicion of the individual who dared to range himself against the community. The Party as Stalin shaped it, disciplined to absolute subservience, with all decisions made at the top, suited a man like Khrushchev. It gave him the political guidance he needed while leaving plenty of scope for his energy in practical matters. The Stalin of this period, moreover, was conducting a brilliant campaign to consolidate the Revolution and his own dominance of it. It was ruthless, of course, but then Lenin too had been ruthless. At the same time he showed far more political skill than his rivals; the erratic Jewish intellectuals, Kamenev and Zinovyev, and even the brilliant Trotsky were no match for him. Stalin's personal rancour against these men (he had long disliked the Bolshevik intellectuals, who made him feel uncomfortable) and his plans for Russia in fact form a whole, and probably he was unable to distinguish between the two himself. How could

Khrushchev, suspecting little of the origins of such hatreds, see any more clearly?

Khrushchev's first experience of the dangerous world of Bolshevik high politics came in December 1925 when he attended the 14th Party Congress as a non-voting delegate from Stalino. The Congress embodied the two sides of Stalin, the constructive and the destructive. On one hand it endorsed the first stages of his programme for socialism in one country – the idea that Russia should not wait for world revolution but consolidate her strength at home – which was to become the basis of Soviet policy and power. At the same time Stalin used the Congress to further his schemes against Zinovyev and Kamenev. The fact that Lenin's revered widow Krupskaya was jeered and heckled for a speech in which she stressed that all Party members should speak 'according to conscience' suggests the tone of the proceedings. The Congress was the first to reflect Stalin's control of the Party organization, and one of his opponents later called it 'a well-rehearsed play, acted just as its producer [Stalin] had planned over several years'. There is no reason to suppose that Khrushchev, with only the humblest of walk-on parts, was dissatisfied with the play.

Khrushchev eagerly endorsed all Stalin's attacks on his opponents. At the 1st All-Ukrainian Party Conference in October 1926 – his first speech on such an important occasion – he declared that the recent public confession of error, made by Trotsky, Zinovyev and Kamenev, was not sincere, and he demanded 'repressive measures' against the opposition, 'regardless of their former merits and positions', if they failed to mend their ways. Then came promotion as head of the Stalino Party's organization department, 'in order to head the battle of the communists of the region against the Zinovyev-ists and Trotskyists'. In early 1928 Khrushchev moved on again, first to Kharkov (then the Ukraine's capital) for a short time and then to Kiev,*

* The Kiev Party was hit by a scandal while Khrushchev was there. The trouble was 'systematic drinking' and 'bad management' according to an article written in a Party journal in 1930 by, of all people, the young Georgi Malenkov, who was then working in the Central Committee apparatus in Moscow. Khrushchev does not seem to have been involved; at any rate, not in any way to damage his career.

where he seems to have worked either in the city or region Party committee. In April 1929 he spoke at the 2nd Ukrainian Party Conference against Stalin's new enemies – the right-wing opposition led by Bukharin, a leading Bolshevik theoretician whom Lenin had called 'the darling of the Party' and who now disagreed with the ending of NEP and the contrary scheme to force industrial growth by rigid central planning.

In all this, Khrushchev followed the leadership of his chief Kaganovich, and so had become a reliable though very junior Stalin man himself. No doubt in his mind the equation was simple: the Revolution equalled the Party, and the Party now equalled its leader, Stalin.

Chapter 3
Moscow

Little is known of the personal relationships between the men who ruled the Soviet Union under Stalin. This is partly because Soviet communists have genuinely believed such things irrelevant to those who are not wilful politicians but the instruments of 'History'. It is also because the Soviet leaders have happened to have the power to frustrate any embarrassing curiosity. This means that very little is known about Khrushchev's relationship with Lazar Kaganovich, who was by far the most important political connexion of his early career. The two men may first have met during Kaganovich's short stay at Yuzovka in early 1917, but they certainly must have met in early 1925 when Kaganovich toured the Ukraine shortly after his appointment as Ukrainian Party chief. Kaganovich had been a Stalin man since before Lenin's death. His constant identification with Stalin makes it only too easy to dismiss him as the dictator's tool, but this is to underestimate both Kaganovich and his colleagues (and to misunderstand the nature of Stalin's rule into the bargain). He was in some ways an attractive man – he reminded one veteran Moscow correspondent of the genial American politician Wendell Wilkie – with a somewhat Rabelaisian sense of humour and a better line in oratory than most of Stalin's men. He is said to have despised intellectuals, and Stalin's chief enemies in the years after Lenin's death were mainly intellectuals. Although he began life as a leather-worker and had little education, Kaganovich developed a great talent for economic organization. As Ukrainian leader he had supervised the early construction of the Dnieproges, the mammoth hydro-electric station on the River Dnieper that became a symbol of the brave new Russia. And in the thirties he was to begin the building of modern Moscow, including its famous subway.

It may be that the young Khrushchev, as he worked his way up the Ukrainian Party apparatus, caught Kaganovich's eye as much by his own practical abilities as by his firm echoing of Stalin's political line. At any rate in the autumn of 1929, the year after

Kaganovich left the Ukraine to help in Stalin's final destruction of open opposition, Khrushchev himself went to Moscow as a student at the Academy of Heavy Industry. The Academy was one of a number established to train Party members of correct proletarian background but little education to replace the old technical intelligentsia, whom Stalin did not trust, at the barricades of the new, industrial revolution. But the purpose behind Khrushchev's transfer may have been mainly a political one.

Stalin's fight with Bukharin, who led the so-called Right opposition against the new policy of the Five-Year Plans and ruthless industrialization, came to a successful end in 1929. Bukharin was then removed from positions of power, but he still had a following in the Party, and particularly within the Moscow organization. And Moscow was of strategic importance to Stalin in his fight for control over the Party, because he was to use it as his base from which to launch later attacks on the two other most important regional Party organizations, those of Leningrad and the Ukraine. Notable among the unreliable sectors of the Moscow organization were institutions of higher education such as the Industrial Academy, where for obvious reasons the arguments of the Right opposition found considerable intellectual support. A Rightist faction was revealed in the Industrial Academy about the time of Khrushchev's arrival in Moscow, although its existence had presumably been at least suspected before then. In April 1930, Kaganovich took over the leadership of the Moscow organization, and the following month the crisis in the Industrial Academy came to a head when it appeared that the supporters of Bukharin were still managing to dominate the Academy's political life. After various alarums and excursions, the errant Party cell was forced to dissolve itself, and a new one was elected with Khrushchev as secretary.

Was Khrushchev brought to Moscow in the first place with such an end in mind, or did Kaganovich just happen to discover his presence at the Academy at this most convenient time? There is no way of telling, but in either case the importance of Khrushchev's link with Kaganovich is clear. His new job as the Industrial Academy's Party secretary brought him into Moscow politics at an excellent moment for his political advancement. The process of weeding out unreliable (from Stalin's point of view) elements from the Moscow Party took time, and Khrushchev, with Kaganovich's patronage, stood only to gain from this. In January 1931 Khrushchev was made Party secretary of the Bauman district where the Academy was situated. His course at the Industrial Academy was meant to have lasted three years, but he had been there for only just over a year, and much of that must have been given over to Party work. Within months he was moved on again to the command of the Krasnopresnensky district, which was of greater industrial importance.

Khrushchev's political rise was now spectacular. In 1933 he became Kaganovich's No. 2 in the Moscow city Party and then himself took over its leadership in early 1934, following this with election to the Soviet Central Committee at the 17th Party Congress in February of the same year. This made him one of the hundred odd most important Party functionaries in the country, a position from which he advanced in March 1935 to succeed Kaganovich as the leader of the Party for the whole Moscow region. In the five years since his arrival in Moscow he had risen from complete obscurity to be the leader of the most important, because most loyal to Stalin, of all the country's regional Party organizations. In the process he had completely overtaken other promising young men like Georgi Malenkov and Nikolai Bulganin, both of whom rose through the Moscow Party at the same time. Bulganin, with a distinguished past as a secret policeman during the Civil War, was now mayor of Moscow but only a candidate member of the Central Committee. The pudgy, baby-faced Malenkov was already personally close to Stalin (almost certainly considerably closer than Khrushchev), but was still not a Central Committee member in 1935.

There is a danger that Stalin's barbarism will dominate our image of the Soviet Union from the 1930s on, to the exclusion of almost everything else. And it is particularly important not to forget that Khrushchev's arrival in Moscow coincided with the abandonment of the easy ways of NEP, and that from now on the years are coloured by the stern but none the less deeply felt romance of industrial revolution. This was Russia's 'Iron Age', when people genuinely believed (as others still do in underdeveloped countries today) that only industrialization would bring happiness and prosperity; when factories, tractors and smoke were the symbols of a nobler as well as richer future. The Soviet Union was to achieve this magnificent end by a unique experiment in centralized economic management which itself added to the excitement. The new age was to be measured by a new calendar which contained weeks of only five days length and abolished the names of the old weekdays. Students and office-workers turned out to do manual work on the (former) Saturdays, and thousands of young people left their homes in the old towns of the west to build quite literally the new world in the savage spaces of the east. The songs which were sung about these new heroes, the books and paintings which recorded their feats, still had a certain freshness and had not yet become the cant behind which a terrible truth was concealed. The heroism of this period was central to the experience of the men in Khrushchev's generation: it is hard to see how they could have survived without it. For a man like Khrushchev, moreover, it was not to be only the justification of his life, but the main daily preoccupation of most of his career.

From 1931 onward, with his appointment to the Bauman district, he was plunged into supervising the construction of a Moscow fit to be the capital of a powerful industrial nation. At the end of the 1920s Moscow was still largely a medieval city with little drainage, few proper roads and grossly inadequate old houses and schools. The size of the problem can be gauged from the observation of Sir E. D. Simon, an English expert who visited Moscow in the mid-thirties when its reconstruction had already been under way for a few years. 'It is safe to say,' he recorded, 'that ninety per cent of the families in Moscow would improve their housing conditions beyond recognition if they could have to themselves one of [the] houses which are being pulled down in Manchester as unfit for human habitation.' Small wonder that most of Khrushchev's published speeches at this period deal with construction problems, as did his first article written for *Pravda*, the main Party newspaper. And it was these problems, too, which occupied the main part of his speech at the 17th Party Congress in 1934, the first speech he made at this the most important of all Bolshevik gatherings.

The most widely hailed building feat in Moscow at this time was of course the subway, where work was rushed to meet impossible deadlines regardless of difficulty and danger. Khrushchev ranks only second to Kaganovich in the official distribution of praise for this, and was awarded his first Order of Lenin for his efforts. But in fact from the time that Kaganovich left the Moscow organization, the subway programme was primarily Khrushchev's responsibility. The prominence that Khrushchev had now achieved allows one to notice properly for the first time the synthesis that he was developing between his own, personal style of work and the demands he put on the Party organizations under his command. His talent for practical organization and his keenness to see and do things for himself come over clearly in the Soviet books on the first years of the subway. We see him telephoning late into the night in order to break through a sudden shortage in the cement supply; visiting once or twice a day any section that ran up against particular difficulties. The extent of his personal control is suggested in an account by George Morgan, the chief American technical adviser on the subway, of how Khrushchev would decide differences of opinion between the engineers by getting them to submit their ideas personally to him on no more than two pieces of paper. He also intervened in such matters as the design of the subway coaches, ordering the first models that were produced to be scrapped.

This eagerness to have a say even in the details of the work under his authority could be seen in other fields too. He was as ready to advise on the correct height for laying bricks as to suggest that the capital's various building organizations be unified (something he was to achieve when he returned to head the Moscow Party once more after the war). He was now sufficiently senior to be able to generalize from his own interests and experience so as to produce an approach to Party work that he expected his subordinates to follow. In 1933, for instance, he told Moscow Party and government officials that a real Bolshevik was not someone who 'repeats again and again' the latest slogans but someone whose 'work is organized, whose machinery works and doesn't lie abandoned under all kinds of rubbish', and who 'each day, each hour controls matters effectively'. What may very well have happened is that Khrushchev was troubled by the problem of delegating authority when he began Party work in Moscow. At any rate in a reminiscence in 1955 he told how during his spell in the Bauman district in 1931 he had been called to the Central Committee and asked how he felt about his work. 'Very badly,' Khrushchev claimed to have replied, 'because I have two hundred cells [the cell is the smallest Party unit] in the district, the secretaries there are elected and re-elected and I only know that I register them. I can't have personal contact with the cells and the people, and if I don't have personal contact I can't influence their work.' Khrushchev's remedy seems to have been to turn the Party organization under his control into as much an extension of himself as possible, with its members sharing, or at least being exhorted to share, his own passion for personal control and knowledge of the work in hand.

It was the combination, from this time on, of his preoccupation with economic construction and his own ideas on the correct style of work for himself and his subordinates that was to form the basis of what many years later, after Stalin's death, can best be described as Khrushchevism.

Chapter 4
The Blood Purge

The history of the Soviet Union under Stalin is like two halves of a puzzle that somehow can never be made to fit together. There is its positive side – the great work of building the material foundations of a new society. But there is also a purposeful disregard of human life that in the 1930s assumed a dimension beyond ordinary human cruelty. Many people have been able to resolve this paradox by refusing to acknowledge its existence and by stressing one aspect to the exclusion of the other. The Soviet Union has accordingly been represented either as the only good society or on the contrary as a land ruled by men intent on keeping their personal power at no matter what cost in human life. While such interpretations may help contemporaries to keep their sanity, they cannot be allowed to explain the Khrushchev of this period. Indeed to expect an 'explanation' at all is to ask for too much. Perhaps some day a Soviet historian with better access to material that is still kept secret may come near it. Until then we must constantly acknowledge the reservations behind any interpretation that is offered, and qualify any judgement that we make.

As its name implies, the Iron Age which dominated Khrushchev's work from his arrival in Moscow also had its grim side. Aided by no foreign capital whatsoever, the Soviet Union had literally to devour its own citizens to provide the mighty investments in heavy industry demanded by the Five-Year Plans. During the first plan a system of rationing was introduced that cruelly penalized those whose work was of secondary importance in the national effort and excluded completely the politically unreliable. Most sensational of all was the campaign to collectivize agriculture. This was both a political and an economic measure: on one hand it was meant to break the power of the better-off peasants, and on the other make it possible to extract food for the factory workers at the cheapest possible price. Khrushchev was himself involved in the later stages of collectivization in the Moscow region. He must have known that peasants died of starvation and were deported to labour camps in millions. He must have seen the droves of stray peasant children who reappeared on Moscow's streets as in the period of chaos after the Civil War. He was himself forced to dance to the sombre tune of the first Five-Year Plan and divert the capital's labour and resources from housing to the building and reconstruction of factories, to the Moscow–Volga canal, and to expensive prestige projects like the subway and the Palace of Soviets.*

Although some Party members revolted against the ruthlessness of these policies, it is not hard to understand how many believed them justified. The vision of a mighty Soviet Russia equal to the great capitalist states appealed powerfully to both the Russian and the communist mind. The fear that these states might attack Russia (their intervention in the Civil War was, of course, never forgotten) seemed doubly justified by the birth and growth of Nazi Germany. Stalin's simple policy to make the Soviet Union strong in as short a time as possible seemed literally a matter of life and death. The age did not apparently allow for pity in the execution of such a policy, but then the Russian political tradition was singularly lacking in pity anyway.

Khrushchev was now personally identified with the régime. It had given him, the son of a poor peasant, power and an intoxicating sense of involvement in great matters of state: the Revolution was proved a success by his own personal experience, and this was the most powerful justification of all. At the same time Stalin's practical mind was to be seen at work in the increasing rewards that were given to men like Khrushchev from the 1930s on. Lenin's 'Party maximum', which had limited Party and government officials to the average worker's wage, was quietly abandoned. Key officials were given priority in housing and in the allocation of scarce food and consumer goods. Privileges like these are the oil which lubricates most authoritarian political

* The cost of the first two sections of the Moscow subway, built in 1932–6, was 1,500 million roubles. This would have provided new housing space of 8 square metres per person for 470,000 people (the actual 1936 average living space per person in Moscow was 4·5 square metres). The excavation of the site of the Palace of Soviets alone cost 30 million roubles. The Palace, designed to be a skyscraper topped by a giant statue of Lenin, was never built because the foundations proved unsafe. After Stalin's death the site was turned into a vast open-air swimming pool.

systems. It would be ludicrous to suggest that they alone kept Khrushchev and men like him loyal to Stalin, but they form the background to Khrushchev's life from now on and cannot be ignored.

No Soviet politician has given, or is likely to give, a first-hand informal account of his attitudes during this period, but there is a roughly analagous description of the state of mind of up-and-coming Party members recorded by a British scholar who spent a year mixing with the students of the Moscow Planning Academy in the mid-thirties. He is, of course, writing of men junior in age and Party position to Khrushchev, but the analysis of their attitudes seems strikingly relevant nonetheless. The Academy's students were all Party members of at least five years' standing but little or no formal education, and possessed, the Briton found, a

> simple-minded and ruthless practicality. Marxist theory and Soviet policy as expounded by Stalin suited them exactly. I could not, and cannot, imagine a leader better suited to them. In the opinion of one of them, there were about 50,000 Party members of their general status and these were the 'masters of the country'. The purge worried them not at all in any way apparent to me, either for their own safety, or for pity.*

One must remember that for Khrushchev, as for these men, the sensational repressions against the Party that reached their climax in 1936–8 were only the last stages in a bloodletting operation of already massive proportions. The purge of the Party has attracted so much attention partly because Khrushchev himself revealed and condemned it in his secret speech of 1956, and partly because of the world-wide publicity accorded at the time to the show-trials of famous Bolshevik figures like Kamenev, Zinovyev and Bukharin. But repression and terror had been used by the Cheka, the first Soviet security service, against both Whites and left-wing opponents during the Civil War. Although the period of NEP was more relaxed, the Iron Age at the end of the 1920s was accompanied by a wave of terror against the old intelligentsia, complete with show-trials. The first of these trials was held in the Ukraine in 1928 when Khrushchev was still

* From an essay by Jack Miller in *Soviet Planning* (London, 1964).

working there. Then came the bloodiest of all measures, the collectivization of peasant agriculture.

Inseparable from the growing use of force as an instrument of policy was the dogma of the inadmissibility of opposition to the Party line, which itself hardened into the terrorist logic that all disagreement was malicious and therefore punishable. In this way support given to Stalin in his battles with his old Bolshevik colleagues in the 1920s led, by the thirties, to acceptance of the Stalinist Party as the sole source of absolute truth, endowed with the right to punish people for their own salvation's sake as well as for the defence of the Revolution. This was accepted not only by the Stalinists. Zinovyev, Kamenev and Bukharin and many other of Stalin's victims seem to have made false confessions at their trials partly because they believed that there could be no real existence outside the Party. This process did not take place in a vacuum: the constant pressure of the outside world on the Soviet Union was vigorously exploited by Stalin, who was able to control, in a manner unimaginable in most West European countries, the information about that world received by even quite senior colleagues like Khrushchev. The ignorance of the Khrushchev generation was always a powerful weapon in its master's hand. Perhaps most important of all, and also curiously easiest to forget, is Stalin's domination of the Soviet Union by his superior will and ability. This small ungainly Georgian had driven the glittering Trotsky into angry but impotent exile; the most brilliant of Lenin's colleagues now prostrated themselves before him like repentant heretics before a Pope. Khrushchev, in that part of his secret speech which reaffirmed his belief in Stalin's positive role in founding the Soviet cultural and industrial revolutions, spoke of the dictator's 'logic, his strength, and his will'. These were real enough: there could have been no Stalinism without them.

Much of the above is, so to speak, the case for Khrushchev. What of the case against him? Perhaps the most damaging accusation that can be made is that he survived the thirties at all, since anyone who was suspected of questioning Stalin's rule did not. The survival rate was meagre: of the nine Moscow district Party secretaries appointed with Khrushchev in January 1931, he was the only one to be still in politics at the end of the decade.

More sensational still, some one hundred of the 139 members of the Central Committee to which Khrushchev was elected in 1934 were arrested, and most of them shot, by 1938. Khrushchev's Moscow speeches are as full as anyone else's of gross praise for Stalin (he was also careful always to acknowledge Kaganovich's part in any Moscow achievement) and as loaded with abuse against Stalin's opponents. He developed with characteristic vigour all the various themes of the purge period. A typical example is a speech made in March 1937 ridiculing economic officials and even people's commissars (i.e. ministers) for not spotting the 'wreckers' in their establishments. 'Sometimes a man sits there,' he said, 'enemies are swarming around him, are almost climbing up his legs, and he notices nothing and puffs: I've got no wreckers in my apparatus.' 'One must criticize,' Khrushchev concluded, 'regardless of persons and the feelings of these persons. To criticize in time – this is to help and sometimes to save a worker.' Many were arrested in the course of such salvation.

There is no evidence that Khrushchev was personally close to Stalin during this period, or indeed even later. He did not become a candidate member of the Politburo until January 1938, when he moved from Moscow to the Ukraine. It is true that he may have come early to Stalin's attention when at the Industrial Academy. Stalin's wife, Nadezhda Alliluyeva, was also a student of the Academy, and it is possible that she supported the rightist faction there which Khrushchev replaced. (Alliluyeva committed suicide in 1932, distressed, it is generally believed, by the increasingly repressive nature of Stalin's rule.) His own wife's involvement in the Industrial Academy affair may well have made Stalin take a close look at the others involved in it, but nothing more personal seems to have resulted. Khrushchev's line to Stalin was rather through Kaganovich.

We do not know which if any of Stalin's close associates were involved in his most sensational crimes, like the murder of the Leningrad Party leader Kirov, a handsome, popular and therefore dangerous man, whose death in December 1934 touched off the great purge of the Party. The machinery of repression was beyond the Party's control, since the Party had to be repressed as much as anyone else. But if Khrushchev did not know some of the appalling details of the blood purge in action, he certainly knew well both Yagoda and Yezhov, the two NKVD chiefs responsible. He had worked with them in the Moscow apparatus and he had co-operated with them in the building of the Moscow–Volga canal. The most damning evidence against Khrushchev is that some senior members of the Party did express open doubts about the repression and the validity of the accusations against loyal communists. These were heard at the Central Committee plenum held in February–March 1937, which Khrushchev attended. The spokesman for the doubters was Pavel Postyshev, then Party leader of the Ukraine but soon to be demoted and then killed for his temerity. Curiously, it is from Khrushchev's secret speech that we know how Postyshev expressed his disbelief in the charges being brought against longstanding Party members. According to Khrushchev, Postyshev said:

> I personally do not believe that in 1934 an honest Party member who had trod the long road of unrelenting fight against enemies for the Party and Socialism, would now be in the camp of the enemies.... I cannot imagine how it would be possible to travel with the Party during the difficult years and then, in 1934, join the Trotskyites.

It was after this meeting that the axe fell with a vengeance on the Central Committee. Many senior Party members – almost the whole of the Ukrainian leadership whom Khrushchev himself was to replace (see next chapter), and Jan Gamarnik, head of the Red Army's Political Directorate and Khrushchev's colleague on the Moscow Committee, to cite some personally connected with Khrushchev – were never even tried publicly, perhaps because they refused to confess to the bizarre and gruesome crimes concocted by the NKVD. Whatever Khrushchev may have thought then about the real guilt of these men, he must have known that action was being taken against them illegally. According to Party rules it was necessary to obtain a two-thirds vote of the Central Committee and the Party Control Commission before a Central Committee member could be excluded from the Party. But, as Khrushchev admitted in the secret speech, no such plenum was held in 1937–8 during the height of the purge when most of the Committee disappeared.

The times did not encourage rational behaviour. As the purges grew, so did personal hysteria. There is certainly a sign that Khrushchev was caught up by this in a speech he made in Red Square after the trial of a group of so-called Trotskyites in January 1937. This achieves a pitch of hysterical demagoguery not equalled by any other of Khrushchev's recorded speeches: 'The Trotskyites,' he said, 'wanted to destroy our seven-hour working day, to destroy our great rights to labour, rest, education; to recreate the horrors of unemployment. . . .' They wanted 'at one level the poverty and hunger of millions, on the other – the riches of a bunch of kulaks'. Their aim was to turn the Soviet Union into a 'colony of German and Japanese imperialism. . . . Raising their hand against Stalin, they raised it against all the best that mankind has, because Stalin is the hope, the longing, the lighthouse of all forward and progressive humanity.'

This was the speech of an excited man: it cannot be dismissed as a politician's deception. The blood purge had corrupted its supporters as much as it killed its declared enemies. It corrupted even Stalin and there is no doubt that it corrupted Khrushchev too. But the signs are that Khrushchev nevertheless came to feel guilty about it. Of all the sacred cows of his own régime, none was more sacred than the supposed ignorance of Khrushchev and his colleagues about Stalin's murder of innocent communists.* Khrushchev never expressed regret for the other repressions before 1934; he sometimes regretted the extreme violence of collectivization but never suggested that most of its victims might have been spared. On the other hand, one senses in his treatment

* To anticipate: Khrushchev gave one of his most explicit self-justifications to a gathering of Soviet intelligentsia in 1963. 'It is asked', he said, 'did the leading cadres of the Party know of, let us say, the arrests of people at the time? Yes, they knew. But did they know that people who were innocent of any wrongdoing were being arrested? No. This they did not know. They believed Stalin and did not admit the thought that repression could be applied to honest people devoted to our cause.' A few weeks earlier the writer Ilya Ehrenburg had suggested in his memoirs 'a theory of silence' about the 1930s repressions which implied that he knew unjust arrests were being made but had to grit his teeth and say nothing. This of course was dynamite: what Ehrenburg knew Party leaders also must have known, and Ehrenburg was savagely attacked for this by Khrushchev as well as by literary critics who had flourished under Stalin.

of Stalin's crimes against the Party in the secret speech not just a political manoeuvre but also an attempt to cleanse his own conscience. And perhaps his own sense of guilt made his condemnation of Stalin all the more bitter.

Chapter 5
The Ukraine

On 28 January 1938 *Pravda* announced that a plenum of the Ukrainian Communist Party Central Committee had elected 'Comrade N. S. Khrushchev as acting first secretary'. Behind this abrupt statement lay a story of remarkable political intrigue which involved Khrushchev more closely than any other episode of Stalinist repression and which in the years to come, when Stalin had been repudiated, caused him more embarrassment than any other part of his career.

Ever since the Revolution the Ukraine had presented Moscow with a special problem in its nationalism. Even the Ukrainian communists, although not supporting the nationalist desire for complete Ukrainian independence from Russia, carried out markedly 'Ukrainian' policies in the 1920s. But even such limited nationalism had its dangers when the whole country was subjected to the tremendous strain of the Five-Year Plans and collectivization: the discontent caused by these policies could only too easily take on nationalist colouring. In 1933, when the chaotic effects of collectivization on Ukrainian agriculture were all too plain, Stalin sent in a Russian communist, Postyshev, to become *de facto* ruler of the Ukraine and to carry out a purge. This he did to some effect, but by the summer of 1937, after Postyshev himself had been purged (see page 48), the Ukrainian leaders were again showing signs of tolerance towards nationalist sentiment.

The punishment that Stalin was now planning for the Ukrainians can only be understood by grasping how important his fear of Nazi Germany was as a motive behind the whole policy of blood purge. If any part of the Soviet Union seemed to be threatened by Hitler, it was the Ukraine with its grain lands and natural resources. Hitler himself had said that Germany would live in luxury if it controlled the Ukraine (Khrushchev had quoted this at a meeting of the Supreme Soviet in 1936 and warned the German dictator against the danger of such dreams). At the same time Russians had not forgotten how the Ukrainian nationalists had allied themselves with Germany in 1917: twenty years later a German invasion still seemed the only thing that might make Ukrainian separatism possible. It is not surprising that if Hitler could help to make Stalin suspicious of Marshal Tukhachevsky and the other Red Army leaders killed in 1937, he should also have destroyed Stalin's trust in the Ukrainian leadership.

The first sign of trouble came in August 1937, when a powerful and ominous trio arrived in the Ukrainian capital of Kiev, composed of Molotov, Soviet prime minister and Stalin's right-hand man; Yezhov, the head of the NKVD; and Khrushchev, the least well known of the three.* The fact that they were accompanied by a special detachment of NKVD troops from Moscow hinted that they were on more than a simple visit of good will. A plenum of the Ukrainian Central Committee was accordingly summoned to meet the guests and met to find that it was being guarded by the Moscow troops. Molotov opened the meeting with a long speech accusing the Ukrainians of mistakes. He demanded that Kosior, the Ukrainian first secretary, and the other leaders be dismissed and that Khrushchev be elected to Kosior's place. The Ukrainians refused. The Moscow trio then retired, and Molotov had a long telephone conversation with Stalin. The meeting was resumed the next day, this time in the headquarters set up by the Moscow NKVD force, but again the vote of non-confidence in Kosior was refused and again Khrushchev's election avoided. Molotov now suggested that the Ukrainians should go to Moscow to discuss the matter with the Soviet Central Committee and a majority agreed, although the Ukrainian premier Lyubchenko and some others voted against even this. In fact the Ukrainians had simply chosen to walk to the scaffold. In Moscow they were seen by Stalin, Molotov and Kaganovich, but not, apparently, by Khrushchev. It is not known what happened at the meeting, but there is no doubt that

* There is only one detailed source for this extraordinary story – Alexander Uralov (real name A. Avtorkhanov), *The Reign of Stalin* (London, 1953), pp. 67–70. Avtorkhanov was a senior Party official before he emigrated to the West and his book is largely based on undocumented recollections. But there is a second, far less-detailed version of this important episode in V. Dedijer's *Tito Speaks* (London, 1953). Tito apparently heard stories about the Ukrainian purge when he lived in Moscow.

it sealed their fate. Kosior disappeared soon after the announcement that Khrushchev had succeeded him as Ukrainian first secretary. Khrushchev revealed in his secret speech that he was in fact arrested, tortured and then killed. He was not brought to trial, presumably because he never confessed to any of the crimes of which he was supposed to be guilty. With Kosior perished most of the senior Party and government officials of the Ukraine. The majority of these seem to have been arrested before Kosior disappeared and before Khrushchev himself arrived in Kiev; at any rate it is extremely unlikely that the Central Committee which was supposed to have elected Khrushchev in January 1938 still had enough free members to form the necessary quorum.

Khrushchev was accompanied to the Ukraine by a completely new set of chiefs. His six-man politburo contained only one Ukrainian, the Civil-War hero General Timoshenko. Its two most important members apart from Khrushchev (and who in fact constituted a considerable restraint on his freedom of action) were the second secretary Mikhail Burmistenko and the NKVD chief A. I. Uspensky. Burmistenko had overall responsibility for Party appointments, a key position at a time of total purge, and was connected with Malenkov, who was now an extremely powerful figure in the Central Committee apparatus in Moscow where he specialized in Party appointments. The most immediate task before the new men was to rebuild the horribly shattered Party and state apparatus as quickly as possible. To this end Khrushchev called the 14th Ukrainian Party Congress in June and summoned a new Supreme Soviet the next month. The former elected the new Central Committee (Khrushchev was until then technically only 'acting' first secretary), and the latter elected a new government. The extraordinary thoroughness of the purge was reflected in the membership of the Central Committee chosen by the Congress. It was about half the size of its predecessor and included only three members of the old Central Committee. Not surprisingly, few of these new men had previously been well known in the Ukraine. Another result of the purge was the need to recruit a mass of new Party members, and this could not be done without telling severely on the educational level of the Party. Nevertheless Khrushchev and his colleagues seem to have done their work satisfactorily, because from 1939 onward the leadership of the Ukraine remained more or less constant for some ten years.

Although it seems extremely unlikely that Stalin would have taken Khrushchev into his confidence in the planning of the Ukrainian affair, there can have been few of its details that he did not eventually come to know. The repression in the Ukraine began in the late summer and autumn of 1937 – that is, some months before Khrushchev's arrival – but he never avoided taking full praise for his work as Stalin's scourge. The NKVD chief Uspensky declared in June 1938 that 'only after the faithful Stalinist, Nikita Sergeyevich Khrushchev, arrived in the Ukraine did the smashing of the enemies of the people begin in earnest.'* And Khrushchev himself rejected the idea of showing mercy when he told the Ukrainian Party Congress in June 1938 that traitors to the Party and government would be executed to a man, just as Gogol's famous Ukrainian hero Taras Bulba had killed even his own son when he fell in love with a daughter of his Polish enemy. Khrushchev was equally active as a Russianizer. He introduced compulsory Russian into all Ukrainian schools and ordered a Russian-language daily paper to be published in Kiev. The Ukrainian 'bourgeois nationalists', he told the 14th Party Congress, had tried to suppress the Russian language because they knew it 'meant the influence of the teaching of Lenin and Stalin on the minds of the Ukrainian people'. These measures were part of a full-scale campaign to destroy harmful Ukrainian nationalist feeling, and there is no sign that Khrushchev, a Russian who can have spoken only very broken Ukrainian at best, then or later doubted his right to treat another nation in this way.† The Ukrainian affair brought out in Khrushchev the self-confident *Russian* communist who was quite as sure of his

* In fact an NKVD prisoner in Kharkov in 1937 noted that the mass arrests began in the late summer and autumn of that year and that the use of violence against prisoners only became commonplace at the same time. He also calculated that about 5½ per cent of the Kharkov region were arrested between February 1937 and February 1939.

† Khrushchev told a foreign visitor in 1958, 'I know Ukrainian pretty well, but I must admit I also want people to slow down when they speak too fast.' Although two of Khrushchev's Ukrainian Politburo – Burmistenko and Korotchenko – had Ukrainian-sounding names, both were in fact Russian.

ability and right to guide lesser nations as any white imperialist of the nineteenth century.

Khrushchev's takeover of the Ukraine is the most blatantly Stalinist episode in his career. In it we see a man who had accepted total ruthlessness as a legitimate political weapon; who, partly from ignorance and partly from a deep if crude faith that appeared to justify any means, was ready to tolerate the large-scale murder and arrest of critics and supposed opponents. One must never forget that Khrushchev the politician was a creature of Stalin's making. He was created to operate in a system in which no hint of opposition was allowed, and he was finally, with others like him, caught up in a crazy logic that led inexorably to the blood purge. It was largely ignorance in the first place that made him go along with Stalinism; but he would have been useless in the Ukraine had he not also possessed a pitiless toughness still fired by the old revolutionary and class feelings.

So much obloquy has been heaped on Khrushchev as the 'butcher of the Ukraine' that very little attention has been paid to the part of his work there that really did have the power to make or break him – the management of the Ukrainian economy. The Ukrainian purge had waned by the end of 1938 and Khrushchev's NKVD chief Uspensky vanished together with his master Yezhov. From then on Khrushchev's reputation depended primarily on his ability to make the Ukraine work.

It was a vast job. In 1938 the Ukraine accounted for 55 per cent of all the pig iron produced in the Soviet Union; for 35 per cent of the steel; and for over half of its total coal production. It had a population of some 40 million, and was by European standards a large and rich country in its own right. For Khrushchev to be given control of it was a sign of Stalin's confidence not only in his reliability as a Stalinist but also in his ability as an adminstrator. His main immediate task in the Ukraine, however, was to restore its agriculture. The Ukraine, then as now, was one of the main grain-growing areas in the Soviet Union and in 1938 provided well over a quarter of the Soviet government's grain purchases. But the growing food needs of an expanding labour force plus the catastrophic effects of collectivization on Ukrainian farming meant that even more effort had to be got out of the farmers as a matter of the greatest urgency. Khrushchev himself admitted later that he had had little real experience of farming before he went to the Ukraine and what he saw there on his first trips round the collective and state farms was certainly not the best possible introduction to his new interest. The Ukrainian peasants had responded to collectivization like the peasants in Russia, by slaughtering their animals. Between 1929 and 1934 they had lost half of their horses; forty per cent of their cattle; half their pigs; and three quarters of all their sheep.

This first serious encounter with agriculture had extremely important consequences for Khrushchev's later career. In the first place agriculture was a matter of far more immediate political importance in Russia than was imaginable in the rich countries of Western Europe. In a land where bread was the staple food, a bad harvest was the surest cause of popular discontent because it had an immediate effect on the already humble level of consumption: there was no question of making good a harvest failure by imports. This anxious dependence of the politicians on the harvest was to remain an important feature of Soviet politics throughout Khrushchev's active life. The experience he gained in the Ukraine was therefore to stand him in good stead after Stalin's death, when he could genuinely pose as the man most likely to solve this apparently chronic problem.

Secondly, agriculture was the one sphere of economic activity that seemed most likely to respond well to active Party interference. In the Ukraine, where many collective farms had no Party members, let alone Party organizations, an extension of Party control seemed to promise nothing but good. Khrushchev appears to have believed then, as later, that he could master the skills of modern agriculture personally and pass them on to the peasants through an expanding network of Party organizations on the spot. Also unlike industry, where key plants were controlled by rigidly centralized Moscow ministries, agriculture offered local Party organizations, from the republican to the district level, far greater scope for initiative and responsibility. All in all, agriculture seemed excellently suited to a man like Khrushchev who had already shown his conviction that Party officials should not just limit themselves to propaganda but be ready to roll up their sleeves and get their hands dirty. In the Ukraine Khrushchev repeatedly told his local officials to get to know the farms in their area thoroughly. He himself was a tireless traveller round the countryside, at one moment investigating some problem for himself and the next subjecting a district secretary to a thorough examination on farming practice. One meeting of Party officials was told that 'the milk yield of cows will not increase however much you wag your tongue', and another was asked 'What sort of a leader is it who can't provide cabbage?'

The Khrushchev formula may have been simple to the point of crudeness, but it paid off. By 1939, after two harvests under his care, Khrushchev was able to declare the grain problem solved and went on to launch an offensive against the wretched state of livestock farming, revealing that only some sixty per cent of Ukrainian collective farms kept cows at all and that most of these had only ten or less. 'Ten cows to a collective farm,' he remarked; 'that's enough to make a chicken laugh.' Moscow thought well of Khrushchev's work, and he was now launched for the first time as a Party agricultural expert on a national scale. His main Ukrainian agricultural speeches were published by *Pravda* at greater length than those by any other senior Party leader, and he was allowed to take the credit for an important new system of incentive payments to farmers first tried in the Ukraine and then applied throughout the whole country. This growth in stature as a national figure was matched by promotion to candidate membership of the Politburo in 1938 and full membership a year later. He was still not a close associate of Stalin, and his work in the Ukraine obviously kept him away from the centre of political power. Nevertheless his talent as an administrator seemed to assure his future now that the madness of the purges was over.

Chapter 6
War

As ruler of the Ukraine, Khrushchev must have given much thought to the threat of Nazi Germany. The general atmosphere of nervousness about Hitler's intentions was well caught by a message to Stalin from the Kiev Party in early 1939 which described itself as 'living here in a frontier zone, on the border of two worlds' and claimed that it had 'spared no efforts to turn the province of Kiev into an impregnable advance post of Soviet Ukraine'. Khrushchev himself responded in public with that bravado which was to become so familiar to the world in years ahead. In 1938 he gave this typical advice to the Germans:

> Don't dream about the Ukrainian lands, don't hanker after Ukrainian fat although it certainly smells and tastes good. We say ... in the words of the proverb: 'It's good, Masha, but it isn't yours'. 'Have a nice look and pass by.' Remember, if you come after Ukrainian fat, we shall feed you with lead and shells.

For all their bold words, however, the Ukrainian leaders most likely met the Soviet-German pact of August 1939 with considerable relief. While the Western democracies, who had never quite been able to bring themselves to conclude an alliance with Red Russia, expressed horror at the pact's cynicism, Khrushchev and his colleagues must clearly have seen how important was the time it won for the Soviet Union. Equally significant for the Ukraine was the secret agreement within the treaty on the division of Poland which extended the Ukrainian frontier substantially westwards. Planning for the incorporation of the so-called Western Ukraine presumably began immediately after the pact was signed, and the operation itself was launched a few days after the Nazi invasion of Poland in September 1939. It was not pleasant to watch two great powers once again combining to remove Poland from the map, but on the Soviet side the expediency of the move doubtless seemed complete justification. Khrushchev supervised the Soviet occupation on the spot, aided by Ivan Serov, the new Ukrainian N K V D chief who was to have a notoriously successful career in the Soviet security services. Khrushchev crossed into West Ukraine the same day as the Soviet troops and made a triumphant entry into Lvov, its main city, shortly after its capture. The military occupation presented few difficulties: Khrushchev's main problem was to incorporate the nine million inhabitants of the area into the Soviet system as rapidly as possible. This meant deportation of all 'unreliable' elements (including some unfortunate Polish communists who thought they had fled to safety from the Germans); the collectivization of peasant farming; and the creation of a completely new administration based on communist cadres. Khrushchev seems to have carried out the work efficiently and went on to manage a similar though far smaller operation in July 1940, when the Soviet Union annexed Bessarabia from Rumania.

History, with an unusual sense of justice, was however soon to teach Khrushchev and his colleagues what it was like to be overrun themselves. On 22 June 1941 the German army attacked the Soviet Union and within four months occupied almost all the Ukraine. The Soviet troops who had performed to such perfection in the West Ukraine were reduced to confusion. The Ukrainian Party's arrangements for an emergency apparently proved quite inadequate, and as the German soldiers advanced local Party organizations simply disintegrated.* The shock of the first disastrous months of the war with Germany had its impact, too, on Khrushchev's relations with Stalin. Up to the war there is no evidence that Khrushchev ever questioned his leader, but this simple relationship was destroyed by the war, and was never re-established. It is possible, although there is no definite evidence for this, that Khrushchev's belief in Stalin's infallibility was first shaken at the very start of the war. For one thing, Khrushchev saw for himself the chaos caused by the German attack. In the first week of the invasion he spent some time near the front, and years later recounted a horrifying incident to show how bad

* Main casualties in the rush were the political prisoners held in the recently occupied areas of the West Ukraine, many of whom, according to Ukrainian émigré sources, were executed to prevent their falling into German hands.

the panic had been among the Soviet forces. On the fifth or sixth day of the war he had sent a Soviet general to the front with orders for a tank corps operating there. The general came back, in Khrushchev's own words, 'in a grave and confused state. "Everything is lost, things are going as they did in France. The end has come. I shall shoot myself," he said. I tried to stop him: "You are mad, come to your senses!" But before I could do anything he drew his pistol and shot himself on the spot.'

Significantly it was in the section of his secret speech blaming Stalin for the lack of proper Soviet war preparations that Khrushchev made his first reference to himself. He recalled how he had telephoned Malenkov in Moscow for rifles to equip the Ukrainian volunteers and had been told, 'We are sending all our rifles to Leningrad . . . you have to arm yourselves.' Khrushchev's picture of a Stalin who simply refused to believe that Hitler could attack can be dismissed as a ploy to make the dead dictator look ridiculous, and there is anyhow good evidence that Stalin telephoned him on 21 June to warn him that Germany might invade the next day. But the truth behind this charge was Khrushchev's own realization, which must have hit him the moment the Germans attacked, that the brilliant Stalin had made a terrible miscalculation in believing war with Hitler could be avoided any longer. It was this belief which made Stalin so anxious not to annoy the Germans up to the last minute, and also explains his rejection of defence measures proposed by the commander of the Kiev Military District, General Kirponos, as a 'provocation'. For Khrushchev, then, it was not only the Soviet armies that were destroyed on the Ukrainian battlefields in the terrible days of June 1941, but also Stalin's infallibility.

The rapidity of the German advance can have left no time to brood over such discoveries. On 3 July Khrushchev was made senior member of the War Council of the South West Directorate under the command of the veteran cavalryman Marshal Budyonny. A little earlier Stalin had emerged from the state of shock which apparently gripped him for the first days of the war (and which must also have shaken Khrushchev's and others' confidence in him) to create a State Defence Committee to direct the war. Its members were Stalin, Molotov, Voroshilov, Beria (who had succeeded Yezhov as NKVD chief in 1938) and Malenkov. Khrushchev was technically senior to both Beria and Malenkov, who remained only candidate members of the Politburo throughout the war, but he was not even brought into the Council when it was later enlarged. His job throughout the war was rather to represent the Party at the highest level at the front.

During the first year of the war a system of dual military and political command was introduced into the Red Army, allowing Khrushchev and other political officers to take part in purely military decision-making. This system was naturally unpopular with the soldiers and was ended as soon as the chaos and demoralization of the first months of the war were over. From then on Khrushchev was technically limited to the fields of political indoctrination and general leadership, but in practice it must have been hard to set limits to a man of his character, particularly since he had to work at extremely close quarters with military commanders.

Not surprisingly it was the early stages of the war, when matters were going badly, that brought Khrushchev's first personal conflicts with Stalin. By September 1941 the German armies had almost surrounded Kiev, the Ukrainian capital. Budyonny and Khrushchev, as military and political chiefs of the South West Directorate which had its headquarters in Kiev, advised Stalin on 11 September that it was useless to try to stop the German advance and recommended a Soviet withdrawal to the east. This was against the orders of the Stavka (the Soviet Supreme Command), and Stalin rejected it. He also had General Timoshenko flown into Kiev to replace Budyonny and execute the no-retreat policy. The situation continued to deteriorate, and Khrushchev then seems to have ordered on his own initiative that an attempt be made to withdraw through the weakest point in the German circle. General Kirponos, the front's commander, faced with an order that contradicted Stalin's command, dallied and then checked back with the Stavka, which finally agreed to the plan late on 17 September – six days after Khrushchev and Budyonny had first suggested it. The delay brought disaster. Only a very few Soviet troops did escape. Several senior military and political officers were killed while attempting the breakthrough, including Kirponos and Burmistenko, Khrushchev's number two in the Ukrainian Party, and 600,000 Soviet troops were captured in the German net. Khrushchev, Timoshenko and Budyonny apparently managed to escape by air.*

This is Khrushchev's version of the Kiev disaster as told in the official Soviet history of the war published during his days of supremacy. It ignores such things as Budyonny's inability to cope with modern warfare, which was certainly one of the reasons for his replacement, and it does not mention the possibility that the holding action at Kiev won valuable time. Biased though the account may be, the picture of a conflict between the man on the spot and the strategist in the rear is convincing enough. In 1941 the Soviet Union could more easily spare men than time, but it was far easier for the Stavka to accept the implications of this than for Khrushchev, whose men had to suffer. Also before the war there had always been a political-ideological 'reason' for any of Stalin's decisions which Khrushchev might have been tempted to jib at. But the language of war was simpler than that of politics and lent itself less easily to devious justifications. The war, in fact, had given Khrushchev no less than his first chance to place his own judgement on virtually even terms with Stalin's.

Within months there was another conflict between the two men. After Kiev the Soviet armies in the Ukraine were in unbroken retreat, and Khrushchev with them. In the early spring of 1942 the Stavka produced a plan for a Ukrainian counter-offensive, but this was soon abandoned in favour of a more modest scheme to retake Kharkov. Khrushchev was a member of the military council of the South West Front (the old South West

* A boy's adventure story account of Khrushchev's evacuation of Kharkov the following month was given by the Soviet paper *Izvestiya* in February 1963. Colonel Starinov, a mine expert, was called in to mine the city before the Soviet abandoned it. Khrushchev insisted that his own HQ, a solid one-storey house at 17 Dzerzhinsky Street, be mined like all the rest. In spite of this Khrushchev refused to leave the HQ until the last moment, although the delayed action fuse had already been set, so as not to arouse the suspicion of the German scouts. The mine exploded on 14 November killing the German Commander-in-Chief General Georg von Braun, cousin of the now American rocket scientist.

Directorate had been reorganized) whose troops, under General Timoshenko, were to be involved in the operation. In the secret speech he described at length how he had tried to persuade Stalin that the plan would fail. In particular he told how he had telephoned General Vasilevsky at the Stavka and 'begged':

'Alexander Mikhailovich, take a map ... and show Comrade Stalin the situation which has developed.' We should note that Stalin planned operations on a globe. Yes, Comrades, he used to take the globe and trace the front line on it. I said to Comrade Vasilevsky: 'Show him the situation on a map; in the present situation we cannot continue the operation which was planned. The old decision must be changed for the good of the cause.'

Vasilevsky replied, saying that Stalin had already studied this problem and that he, Vasilevsky, would not see Stalin further concerning this matter, because the latter didn't want to hear any arguments on the subject of this operation. After my talk with Vasilevsky I telephoned to Stalin at his villa. But Stalin did not answer the telephone and Malenkov was at the receiver. I told Comrade Malenkov that I was calling from the front and that I wanted to speak personally to Stalin. Stalin informed me through Malenkov that I should speak with Malenkov. I stated for the second time that I wished to inform Stalin personally about the grave situation which had arisen for us at the front. But Stalin did not find it convenient to raise the phone and again stated that I should speak to him through Malenkov, although he was only a few steps from the telephone.

After 'listening' in this manner to our plea, Stalin said, 'Let everything remain as it is.'

The Kharkov operation ended in the rout of three Soviet armies and the capture of 200,000 Soviet prisoners, a terrible enough justification of Khrushchev's warning. The almost ridiculous detail with which Khrushchev described the incident in the secret speech suggests that it had rankled with him for years, although it is also true that anxiety to discredit Stalin led him into absurd exaggerations, like the claim that Stalin used only a globe for military planning. (In memoirs published after Khrushchev's fall Marshal Konyev went out of his way to describe Stalin working with large-scale maps.) But whatever the exact extent of his feelings at the time, they must certainly have contained, as after the Kiev débâcle, a suspicion of Stalin that would have been unimaginable before the war.

Shortly after the defeat at Kharkov the Stalingrad front was established, and Khrushchev became political representative on its Military Council. Stalingrad was to occupy a unique place in Soviet recollections of the war, being popularly considered the war's turning-point and the high point of Soviet heroism. Stalin, who for the first unsuccessful year of the war had remained uncharacteristically out of the limelight, began to develop the cult of his own military genius after Stalingrad, thereby diminishing the glory of his lieutenants. After Stalin's death Khrushchev in turn influenced the histories of the battle so that political enemies like Malenkov and Marshal Zhukov mysteriously disappeared, while exaggerated attention was given to his own part in the victory. His distortion of events at Stalingrad was all the more absurd because there is no doubt that he had a very real claim to a share in the glory.

Khrushchev was with the Soviet armies as they were pushed back to the city on the west bank of the Volga in the summer of 1942. It was then perfectly clear that if Stalingrad was lost, German possession of the invaluable Caucasian oilfields would be complete and that even the great defence industries of the Urals would be threatened. Stalingrad, partly because of its name, had also come to stand for the whole of Soviet resistance to Germany, and Hitler in turn was obsessed with its destruction. By August the situation was so grim that even the commander on the spot, General Gordov, seems to have lost heart. He was replaced in that same month by General Yeremenko, with whom Khrushchev worked closely throughout the rest of the battle. In his memoirs Yeremenko described the impression Khrushchev made on him – the two men had not met before. With due allowance for the fact that the memoirs were published during Khrushchev's days of power, when a more critical appreciation was out of the question, they probably contain enough of Yeremenko's real feelings to be worth citing:

> At first sight N. S. Khrushchev seemed to me weary and tired, but the preoccupation and agitation with which he carried on the conversation spoke of the fact that he was full of energy.... His worker's simplicity and sincerity at once won over the person he was talking to. He gave the impression of a gifted man of great intelligence who knows

something particularly important which gives him the ability to solve the most difficult problems.

On 23 August the Germans launched a heavy attack on the city accompanied by intensive bombardment. The damage to Stalingrad, which had had no rain for two months and had many wooden buildings, was appalling. Yeremenko and Khrushchev spent most of the day at their Command Post in the city, surfacing occasionally to survey the ruins. 'One had to undergo a great deal in the last war,' Yeremenko comments in his book, 'but what we saw on 23 August struck us as an oppressive nightmare.' Khrushchev's work was considerably increased by Stalin's decision made the same night that neither Stalingrad's civilians nor its industry were to be evacuated; he is reputed to have said simply, 'I shall not discuss the matter.' In the event the city's factories continued to turn out tanks and guns even during street fighting.

Khrushchev's importance in the Stalingrad battle was as one of a team. Apart from the direction from Moscow, Stalin was represented on the spot from August to December by Malenkov, who as a member of the Defence Council had seniority over everyone else. And there were also visits by Generals Zhukov, Vasilevsky and others from the Stavka who were finally responsible for the brilliant counter-offensive which destroyed the German forces. But it is very likely that Khrushchev brought his own methods to the 'political work' that was in theory his preserve. Just how much he included under this heading is suggested by advice he gave to heads of political departments on the Voronezh front in 1943: 'Political work is everything by which the fighting man lives – the conditions of his weapons, his training, his food – all this is included in the political officers' field of work.' The man who before the war had told Ukrainian Party officials to get mud on their boots is instantly recognizable. Yeremenko also describes the sort of on-the-spot work done by Khrushchev during the last two weeks before the great counter-offensive was launched, and it has a familiar ring. 'From the beginning of November right up to the attack Nikita Sergeyevich was almost never at the Command Post, spending all the time among the formations and units. It was necessary to check the placing of Communists and Komsomol [Communist Youth Organization] members, to direct tested Soviet people to the most responsible sectors.'*

The most apt comment on Khrushchev's part in the Stalingrad battle was made after it was all over. At a dinner given to celebrate the victory General Shumilov, commander of the Soviet 64th Army which captured the German commander-in-chief Von Paulus, presented Khrushchev with the German's personal revolver, and Khrushchev later gave it to Yeremenko, who was ill at the time of the dinner. The honour was to the men under Yeremenko's and Khrushchev's command, but there is no doubt that their leaders were worthy of them.

Shortly after Stalingrad Khrushchev was made a Lieutenant-General, which was apparently a formalizing of his status rather than promotion, and as a member of the Military Council of the Voronezh front took part in the battle of the Kursk Bulge, one of the most fearsome of all German-Soviet encounters. But with the Soviet army now advancing, Khrushchev's work as leader of the Ukrainian Party also increased. He was ultimately responsible for the organization of the Ukrainian partisan movement and of the clandestine Party organization behind the German lines in the Ukraine which now began to flourish. At the same time the land freed by the Soviet troops demanded immediate attention. In August 1943 Kharkov, the second city of the Ukraine, was liberated, and the capital Kiev in the following November. By the next July, when Khrushchev entered Lvov with the Soviet army, the whole of the Ukraine was free of German troops. The war had left the Ukraine so devastated that it seems almost cruel to talk of the benefits it brought Khrushchev. But in two important ways it left him a bigger man. First he had learnt that it was possible to look at Stalin critically. And second, he had experienced modern warfare with an intensity

* Marshal Chuikov, in his reminiscences of Stalingrad, gives a more curious example of the work required of Khrushchev. Chuikov wrote that in November the Deputy Chief of the Rear of the Soviet Army, General Vinogradov, insisted on supplying Stalingrad with mountains of clothing and food although what the troops needed most was ammunition. 'Only the interference of N. S. Khrushchev,' according to Chuikov, 'stopped the flood of fur hats and felt boots into Stalingrad. Soon Vinogradov went away and we breathed a sigh of relief.'

that few professional politicians outside the Soviet Union could match. In years to come, and in a way then quite unforeseeable, this experience was to mean a great deal to the world.

Chapter 7
The Ukrainian Phoenix

Almost immediately after the liberation of Kiev in 1943 Khrushchev sent a letter to the Central Committee in Moscow describing the chaos and destruction that he had to repair:

> The Germans have plundered almost all the houses in the city; from some even the door handles have been removed, the window sills pulled out, doors, window frames, parquet and marble tiles torn up. . . . Kiev gives the impression of an extinct town. The inhabitants are now coming back in large groups from the surrounding woods, marshes, ravines and cemetery crypts. They make a heavy impression from the horrors, humiliations and deprivations that they have undergone. . . . We are now occupied with establishing order in the city, with checking the property that has survived, and with the re-establishment of the most important sectors of the city's economy.

For the second time in his life, though now of course on a scale many times larger, Khrushchev had to put together what war had shot to pieces. The years spent rebuilding the Ukraine after the Second World War formed as essential a part of Khrushchev's experience of war as the months spent at the front itself. When this experience was later combined with knowledge of the facts of nuclear warfare, it was to produce a statesman deeply committed to the preservation of peace on Soviet soil.

Khrushchev had already felt the horror of war at the most personal level when his eldest son, a fighter pilot, was killed in action. More mixed emotions were stirred by a visit at the end of the war to his native village, Kalinovka (made apparently at Stalin's suggestion). He found that the peasants got no pay for work on the collective farm and consequently did nothing. When he procured some horses for the farm, they had to be sent away because there was no food for them. Khrushchev recalled:

> On one hand, it was sad to see a completely destroyed village. . . . On the other there was a feeling of anger against the indifference of people. I made a speech to the kolkhozniks . . . but for them I was just like some sort of Martian, coming from who knows where and trying to make

people believe in their own capabilities. I think there were . . . some who waited for me to go and stop rubbing salt into their wounds.*

In a way the Ukraine was Kalinovka writ large, because there too the work of reconstruction was hindered by the many Ukrainians who were not only indifferent but even hostile to these efforts. This was partly because of the exhaustion inevitable after such a war, but it was also caused by the old Ukrainian antagonism to Russia which the war had released and which might well have helped the Germans considerably had Hitler not alienated all potential support by his barbaric racial policies. Ukrainian nationalist guerrillas nevertheless continued to operate on some scale after the war, claiming among their victims the gifted Russian liberator of Kiev, General Vatutin. Stalin, according to Khrushchev, would have deported the whole Ukrainian people as a punishment for collaboration (as he did some of the small nations of the Caucasus) and was only prevented 'because there were too many of them and there was no place to which to deport them'. But the Ukrainians in fact got no more sympathy from Khrushchev. At a meeting to celebrate Kiev's freedom in 1943 Khrushchev had inspired the acceptance of a 'letter' from the Ukrainian to the Russian people which read in part: 'On the high hills of Kiev . . . we stand and look to the East. There is the land of the great Russian people. From there came freedom.' Khrushchev had no doubt that the sort of freedom he brought as a Russian and a communist was the best, and he showed no toleration towards Ukrainians who thought otherwise.

The Ukraine suffered more war damage than any other part of Europe. The Soviet authorities had evacuated a remarkable amount of its most important industries before the German advance. The Germans in turn sent two million Ukrainians to forced labour in Germany, and took with them millions of farm animals and as much industrial equipment as possible when

* Khrushchev was the only Soviet leader of his day who publicly admitted that peasants could be sullen and discontented. After Stalin's death he told how in 1951 he had visited a collective farm near Moscow where potatoes were being planted according to a method he had suggested. 'The kolkhozniks looked at me suspiciously,' he said, 'as if to say "Here's the one who thought up the new method". . . . I began to joke but there was no answer as though they were thinking "It's all very well for you to joke."'

they in turn retreated. Ten million Ukrainians were left homeless. In early 1946, an UNRRA report described the situation:

> The pattern is fairly uniform. Many plants were completely destroyed and those which still stood were usually heavily damaged and almost universally gutted of all modern equipment.... So great is the destruction that there are competing calls upon the limited supplies of manpower, equipment and materials. We observed many instances of ingenious adaptation and salvaging of old and antiquated machinery; yet restoration was everywhere complicated by lack of equipment.... Low calorie diets, caused by lack of foodstuffs, cause low efficiency and slow production.

The reliance of the whole Soviet Union on the Ukraine for so much of its grain and coal (at that time still the main Soviet fuel) as well as the importance of its heavy industry made its restoration a major national undertaking, and one third of the capital investment of the Soviet Five-Year Plan of 1946 was assigned to the Ukraine. For Khrushchev it was a major sign of Stalin's confidence in his ability to be given the job of supervising this work in the double role of Ukrainian Party leader and Prime Minister – a post he had held since just before the war's end. As before the war, agriculture offered him his biggest chance, because a good deal of the industrial reconstruction was directed by Moscow. It was his second experience of having to cope with an agricultural crisis, and although he was to have others, this was by far the most challenging. The collective farm system had literally disintegrated, particularly in the West Ukraine, where it had never had a proper chance to take root, and the problem of the Party's presence on the farms was more acute than ever. In 1945, the first complete year of Ukrainian liberation, only half of the pre-war grain area was sown. The poor yields were largely reaped and threshed by hand, and by women. That autumn Khrushchev told Party officials that cows should be used for farm work where no tractors or horses were available. After the war as before it, Khrushchev believed that he saw in the Ukraine proof of the direct relationship between increased production and the Party's presence on the farms. At the same time everything he learnt in these situations of agricultural crisis encouraged a method that was energetic and crude rather than restrained and subtle.

Khrushchev spent in all ten years of peace and war in the Ukraine. It has been suggested that the war provoked for the first time in him a critical attitude towards Stalin. Similarly his relative independence from Stalin and from the cramping stuffiness of Moscow that he enjoyed in the Ukraine seems to have allowed him to develop both his own political personality and style. While in the years after the war Stalin's autocracy approached the point of paranoia, and even his senior colleagues were plunged into mutual suspicion and fear, Khrushchev ran the Ukrainian Party on more or less legal Party lines. Its Central Committee met regularly, unlike the Soviet Central Committee, and something not unlike collective leadership seems to have existed. When the time came for Khrushchev's own fight for power after 1953, he seemed far fresher than his rivals who had languished for so long in Stalin's Kremlin.

This difference in Khrushchev was sensed by a Yugoslav Communist delegation that passed through Kiev at the end of the war. Its impressions were recorded by Milovan Djilas, who was then very close to Tito, and they are so vivid as to be worth quoting at length. The Yugoslavs found that Khrushchev, unlike other Soviet leaders,

> was unrestrained and very talkative, although like them he was fond of using folk proverbs and sayings. This was a kind of fashion at the time and proof of one's ties with the people. With him, however, there was less artificiality about this because of his naturally simple and unaffected behaviour and manner of speaking. Unlike Stalin's humour, which was predominantly intellectual and, as such, cynical, Khrushchev's humour was typically folksy and thus often almost crude, but it was lively and inexhaustible.... The commonplaces with which his conversation abounds are the expression of both real ignorance and Marxist maxims learnt by rote, but even these he presents with conviction and frankness.

A member of the UNRRA team that worked in the Ukraine after the war had been impressed by Khrushchev's concern for the smallest details of the work under his care – even to the extent of keeping on his desk an assortment of tiles, cinder blocks and other building materials – and Djilas also noted this.

> He was the only one among the Soviet leaders who delved into details, into the daily life of the Communist rank and file and the

ordinary people.... He did not do this with the aim of changing the system, but of strengthening and improving things under the existing system. He did look into matters and remedy them, while others issued orders from offices and received reports.

None of the Soviet leaders went to collective farms, except occasionally to attend some feast or parade. Khrushchev accompanied us to a collective farm and, without harbouring in any little corner of his mind the slightest doubt of the justice of the system itself, he not only clinked huge glasses of vodka with the collective farmers, but he also inspected the garden hotbeds, peeped into the pigsty, and began discussing practical problems. During the ride back to Kiev he kept coming back to the question of the collective farms and openly talked about their shortcomings.

We could see his extraordinarily practical sense on a grand scale at a meeting of the economic sections of the Ukrainian Government. Unlike Yugoslav ministers, his commissars were excellently acquainted with matters and, what was more important, they assessed possibilities realistically.*

Djilas's picture of Khrushchev in 1945 has a striking likeness to the Khrushchev of the post-Stalin era, and indeed this is not surprising. Khrushchev was now fifty-one, and although he retained throughout his career a great ability to adapt ('like all practical men', Djilas noted), his personality was by now obviously set. But the relative freedom to develop in his own way that this period in the Ukraine (including his work at the front in wartime) had given him was not without its dangers, and in 1947 he was caught in a storm that threatened to end his career and perhaps even his life.

* This description of how the Ukrainian Government worked under Khrushchev compares curiously with the latter's account – no doubt exaggerated – of how Stalin on one occasion in his last years forced his ministers to approve a draft plan they had not even seen by asking: 'Who is against it?' Stalin then went off to watch a film, remarking with evident pleasure, 'We took them for a good ride.'

Chapter 8
First Crisis

The trouble began, as it so often does in the Soviet Union, with the peasants and the land. After a winter of little rain or snow the Ukraine was hit in the summer of 1946 by the worst drought since 1891, and the harvest was disastrous. There was already strict food rationing, but even this was possible only because of UN Relief Agency (UNRRA) supplies that were soon to end. By October the honouring of ration cards had become very irregular, and by December the only food to be found in Kiev was bread, sugar and tinned vegetables. An UNRRA report that winter said that its medical officer had already discovered clinical starvation in some smaller villages and commented, 'Everything depends on the 1947 harvest. Meanwhile the next three or four months are expected to be the worst period since the famine of 1922.' The agricultural crisis might alone have been enough to justify Khrushchev's replacement as Ukrainian Party leader by his old patron Kaganovich in March 1947. A failure in the 1947 harvest would have meant serious political as well as economic trouble, and Kaganovich, with his past Ukrainian experience, his proven skill as a troubleshooter and his special relationship with Khrushchev, was certainly the obvious choice for new overlord of the Ukraine.

But nothing was as simple as this in post-war Soviet politics. At various times after the war Stalin's behaviour towards his colleagues appeared alarmingly like that of a lion-tamer stepping back and watching his animals maul each other so as to lessen their threat to him. In 1946 he seemed to be tolerating in just this spirit a battle between his close associate Malenkov and the tough and dogmatic Andrei Zhdanov. In this year Zhdanov issued the famous decrees on ideological purity that were to blight Soviet cultural life for years ahead, and it is possible that he even managed for a time to push Malenkov out of his key job as Central Committee secretary. Their rivalry may have begun during the war when Malenkov was appointed to the State

Defence Committee over the heads of full Politburo members like Zhdanov (and Khrushchev). After Zhdanov's death in 1948 – from natural causes, as far as is known – Malenkov was to purge all Zhdanov's supporters in Leningrad, where the latter had been Party leader for ten years.

Stalin's reasons for allowing this rivalry are obscure. Perhaps he thought Malenkov was becoming too powerful; perhaps he even considered removing him altogether and then changed his mind. There is similar doubt about what Stalin meant to do with Khrushchev. He too was almost certainly found wanting by the stern test of Zhdanovism. But it is also probable that Malenkov was trying to undermine Khrushchev – although Malenkov's own influence was apparently on the wane. Khrushchev himself later suggested that Malenkov tried to damage him during the Ukrainian crisis, but he also claimed that he had been the victim of Stalin's capriciousness. The incident is so important as a stage in Khrushchev's relations with Stalin and as one of the sources of his conflict with Malenkov which was to dominate Soviet politics after 1953 that it bears examining in some detail. It also has surprising relevance to other episodes in Khrushchev's career and in particular to his final removal from power.

Apart from the agricultural crisis, of which there was no open talk, Khrushchev's leadership was publicly criticized on two other counts in 1946. The first clearly related to the Zhdanov decrees earlier in the year. In August Khrushchev had to tell the Ukrainian Central Committee that Moscow considered they had 'underestimated the particular importance of ideological work' to the extent of tolerating instances of bourgeois nationalism. The next month the Soviet central press launched an attack on nationalism in Ukrainian cultural life, and some well-known Ukrainian writers and academics were accordingly removed from their posts in the cultural bureaucracy. Was Zhdanov gunning for Khrushchev as well as Malenkov? Khrushchev in later years never said anything about this, but then the accusation that Malenkov had destroyed Zhdanov's supporters in Leningrad was an important part of his own campaign against Malenkov, and it would scarcely have served his interests to reveal that he too had been an enemy of Zhdanov.

But Moscow's quarrel with the Ukraine was not just related

to agricultural and ideological matters. Khrushchev also disclosed in August 1946 that he had had to give the Soviet Central Committee earlier that summer an account of all aspects of the Ukrainian Committee's work and that Moscow believed that 'serious faults and mistakes' had been committed in the important field of cadres' policy. Cadres' policy concerned everything to do with Party appointments and personnel, and it was the key department of power in the Soviet and republican Central Committees. Malenkov had controlled overall cadres' policy from Moscow for several years and even during his eclipse in 1946 probably kept tabs on it through his associate N. N. Shatalin, who was officially the head of the Cadres' Directorate in Moscow. An attack on Ukrainian (i.e. Khrushchev's) cadres' policy was therefore very probably inspired by Malenkov.

Khrushchev's position by the late summer of 1946 was clearly precarious, but the final stage of the crisis apparently did not come until a meeting of the Soviet Central Committee in February 1947, when it appeared in the unlikely shape of a dispute over the respective merits of spring and winter wheat. Shortly after the 22nd Party Congress in 1961 Khrushchev gave his own account of this plenum which, though far from frank, suggests that both Stalin and Malenkov were out to damage him. According to Khrushchev Stalin was greatly impressed by the argument of an agronomist at the plenum in favour of spring wheat, and it is likely (though Khrushchev did not say this) that Khrushchev's own preference for winter wheat was held against him in the light of the 1946 harvest failure. Khrushchev argued that spring wheat was suitable for the Urals and Siberia but not for the Ukraine, only to be sharply rebuked by Stalin with the words 'Incorrect. ... You've also got black earth.' The plenum then went on to include in its resolution a section criticizing the Ukrainians for ignoring spring wheat, which was the nearest anyone came to admitting the Ukrainian harvest disaster. 'True,' Khrushchev added, 'my name was not mentioned, but everyone who knew something of the heart of the matter understood that it was directed against me personally.' He said he had tried to persuade Stalin to criticize the other areas guilty of the same neglect, but Stalin refused. 'It was clear that he only wanted to hit the Ukraine. And then Kaganovich came....'

Khrushchev was clearly implying that Stalin wanted to damage the Ukraine and himself for reasons other than a mere dispute over agriculture, but he did not elaborate on this. Although it was in Khrushchev's interest in 1961 to show himself as an innocent victim of Stalin's plotting there is some evidence to suggest that he really was threatened in 1947. He had tried hard in the latter part of 1946 to put right the faults Moscow had discovered in the Ukraine by a massive turnover of Party personnel and probably by a good many arrests of suspected 'nationalists', but it was clear that worse was to come after the February 1947 plenum. The blow fell at the beginning of March with the announcement that the posts of First Secretary and Premier were to be divided and that Kaganovich was to take over the former and by far the most important, while Khrushchev kept the premiership. At the same time Khrushchev had to give up his first secretaryship of the Kiev city and region Party committees. Kaganovich brought with him a man from the Central Committee in Moscow, Nikolai Patolichev (later Foreign Trade Minister under Khrushchev), to be second secretary in charge of agriculture – another obvious slap at Khrushchev. Khrushchev was still allowed to give a long report on agriculture to the Ukrainian Central Committee on 10 March and to put the blame for ignoring Stalin's sudden appetite for spring wheat on the Ukrainian Minister of Agriculture. He even put in a good word for winter wheat, saying that spring wheat sowings should not be increased at the latter's expense. But from early May to early September Khrushchev did not appear. His presence was not reported at occasions like meetings of the Supreme Soviet which the Prime Minister would normally have attended, although his name did not vanish entirely from the Ukrainian press. Then, in the first week of September, papers carried a photograph of him with the rest of the Ukrainian leadership, and perhaps significantly Patolichev was moved to another job about the same time. Khrushchev now edged his way back to safety and in December 1947 took over the first secretaryship from Kaganovich.

If Khrushchev really was in dangerous disgrace in mid-1947, his recovery was quick and complete. The most likely explanation for his troubles is that he had fallen foul of Stalin's campaign against Ukrainian nationalism. This was suggested by Khrushchev himself in a 1957 speech which told how he defended the well-known Ukrainian poet Maxim Rylsky from Kaganovich's charge that he was a 'Ukrainian bourgeois nationalist'; an accusation, Khrushchev added meaningfully, that 'could have led to drastic consequences not only for literature'. A few years later he elaborated on this. 'Stalin', according to Khrushchev, 'intended to wipe out a considerable part of the creative intelligentsia' of the Ukraine. On the 'instigation' of Beria and Kaganovich, he had made plans towards this end, 'and if the Ukrainian Bolsheviks had yielded to Stalin's intentions at the time, the intelligentsia of the Ukraine presumably would have experienced great losses, and in all probability a "case" of Ukrainian nationalists would have been created.' The implication is that Khrushchev himself was largely responsible for stopping this, but it is hard to see how his own position in 1947 was strong enough to allow such a daring stand. It is by no means impossible that Stalin should have suspected Khrushchev of softness towards Ukrainian nationalism. He was now a very suspicious man and in a few years' time he was to have doubts about men much closer to him than Khrushchev ever was and even probably to consider their elimination. More curious still there is a story recorded by the American journalist C. L. Sulzburger – told him by the King of Greece, who had heard it from Marshal Tito in 1955, who in his turn said that he had heard it from Khrushchev on his Yugoslav visit earlier that year – that Khrushchev had 'almost been purged by Stalin as a Ukrainian separatist'. This certainly does suggest that Stalin was contemplating a 'case' against Khrushchev as well as the Ukrainians; but acceptance of the story must be qualified, since in 1955 it was obviously useful for Khrushchev to persuade Tito that he had nearly been Stalin's victim too.

Whatever the truth, Stalin must have changed his mind. But Malenkov, on the other hand, continued to intrigue against Khrushchev – according to Khrushchev. In his account of the February 1947 plenum, Khrushchev said that eventually (presumably in 1948) Stalin agreed to change his policy on spring wheat for the Ukraine but that Malenkov and A. I. Kozlov, then head of the Central Committee's Agricultural Section and later Minister for State Farms, 'forced' the well-known geneticist Lysenko and one of his pupils to write an article in favour of spring wheat and against winter wheat. It was in devious ways like these that the Soviet politicians pursued their squabbles under Stalin and even later; the persistence with which Khrushchev hounded Kozlov after 1953, finally removing him after Malenkov's defeat in 1955, adds credibility to this story. But why should there have been antagonism between Malenkov and Khrushchev in the first place? Although there is no evidence of earlier quarrels between them, there were many occasions when their respective authorities could have clashed. Malenkov's word stretched into the Ukraine when Khrushchev first went there in 1938 through Mikhail Burmistenko (see page 53). Khrushchev could well have felt, along with Zhdanov, that his own seniority was snubbed by Malenkov's appointment to the State Defence Committee in the war. The two men spent the critical months at Stalingrad in 1942 together, which gave opportunities enough for Malenkov's new seniority to irk Khrushchev. And after the war Malenkov, as chairman of a committee supervising the rehabilitation of Soviet territory occupied by the Germans, again had a chance to collide with Khrushchev.

It is easier to understand Khrushchev's resentment of Malenkov at this time than *vice versa*. Malenkov's closeness to Stalin over many years, which gave him an importance above his official seniority; his control, before and after the war, of Party cadres throughout the Soviet Union; his qualities as an 'intellectual' – these were all reasons why Khrushchev should fear and dislike him. But just why Malenkov should have wanted to damage Khrushchev at this moment is not so apparent. Khrushchev certainly did not threaten him as Zhdanov had done. Yet Khrushchev's story does have the ring of truth. If he had simply wanted to produce an anecdote damaging to Malenkov, surely he could have thought of something more sensational.

The next act in the Khrushchev-Malenkov drama was to take place after Khrushchev's transfer to Moscow in 1949. But the story of his 1946–7 troubles is not yet over. In Khrushchev's account to the Ukrainian Central Committee in August 1946 of Moscow's analysis of Ukrainian shortcomings, he detailed a list of faults in the technique of Party work and management. He came back to this theme in one of his first speeches after his restoration in a way that made it clear that he was expiating his own personal sins. These sins went to the very core of Khrushchev's style of work as we have watched it develop. Moscow's central criticism was that the Ukrainian Party under Khrushchev had become too deeply involved in the economic management of the republic, to the extent of even 'replacing' government and economic organs. Many Ukrainian Party workers, according to the Soviet Central Committee's resolution, had 'taken on themselves the solving of all current, even petty, questions', and political work had as a result been ignored. The most sensational example of fusion between Party and government bodies cited was the payment of premiums to Party workers, by factories and economic organs, according to production results, as though they were managerial staff. There is no doubt that Khrushchev had led the way in this. As both first secretary and Prime Minister, he had every chance to push the Party deeper and deeper into the work which personally absorbed him most – the concrete management of economic construction. In doing so he clearly distorted the division of functions among the Party, government and economic bureaucracy, a division which was – and still is – central to the Soviet system.* Khrushchev had not been content to stick to the traditional sphere of Party activities, which included the selection of personnel for all important jobs, political education of the masses and organizing support for the execution of Party and government decisions. This 'deviation' was clearly shown in his handling of the plenums of the Ukrainian Central Committee: too many people outside the Central Committee were invited to them, and they discussed too often economic matters, with the result (in the words of the Soviet Central Committee's resolution) that 'the plenums were turned from directive organs into instructional meetings'.

* A few other local Parties besides the Ukrainian were accused of the same fault. Malenkov mentioned this in a speech in September 1947: 'During the war Party organs were frequently compelled to engage in operational work in directing the economy. This was correct under the circumstances. One cannot help but see, however, that this engendered certain negative features in the work of Party organs, resulted ... in the replacement of state and economic organs. One of the fundamental tenets of Bolshevik leadership was violated.' In Khrushchev's case the conditions during and immediately after the war which had demanded increased Party activity simply justified methods that he already preferred.

Khrushchev's idiosyncratic approach might have passed uncriticized had it not been for the increasing attention paid in 1946 and 1947 to political and ideological work under Zhdanov's inspiration, and had the Ukraine not particularly called for active political work because of its special national – and in the West Ukraine even class – problems. Khrushchev may have moderated his methods when he returned to power at the end of 1947, and certainly his opportunity to apply them was somewhat limited by the continued division of the jobs of first secretary and Premier. But these methods were to reappear in his struggle for power after Stalin's death and in the years of his supremacy, right down to the handling of Soviet Central Committee plenums as he had once handled Ukrainian ones and to suggestions that premium payments geared to production increases be introduced for Party workers throughout the Soviet Union. This is not surprising, because Khrushchev would not have been Khrushchev otherwise. His style of work reflected his experience, his abilities and his weaknesses, and it is hard to see how he could have changed it at this stage. The Ukrainian episode for the first time showed the dangers involved in his methods, dangers which were to threaten him again in the future and finally contribute to his downfall.

Chapter 9
Moscow and Stalin

The rest of Khrushchev's stay in the Ukraine passed off successfully and uneventfully. However deep Stalin's distrust of Khrushchev had been in 1946 and 1947, he was now apparently prepared to forget it sufficiently at the end of 1949 to bring him to Moscow as head of the Party organization there and at the same time include him in the Central Committee secretariat. For the next three years Khrushchev was to be nearer than he had ever been to Stalin and better placed to pursue the struggle for power among the other Soviet leaders. But these were by no means unqualified advantages. Stalin was now a capricious and extremely suspicious man, and typically his purpose in bringing Khrushchev to Moscow was to counterbalance Malenkov, who after the death of Zhdanov had acquired perhaps too much power. Khrushchev's old disagreements with Malenkov very probably increased his qualifications for the new job in Stalin's eyes. Once again the lion-tamer was standing back to watch his animals spend their fury on each other.

Khrushchev was later to give lurid accounts of Stalin at this period. He was, Khrushchev said, 'a profoundly sick man who suffered from suspiciousness and persecution mania....' In his secret speech Khrushchev described how Stalin 'could look at a man and say, "Why are your eyes so shifty today?" or "Why do you turn so much today and avoid looking me directly in the eyes?"' This picture of Stalin as a half-crazed ogre was an essential part of Khrushchev's explanation, in 1956 and after, that the terrible abuses of Stalinism were basically the responsibility of Stalin alone. But however much he may have exaggerated to this end, it is certain that Khrushchev's three years in Moscow did involve a further deterioration in his relations with Stalin and perhaps – though this can only be speculation – even some painful heart-searching about the course of Soviet development.

There was of course no sign in public that Khrushchev or any other Soviet politician disagreed in any way with the Stalin line.

Together with the rest of his colleagues Khrushchev paid fulsome tribute to his leader in the columns of *Pravda* on Stalin's seventieth birthday in December 1949: 'Glory to our dear father, our wise teacher, to the brilliant leader of the Party, of the Soviet people and of the workers of the entire world, Comrade Stalin,' Khrushchev concluded his article. Without such ritual praise no politician could have hoped to survive. But in Moscow the personalities of the two men must surely have ground against each other. Khrushchev was energetic and extrovert and even in those days thrived on contact with people in a way more suited to American than Stalinist Russian politics. Stalin was the antithesis. Khrushchev's descriptions of Stalin's secluded life reflect his astonishment that a leader could live as he did. Stalin's only trips, said Khrushchev, 'were to his dacha and the Kremlin.... And he was afraid to go around the town, he was scared of people. The man shut himself up in an armour-plated box. What sort of a life is that without links with the people?' It is very likely that Stalin in turn found Khrushchev an extremely able and tough administrator but at the same time despised him for his intellectual clumsiness and even found him slightly ridiculous. The story that he made Khrushchev dance the gopak to amuse him has the ring of truth about it. Khrushchev once told how Stalin would say 'of people who had come from a working-class background ... "This one's come out from under a machine. Where does he think he's going?"', and perhaps he may have suffered from this attitude himself. (By comparison Malenkov was something of an intellectual – he even used classical references in his speeches – and came from a middle-class family.)

To make matters worse, there seems to have been almost from the start of Khrushchev's work in Moscow a basic difference in the attitude of the two men towards agriculture, which was to be Khrushchev's main preoccupation on the national scale until he provoked Stalin's open opposition. Khrushchev had come from the Ukraine full of ideas about farming, especially the need to amalgamate small collective farms into large ones. The purpose of this was to strengthen Party control over the farms and create more efficient production units (there were far too few rural Party members to go round a large number of small farms) and at the same time to improve the living standard of the peasants by grouping them in larger villages with the comforts and services of a small town. It was this latter aim that was to cause all the trouble, because, unlike Khrushchev, Stalin was apparently indifferent to the deplorable state of peasant life in spite of Khrushchev's efforts to rouse him. Khrushchev later recalled how after his first tour round the Moscow region farms Stalin asked for his impressions. 'I answered, "Many buildings and houses are dilapidated. Here and there windows are stuffed up with straw.... What's more important – many peasants have no incentive to increase collective farm production. The young men have left for the cities, leaving the girls alone with no one to marry."' Given such conditions it must have been difficult to put up with Stalin's unconcern, and part of Khrushchev's frustration evidently overflowed into his later descriptions of Stalin's ignorance about the real state of affairs in the countryside. Certainly Khrushchev's story that Stalin was taken in by films of peasants eating plump turkeys until Khrushchev told him they were actors gorging themselves on food bought by the Ministry of Cinematography is ridiculous. The truth was that Stalin was interested in getting as much out of the peasants in return for as little as possible, and that he found Khrushchev's genuine concern for the peasants irrelevant and possibly dangerous. Interestingly, Khrushchev once remarked that Stalin shortly after the war had called him a 'narodnik'* who was 'losing the proletarian class sense' for suggesting that peasants were taxed too high. This different attitude of Khrushchev towards the peasant and the village was at the bottom of the row which broke out in 1951.

Quite soon after his arrival in Moscow it was apparent that Khrushchev had upset the balance of power in the Party leadership to the detriment of Malenkov. Apart from Stalin, they were the two most powerful members by far in the five-man secretariat which looked after the day-to-day running of the Party, and when Khrushchev took over responsibility for agriculture in 1950, a counter-move by Malenkov was perhaps inevitable. Khrushchev gave a hostage to fortune, as he was to do again and again in the future, not only by launching in April 1950 a campaign to

* Narodniks were nineteenth-century Russian populists who believed that peasants could achieve socialism by themselves. Stalin's use of it implied that Khrushchev was a 'peasant-lover'.

increase the size of collective farms throughout the country but by announcing grandiose schemes for the new enlarged villages or 'agrotowns'. It was obvious from a plan of his published in a Moscow paper a few weeks later that he had begun to experiment with the idea of 'agrotowns' while in the Ukraine, where ironically the first projected settlement was to be named after Stalin. In January 1951 Khrushchev made another speech in which he described in detail the facilities that the new villages would have: 'club, farming study centre, school, hospital, village Soviet, store, park, stadium, cinema, public baths . . . gradual installation of water mains, power lines, street lights and pavements' and possibly houses with two or four apartments each rather than the traditional peasant huts.

Khrushchev must have known from his own experience how poor the majority of collective farms were, and yet he saw nothing unrealistic in these magnificent plans which were to be achieved with no more than the resources of the farms themselves. Was he really swept off his feet by the prospect of such a splendid future for the countryside? Or was it the politician in him, hoping to catch support for himself as well as his plans? Almost certainly it was a bit of both. In the years ahead he was again and again to announce breathtaking plans – to overtake America, to produce *x* million more tons of grain – which really did seem to convince him but left many of his colleagues sceptical, and which at the same time he used with great shrewdness as weapons in his political battles. In some curious way the very announcement of a grandiose scheme seemed to persuade Khrushchev that its realization was at hand. Perhaps he would have been a far less energetic and successful man without this optimism so sweeping that it bordered on self-deception. It certainly gave him tenacity too, because in spite of all the attacks that were to be made on the agrotowns, they were to remain his ideal for rural development.

The episode also reveals another side of Khrushchev's political technique: his fondness for making a daring move when his own security seemed most threatened. There is evidence that Khrushchev had already incurred Stalin's disapproval for suggesting that the equipment of the state-owned Machine Tractor Stations be sold off to the collective farms. Stalin later denounced this idea as heresy. At the same time Khrushchev was certainly aware of the opposition that his agrotown proposals had already provoked. It was probably with this in mind that he admitted in his January speech that the word 'agrotown' was too grand. 'The word town implies a great deal,' he said, '... The question must be approached more modestly; imposing titles should not be sought. In my opinion the name "collective farm settlement" would be very fitting.' But the name was all that he changed, and he could scarcely have hoped to appease his critics by that. After Stalin's death he often behaved like this, a diver making his most sensational dive just when the board is being sawn from under his feet. But in 1951 Stalin obviously decided against him, and Malenkov and his allies were allowed to turn on Khrushchev in public.

The offending speech was not published until March, and the very next day *Pravda* announced curtly that Khrushchev's article had been published 'only as a basis for discussion' – a clear sign that the ideas it expressed were questionable. Some critics immediately dismissed the scheme as a fantasy, but Khrushchev's main opponent, Malenkov, did not speak out in public until the next year. In private however he was very active. He was probably behind the *Pravda* editorial announcement, and he also prepared a secret Central Committee document attacking Khrushchev's article as 'anti-Marxist' and 'harmful'. Malenkov's open criticism of Khrushchev came at the 19th Party Congress in October 1952. He made it plain that Khrushchev's 'narodnik' ideas were at the root of the trouble by attacking Khrushchev's plan as the 'consumer approach' which ignored 'the major production tasks of the collective farms' and gave prominence instead to 'tasks that derive from them, consumer tasks connected with welfare amenities in the collective farms'. In other words the Party intended to do nothing to improve the wretched conditions of the peasants, who were to continue their existence as low-cost production machines.

Khrushchev's scheme certainly lacked adequate thought and was clearly premature, but it does seem to have been connected with the general critique of Stalinist farm policies that he was to make after the dictator's death and which must have developed in the privacy of his mind before 1953. At the heart of this critique was the realization that the policy of getting food on the cheap threatened the supply of food and was in the long run extravagantly inefficient. But to entertain such thoughts while Stalin lived was risky. As a result of the agrotown affair Malenkov took over Party supervision of agriculture from Khrushchev, who was himself forced to retire into the shade for some time. Yet although Malenkov had the powerful support of Beria, the security chief, in his attack on him, Khrushchev does not seem to have been in serious danger. Stalin very likely still needed him too much as a check on Malenkov. Khrushchev kept his post on the secretariat and took over control of Party organizational matters, which allowed him to begin putting his own men into key positions of the Party apparatus. His leadership of the Moscow region Party, in itself an extremely important job, also gave him the chance to build up personal support in this most important of all the regional Party organizations, just as he had already done in the Ukraine.

Malenkov was nevertheless obviously on top, and he continued to feud with Khrushchev. In his keynote speech to the 19th Party Congress, he criticized a number of Party organizations for paying insufficient attention to ideological matters and for being 'carried away by economic matters', but named only the Moscow one. The similarity to the charges brought against Khrushchev's Ukraine in 1946, with which Malenkov was also most likely associated, is striking. The odds are that Malenkov was trying another line of attack against Khrushchev and this time had come near to finding his opponent's weakest point. Khrushchev's tendency to be 'carried away by economic matters' at the expense of ideological work was real enough. But Malenkov's attack did little damage, because it was not in Stalin's interest that it should. On the contrary, Malenkov's boast in the same speech that the grain problem was 'solved' offered Khrushchev a chance to counterattack. It was an extraordinarily rash claim to make and could only be substantiated on paper by using an extremely deceptive method of estimating the size of the grain crop. Khrushchev obviously knew the claim to be nonsense but was not able to say so in public. What he seems to have done is to try to persuade Stalin privately that it was nonsense. Khrushchev later claimed that at a discussion in the Central Committee he told Stalin that 'the Ukrainians are very dissatisfied that they are not given white bread. At the Party Congress it was said that the grain problem had been solved, but the Ukrainians, who have always eaten white bread, now do not have any of it.' There is no evidence that Stalin in any way responded to such hints and the only effect Khrushchev's jabs at Malenkov can have had was to exacerbate still more relations between the two men.

The Khrushchev-Malenkov feud might possibly have become bloodier had Stalin not had conflicting plans of his own. At the 19th Party Congress the small Politburo, till now the Party's ruling body, had been turned into a twenty-five-man Presidium. Khrushchev in the secret speech declared that this was a move preliminary to a purge of some of the old-established Soviet leaders, and he named Molotov and Mikoyan as likely candidates for the executioner. Both these men were veteran Bolsheviks, had been close to Stalin for years, and were in their very different ways extremely able. Khrushchev gave no reason for Stalin's suspicion of these two, but he did say that the dictator 'toyed with the absurd and ridiculous suspicion that Voroshilov was an English agent.... A special tapping device was installed in his home to listen to what was said there.' Voroshilov had also been loyal to Stalin for years. He was perhaps the most genuinely liked of all Soviet leaders, keeping the glamour he had won by his exploits in the Civil War despite his patent failure to cope with modern warfare. If Stalin had really turned against these men, there was safety for no one in the Soviet Union. The announcement the following January of a plot by eminent doctors, mainly Jewish, to kill leading Soviet figures was all that was necessary to recreate the atmosphere of the blood purge in the late 1930s.

Khrushchev does not seem to have been on Stalin's elimination list, nor is it possible to link him specifically with the preparations for the purge. The same seems to be the case with Malenkov. In 1963 Khrushchev claimed that he and other Soviet leaders had managed to restrain Stalin in this last period. There would have been more 'cases', he said, 'if everyone who worked beside Stalin at that time had agreed with him in everything.' He mentioned in particular that Stalin had wanted to create 'the so-called case of the Moscow counter-revolutionary centre. But as is known, he found no yes-men,' and so there was no mass repression of Moscow Party cadres. The story is probably true in that most of the Soviet leaders were almost certainly worried – and some even frightened – by Stalin's plans, and they may well have dragged their feet whenever possible. But it is hard to see how Khrushchev or anyone else would have dared open opposition. Moreover Stalin needed no help from his colleagues in preparing the purge. He controlled the security services through his own private secretariat and was even able to bypass Beria, who was very probably one of the planned victims. Khrushchev himself told how Stalin simply presented his colleagues with the documents showing the doctors' guilt, giving them no chance to look into the matter themselves.

The odds are that by 1953 Stalin had lost the confidence of many of his close associates. Khrushchev's own development gives as clear an explanation as one is likely to get of how a man who had stood by Stalin throughout the terrible thirties should at last have turned. In the 1930s Khrushchev had been comparatively young, ambitious and, for all his ability, ignorant. The world he lived and worked in had been virtually created by Stalin, and except for the wretched villages and mining settlements of his childhood and youth he knew no other. His lack of formal education and naturally unspeculative mind had made escape through books and ideas impossible. He had little idea of what the world of the early Bolsheviks, men of great culture as well as passionate revolutionaries, had been like. His work brought him close to the exciting rhythms of the Russian Iron Age, and he undoubtedly felt the intoxication of being able to identify himself with his country's gigantic labours, and to satisfy his own ambition as he satisfied his ambition for Communist Russia. He had been brought up under the Stalinist dogma that all opposition was objectively hostile, and he lacked the natural squeamishness to be revolted when this developed to its logical conclusion in blood purge.

The Ukraine and the war brought many changes. He spent ten years away from Stalin, and this allowed his own political personality to develop. He could within limits experiment and develop his own methods. The war itself helped to begin the destruction of his total belief in Stalin. And in the Ukrainian incident of 1946–7 he had the shattering experience of seeing himself for the first time as a potential victim of Stalin. The war, its devastation and his part in rebuilding the Ukraine afterwards released all his constructive energies and at the same time gave him a valuable sense of what had to be avoided in the future. Stalin's policies in his last years did not accord with the way Khrushchev was developing. Latter-day Stalinism frustrated his energies, ignored his ideas and proposed yet more destruction, as though the blood purge and the war had never been. Stalin was still in the grip of his terrible logic, but Khrushchev had by 1953 to a considerable extent broken free of it.

Chapter 10
Russia without Stalin

Few great men's deaths have been as timely as Stalin's. It saved Russia from the horror of yet another purge, and what in the long run was even more important it released badly needed ideas and energies which the dictator had feared and suppressed. But the announcement on 4 March 1953 that Stalin had had a stroke and the news two days later of his death caused at first as much disarray as relief among the Soviet leadership.

The circumstances of Stalin's death are obscure, but Khrushchev gave one vivid (though scarcely complete) account of it to the American diplomat Averill Harriman:

> One Saturday night, he invited us all to his dacha in the country for dinner. Stalin was in good humour. It was a gay evening and we all had a good time. Then we went home. On Sundays Stalin usually telephoned each of us to discuss business, but that Sunday he did not call, which struck us as odd. He did not come back to town on Monday, and on Monday evening the head of his bodyguard called us and said Stalin was ill. All of us – Beria, Malenkov, Bulganin and I – hurried out to the country to see him. He was already unconscious. A blood clot had paralysed an arm, a leg and his tongue. We stayed with him for three days but he remained unconscious. Then for a time he came out of his coma and we went into his room. A nurse was feeding him tea with a spoon. He shook us by the hand and tried to joke with us, smiling feebly and waving his good arm to a picture over his bed of a baby lamb being fed with a spoon by a little girl. Now, he indicated by gestures, he was just as helpless as a baby lamb.
>
> Some time later he died. I wept. After all, we were his pupils and owed him everything. Like Peter the Great, Stalin fought barbarism with barbarism but he was a great man.

Khrushchev's reaction to Stalin's death was almost certainly as ambiguous as his description of it. He undoubtedly felt a sense of loss to the point of feeling lost himself: many thinking people in Russia who were far from being 'Stalinists' felt the same. But the reverse of this was a sense of liberation. Khrushchev must have realized that there was now a quite unparalleled freedom of action for him and his colleagues in Soviet politics. Stalin's death, however, also had a more immediate and possibly unpleasant consequence: it brought Malenkov's rivalry with Khrushchev to a critical point. With no Stalin to hold the ring between the two men, there was little chance that they could both remain indefinitely at the top of Soviet politics.

The advantages seemed all to lie with Malenkov at first. On 7 March it was announced that he was to be Prime Minister as well as senior Party secretary, more or less a case of the Dauphin becoming King. At the same time Khrushchev lost control of the Moscow Party, but kept his post in the secretariat. The importance of the Malenkov-Khrushchev rivalry was, of course, not clear at the time, probably even to the Soviet politicians themselves. Khrushchev was after all the least well known (though technically not the junior) of the eight men who formed the ruling nucleus after Stalin's death. But this feud was nevertheless to provide the framework of political life in the Soviet Union for the next two years because no one came forward to provide another. To understand why this was so, one must take a closer look at these colleagues of Khrushchev. Molotov was the most genuinely Stalinist of them all. In spite of his master's intention to remove him, he was the only one of the new Soviet leaders to show signs of grief at Stalin's funeral. He was patient and tireless (his name, a revolutionary pseudonym, aptly meant the hammer), and his unsmiling face decorated by austere pince-nez had become famous throughout the world during his years of service as Stalin's Foreign Minister. But his considerable abilities, when applied to the loyal service of Stalin's ideas after Stalin's death, were of far less use in the era of change that the Soviet Union had now entered. What his conservatism did make him was an inevitable tactical ally for Khrushchev against Malenkov when the latter went too far in abandoning old shibboleths.

Voroshilov and Kaganovich had, like Molotov, long been closely associated with Stalin. Voroshilov was now in many ways little more than a figurehead, and was at his most impressive when on his horse reviewing troops in Red Square. He had little real political power, but he was popular and so still a useful friend. He was most unlikely to take the political initiative himself, and as an elderly man was almost sure to find Malenkov's new ways disturbing. Kaganovich, too, was less impressive at second glance. Perhaps he had been too close to Stalin for too long, because he seems by 1953 to have lost the spark he certainly once possessed. It is hard to see how Khrushchev could have been close to him after the Ukrainian affair, and very likely he regarded Kaganovich with something of the contempt of a brilliant and now successful student for his one-time master. But Kaganovich, together with Molotov and Voroshilov, had no reason to like Malenkov, a young man who had pushed past them. Kaganovich also largely shared with Molotov those Stalinist ideas which Malenkov was to offend. In this way three of the most important Soviet politicians were in fact potentially Khrushchev's allies in his quarrel with Malenkov. Of course they almost certainly did not look at it in this way at all. They saw Malenkov as a threat to their own positions, and Khrushchev as a necessary counterweight. What they failed to see was that with Malenkov gone, the problems of post-Stalinism would remain, and that whereas they had no solution for them, Khrushchev thought he had.

If Khrushchev's 'allies' were more pliable in his hands than seemed possible at first sight, Malenkov's allies were in turn less substantial than they looked. Undoubtedly his greatest asset was the support of Lavrenti Beria, the Georgian who took over control of all security matters in a unified Ministry of Internal Affairs (MVD) on 7 March. Khrushchev later hinted that the appointments made that day had been presented by Malenkov and Beria as a *fait accompli* backed up by the presence in Moscow of security troops under Beria's command. But paradoxically, Beria's power was his greatest weakness: the fear he inspired in his colleagues soon led them to destroy him.

Anastas Mikoyan was quite another matter. An Armenian with an uncharacteristic capacity for survival, he was in many ways the opposite of Molotov. He was flexible and undogmatic. As a trade expert he knew the outside world probably better than any of his colleagues. Slight and dark, he looked nimble beside the heavy Russians. Unlike Molotov, Mikoyan clearly reacted against Stalinism and he was ready for experiment and accordingly well disposed towards Malenkov. But at the same time his sense of political survival made him a less than sterling ally; he seems to have had no intention of sticking with Malenkov in defeat. The eighth member of the ruling group, Nikolai Bulganin, had risen through the government apparatus and served as Defence Minister. Foreign observers often commented on how much he looked, with his goatee beard, like an affable German bandmaster. There was never any doubt of Khrushchev's ability to dominate Bulganin personally. The two men had been associated in the Moscow of the thirties, and Khrushchev had been top dog then. Malenkov was to do nothing that would encourage Bulganin to break away from this old pattern.

It is not surprising, given these attitudes to Malenkov among the Soviet leaders, that they should have had second thoughts about giving him so much power, and on 14 March they got him to surrender his post in the Party secretariat.* This episode is extremely obscure. There is no way of telling whether Malenkov was forced or persuaded to relinquish one of his jobs, or why his colleagues should have been able to achieve on 14 March what had been beyond their power a week before. Whatever lay behind it, the episode was crucial for Khrushchev, because it meant that he took over virtual control of the Party apparatus (although Malenkov left behind him some supporters in important positions on the Central Committee). The Party was the piece of Soviet machinery that Khrushchev knew best of all. He had strongly developed ideas about how it should function, and these ideas, combined with his own reliance on the Party as his instrument for acquiring personal power, gave him an estimate of the Party's importance that was far above its real power in 1953. At the 15th Ukrainian Party Congress back in 1940 he had said:

> The Party is responsible for everything. Whether it is Army work, Chekist work, economic work, Soviet [i.e. government] work – all is subordinate to [the] Party leadership, and if anyone thinks otherwise, that means he is no Bolshevik.

* Membership of the leading Party organs was now as follows:
The Presidium (in Soviet order of seniority): Malenkov, Beria, Molotov, Voroshilov, Khrushchev, Bulganin, Kaganovich, Mikoyan, Saburov, Pervukhin. The latter two, aged 53 and 49 respectively, had risen through the economic apparatus and thus were linked with Malenkov as Prime Minister. The Secretariat: Khrushchev, Suslov and Pospelov (both ideological experts), Shatalin (Malenkov's man) and Ignatyev (removed in April 1953). This probably gave Khrushchev a dominant influence in the Secretariat.

This was not how Stalin had come to see the Party. He had turned the secret police against its leaders as against everyone else. Perhaps more important, Stalin himself had stood over the Party as an absolute dictator, ignoring its rules and even its supposedly sovereign bodies like Party Congresses and Central Committees. He had also greatly increased the power of the government apparatus, probably out of traditional divide and rule motives, and through the mighty industrial ministries based in Moscow this apparatus had been able to function almost without Party, as opposed to Stalin's own, supervision. Malenkov's readiness to settle for just the premiership on 14 March can almost certainly be taken as another sign of the diminished importance of the Party. The odds are that he was strong enough to have kept his secretariat post and given up the premiership had he wanted it that way. It is, however, inconceivable that Khrushchev, faced with the same choice, would have chosen as Malenkov did. What in fact Khrushchev was going to do in the years ahead was to build the Party up to fill the power vacuum caused by Stalin's death: where Stalin had dominated, the Party was now to dominate. In feeling the need for this 'Supreme Authority', Khrushchev had much more of the Stalinist in him than Malenkov, who was possibly ready for more daring experiments with the Soviet system.

Stalin's death did not just throw the relationships of the surviving leaders into confusion: it seemed to threaten even the system he had created. Russia after the war was like a carthorse, forced to pull as far and fast as it could, and fed only the minimum necessary to keep it pulling. Once its driver was gone, who was to be found with an equally terrible will to replace him? The feeling that there could not be another Stalin and that there must now be some sort of release was caught in a poem written at the time but not published till some years later. It describes how the poet walked round Moscow looking at what Stalin had built and thinking:

> The age of shows has ended,
> The age of bread has come.
> A break for smoking's been declared
> For the people who have stormed the sky.

Many people had thought that the 'break for smoking' would

come after the war, but in fact Russia had never felt the force of Stalin's will to such effect as in the post-war years. Determined to make the Soviet Union impregnable in the cause of socialism, he had isolated it from the rest of the world as Russia had perhaps never been isolated in the past. The Soviet proletariat worked under stringent discipline, and the prisoners of the security police comprised the country's single largest labour force. The peasants, who accounted for over half the population, had no right to social security benefits and were paid prices for their food that were usually below production cost. As the preparation of the final purge showed only too well, terror was an important weapon of government. And it was held that the only correct policy towards the outside world was one of implacable hostility.

It is quite clear that even while Stalin was alive some of his colleagues had begun to question these policies, and had fretted under his refusal to consider any change or to delegate authority. Khrushchev once described how Stalin in his last years had been 'unable to direct everything himself but refused to allow us subordinates to do anything,' and added, 'It was only after his death that we were able to develop initiatives.' Khrushchev's main concern had been Stalin's stubbornness over agriculture. Within months of Stalin's death Khrushchev was to make a devastating public analysis of the faults of Soviet agriculture (see next chapter), and certainly much of the thinking that went into it must have been done while Stalin was still alive. In 1952 he had been a member of a commission set up to study ways of increasing livestock production, and this had recommended a slight rise in prices paid for animal products to give the peasants more incentive. According to Khrushchev Stalin rejected this out of hand and told the commission to work out new proposals, taking into account that the tax on the collective farms had to be increased by forty billion (old) roubles. Khrushchev claimed that this was only two billion roubles less than the total collective farm income at that time. Whether he exaggerated or not, the story probably gives an accurate picture of the frustrations involved in working under Stalin during these last years.

Agriculture was of course already a Khrushchev speciality, but it is not clear how well informed he was on other equally important matters. Stalin had a way of keeping much to himself and certainly did not discuss everything with the full Politburo. For Khrushchev, because of his long absence from Moscow, much of the months following Stalin's death must have been spent in informing himself as far as possible on the real state of affairs in the Soviet Union and – equally important – in the outside world. Of course the whole of the leadership was to a large extent also occupied in this. One of its first decisions was significantly to send a team of Soviet experts into Eastern Europe to investigate conditions there. The non-communist world, too, was to be examined in a completely new spirit, and many dogmas were to be revised with remarkable speed. Behind these moves lay the feeling that to keep the Soviet Union as a sort of fortress under military discipline was no longer in the national interest. Some of Stalin's colleagues had flirted with new foreign policy ideas during Stalin's lifetime, and there are signs that he knew of this. Once he was dead, their conviction that Soviet national interest and the cause of socialism could best be served by different policies helped them to go some way at least towards meeting the general desire in the country for relaxation. The main fact that Khrushchev and his colleagues seized on was that while the Soviet Union may have looked forbidding enough, the basis of its strength – its economy – was in fact dangerously faulty. Inevitably, it was around this issue that Khrushchev and Malenkov were largely to conduct their fight against each other.

Before the Khrushchev-Malenkov struggle got properly under way, however, another political storm blew up that was to have considerable significance for Khrushchev. Beria, who had helped to install Malenkov in power immediately after Stalin's death, began to develop his own political support outside the security services already under his control. At the same time he apparently entertained some radical ideas about general policy matters, including the belief that communist East Germany should be sacrificed as too great a liability. (Khrushchev later suggested that Malenkov partly went along with Beria on this but stopped just in time.) In June 1953, shortly after the abortive East German revolt, Beria was arrested by his colleagues. Khrushchev later asserted that Beria was preparing a coup: he told a foreign politician in 1956 that a special session of the Presidium was called at which Beria was cross-examined for four hours. Then Beria was left alone while his colleagues discussed what to do with him. They were convinced of his guilt, Khrushchev said, although there was 'not enough juridical evidence' to prove it. But it was impossible to let him go free, and so 'we came to the unanimous decision that the only correct measure for the defence of the Revolution was to shoot him immediately. This decision was adopted by us and carried out on the spot.'

Thus did the Party finally revolt against the tyranny of the secret police. For Khrushchev personally it meant the destruction of the most important rival centre of power to his own chosen weapon, the Party. Beria's successor was a professional policeman of no political standing, and Khrushchev was from now on to have little difficulty in controlling the security services as he rose to power. And Beria's death also robbed Malenkov of the one source of support that might have saved him from Khrushchev's stratagems.

Chapter 11
The Struggle with Malenkov

Khrushchev's struggle with Malenkov concealed the remarkably similar analysis made by the two men of the problems facing their country after Stalin's death. Malenkov very likely thought faster and deeper than Khrushchev: as things turned out, this was to be a disadvantage. And an artificial difference was created by the logic of political battle which compelled Khrushchev to take a publicly opposing view. But fundamentally both men agreed that the Soviet Union could not go on as it was. They saw above all that its economy was seriously out of balance. The reconstruction after the war and the creation of a new defence potential had meant that everything had been sacrificed to heavy industry. Stalin, as before the war, had achieved monumental successes here: steel production had almost tripled since 1945; coal and electricity production had doubled. This, however, had left few resources for investment in the consumer goods and other service industries, with the result that the Soviet worker was badly housed, badly dressed and badly fed. And even in heavy industry the highly centralized methods of planning and control that had achieved such marvels of gross production involved increasing waste and excessively high costs. At the same time the discipline, backed up by terror, that controlled the industrial labour force was scarcely suitable to an economy faced with increasingly sophisticated problems and therefore needing an educated and comparatively free technocracy.

The situation was even worse in agriculture. The peasant revolt against collectivization by the slaughter of their animals, the destruction of war and finally the refusal of Stalin to pay farmers anything like proper prices for their food had produced a very grave crisis. In 1952 the Soviet Union possessed less cattle than Tsarist Russia had done in 1916, and in the last years of Stalin's rule it produced just ten per cent more grain than the same territory under the Tsars in the years before the First World War. The difference was that Stalin had thirty million more people to feed than Tsar Nicholas II. Yet even to produce this inadequate supply of food took the energies of well over half the Soviet population. No other industrial nation had such a wasteful agricultural system.

On top of this unbalanced economy Stalin had built in the conditions of the cold war a harsh foreign policy that had united his enemies, but which at the same time had won him few friends outside the circle of loyal communists. In this, as in his extension of communism to Eastern Europe after the war by means of the Soviet army, his purpose was to make the Soviet Union safe from attack. He was the master defence strategist of the Revolution, for whom socialism was still a beleaguered city. But Khrushchev and Malenkov, in their new approach to Soviet domestic policies, were also to lay the ground for a completely different, and far more subtle Soviet foreign policy (although Malenkov was not to survive in power to see this). The core of their ideas on the Soviet economy was to restore a balance to investments, allowing them to go some way towards meeting the people's demand for more consumer goods and a generally higher living standard. Although both men realized that this could not be done quickly, they must also have grasped that once the satisfaction of the Soviet population's needs became hallowed in this way, it would alter the whole tone of the country's relationship with the rest of the world. For one thing the Soviet Union would seek to avoid conflicts that would waste its men or money (significantly the Korean armistice was signed in July 1953). More important, it meant that the day was not far off when the Soviet Union would sell communism as above all a philosophy of plenty.

The combination of Khrushchev and Malenkov's personal rivalry with their mutual agreement that more attention should be paid to the needs of the ordinary Soviet citizen resulted in the unique sight of two Soviet politicians bidding for popular support. There had already been a hint of this in their relationship before Stalin died, when Khrushchev had launched his agrotowns and Malenkov had claimed that the grain problem was solved, but neither of these moves had made a lasting impact. Now Khrushchev had to watch Malenkov take the initiative at a Supreme Soviet meeting in August. The Prime Minister told the people that they had a 'right to demand' high-quality consumer goods and promised that the production of these would be increased 'very considerably'. Malenkov also announced that increased prices would be paid to farmers for their produce and that there would be a relaxation of the strict limits on the private holdings allowed to peasants.

It was not only what Malenkov said, however, that was remarkable. Khrushchev was no doubt among the first to notice that he made only the briefest references to the Communist Party in his speech, which clearly implied that Malenkov believed that the government (his government) was able and entitled to take on its shoulders the task of coping with the Soviet economy. Like the decision to relinquish his job on the Party secretariat, the speech raised again the question of just what role Malenkov had in mind for the Party. All one can be sure of was that he did not mean it to be a commanding one.

The next month, September, Khrushchev made his bid for public attention with a report on the state of Soviet agriculture to a plenum of the Party Central Committee. Both the subject and the audience were significant. We have seen how Khrushchev had already for many years dealt in detail with agricultural problems, turning much of the Party apparatus under his control to their solution. But now for the first time it was in his power to make agriculture a publicly acknowledged national problem. Once he revealed the real facts, which had for so long been hidden under a mass of Stalinist non-statistics, it would be very hard for anyone else to push agriculture into a back place as Stalin had done. And having thus revealed the giant, Khrushchev was able to step forward and present himself and the Party in the role of the giant-killers. Khrushchev knew from long experience that the structure of Soviet farming laid itself open to guidance and control by the Party more than any other aspect of the country's economic life. This coincidence – that the weakest part of the economy was the one that was most easily dominated by the Party – was to be central to Soviet politics as long as Khrushchev was in power. Finally, the rewards of success promised to be immense. The Soviet politician who could bring food in plenty to the deprived Soviet consumer would be a popular man indeed.

The big shock of Khrushchev's speech came in the figures he gave to show that Soviet farm production in 1953 was little more, and in some instances even less, than it had been before the

Revolution. The statistics that made such a comparison possible had simply not been released in Stalin's day. Khrushchev's main remedy was to restore the principle of material incentive to farming, and to this end he said that the price the state paid for meat and animal products would be greatly increased – by as much as five and a half times in the case of meat supplied compulsorily by the farms to the government (a figure that alone tells much of the appalling condition in which Stalin kept the collective farms). The price increases were moreover part of a general attack by Khrushchev on bad farm management. Wherever he looked – in the agricultural ministries, in the Machine Tractor Stations which controlled agricultural machinery, and in the farms themselves – Khrushchev saw ignorance and inefficiency. Less than a quarter of the MTS directors had higher education. A third of the state farm directors did not even have secondary education. Each year a third of the country's collective farm chairmen left their jobs.

In view of his relations with Malenkov, it is not surprising that Khrushchev aimed much of his invective at the agricultural ministries, which as they stood were in a position to frustrate Khrushchev and the Party's direction of agriculture. He demanded that these ministries be cut down in size and not involve themselves in the detailed supervision of daily farming which, he claimed, they did badly. He ridiculed the ministries' planning methods, declaring that the arable and livestock sections alone in the plan given to a collective farm contained between 200 and 250 indicators that had to be met. And he quoted Lenin to the effect that 'It would be a mistake if we wrote decrees on one pattern for every place in Russia.' Finally Khrushchev left no doubt that the Party's role in tackling this problem was to be dominant. He suggested that 50,000 Party members should be sent at once from the towns to work in the countryside. He emphasized that the Party would have to throw all its weight into agriculture. Some Party members, he hinted, still thought it a matter of only secondary importance, but he reminded these people that a 'Communist society cannot be built without an abundance of bread, meat, milk, butter, vegetables and other agricultural products.'

Khrushchev's agricultural schemes were not made easier by the fact that many senior Party officials who had risen under Stalin had little desire to take up farming in their old age. In the Ukraine and elsewhere, furthermore, Khrushchev had demanded a 'mud on the boots' style of work from his subordinates, and this also was unlikely to attract Stalinist Party dignitaries. Yet if Khrushchev's plans were to succeed, he now had to remodel the Soviet Party on a national scale, and to do this properly he needed to control Party appointments. The September plenum had given him the official title of first secretary, which was an important gain in prestige for him. But Malenkov still had supporters in key departments of the secretariat who were probably able to keep Khrushchev in some check. Nevertheless soon after the September plenum he began to use the new agricultural schemes as a pretext for examining the attitudes of senior regional Party officials. At meetings in the Central Committee offices in Moscow and on journeys round the country Khrushchev took a stern look at all Party bosses of regions with an unsatisfactory agricultural performance. The tone of these meetings and the general anxiety in the Party apparatus over Khrushchev's new ideas are well caught in an account he himself gave of the process.

> I know that after the death of Stalin, when I began to work in the Central Committee, some comrades were displeased that they were asked in the Central Committee about so-called trifles. . . . One regional secretary was reporting to the Central Committee about the work of his region's collective farms, and when he was asked if he knew just one leading kolkhoznitsa who grew record cabbage crops, he replied, offended, 'I'm not a kolkhoznik, I'm the regional Party secretary.' . . . 'My dear chap,' I said to him, 'it's true you're a regional secretary but surely you eat cabbage. Why shouldn't you be interested in how cabbage is grown?' Well, then there was talk in the Central Committee that Khrushchev wants us, the Party workers, to study agronomy. . . .

It is easy to understand the indignation of the offending secretary. He was a man with authority over a few million people. He had much dignity and many privileges. He could not see why he should be concerned with cabbages. Khrushchev's purpose in this and similar interviews was to destroy the old attitude of indifference to agriculture that had been created by Stalin's relegation of farming to a low priority. At the same time an official's attitude to agriculture must have been something of a political touchstone for Khrushchev. If he took offence at the idea of showing interest in cabbages, was he the kind of man who could function well in the sort of Party that Khrushchev wanted to have? As Khrushchev had asked in the Ukraine before the war, 'What sort of a leader is it who can't provide cabbages?' In this the interests of Khrushchev's own struggle with Malenkov and the governmental machine coincided with his ideas on Party work. A Party stocked with the right sort of men would leave no room for Malenkov and would hold the state apparatus firmly in its place.

Khrushchev followed up his plenum speech with another and even more sensational plan to restore the nation's farming which at the same time he used to undermine Malenkov. In January 1954 he addressed a secret memorandum to his Presidium colleagues which claimed that 'The solution of the grain problem announced by us does not quite correspond to the actual state of affairs.' On the contrary the situation was so grave that Soviet grain exports had had to be cut. The 1953 harvest fell far short of what was needed and had had to be supplemented from the grain reserves. The implied criticism of Malenkov was obvious and was indeed rubbed home by figures which Khrushchev produced to show that the method Malenkov had used in 1952 to calculate the harvest produced an answer almost double the reality. There were two ways of increasing grain production rapidly, Khrushchev said. One was to extend the area of arable land, and he proposed that in 1954–5 thirteen million hectares (equal to the entire cropland of Canada) of virgin land in Kazakhstan and Siberia be brought under grain. The other was to grow more productive crops, and here the Soviet Union should learn from the United States, where maize accounted for 36 per cent of the country's grain production, compared to only 3·6 per cent in Russia. The maize proposal had long been popular with Khrushchev, who had already had it planted over considerable areas of the Ukraine and had firm ideas about its treatment. There was obviously much to be said for it, and it seems to have caused little immediate opposition. The virgin lands were quite another matter. Molotov, it was revealed later, exclaimed with horror 'It's a gamble', when he heard of the plan, and there seems to have been not one member of the Presidium who was ready to support Khrushchev actively.

The idea was truly Khrushchevian in both its scope and timing. He risked alienating Molotov and others just when he had to have their support if he was to deal with Malenkov. Again and again in the future he would announce his most controversial policies just when most men would have preferred to play safe. Equally typical of Khrushchev was the size of the project: it was certainly worthy of the man who had thought up the agrotowns. Seventy thousand workers were needed to man the new state farms that would be set up on the virgin steppe, and in two years they were to produce close on a fifth of the nation's total grain. Such an operation was unprecedented in the agricultural history of the world, and the political rewards it promised if successful were immense. Given the lack of enthusiasm in the Presidium for the scheme, it is at first sight surprising that Khrushchev was allowed to go ahead and make it public at another Central Committee plenum at the end of February. This must partly be explained by the extent to which Khrushchev had seized the initiative over agriculture. He had already made it a national problem of the first importance; and he was now proposing suitably radical schemes to solve it. Although there were many reasonable objections to be made against the virgin lands scheme, none of the Presidium could apparently back them up with the knowledge and energy that Khrushchev deployed in its defence. Between his memorandum and the February plenum, the leadership held a number of agricultural conferences in the Kremlin (very likely inspired by Khrushchev, who spoke at all of them) which stressed the seriousness of the situation. The need to do something quickly was clear, and Khrushchev alone had put forward a plan that claimed to take care of everything. Both as a politician and as an international statesman Khrushchev was to win many more battles by seizing the initiative while others failed to make up their minds.

It is very likely that Malenkov himself believed the virgin lands would be the cause of Khrushchev's downfall. As head of the government he had considerable power to frustrate the scheme's execution, and he could expect help in this from two of his senior colleagues in the Council of Ministers, Molotov and Kaganovich, with at least neutrality from the other two, Mikoyan and Bulganin. Khrushchev for his part made no attempt to win the support of the powerful bureaucrats in the Moscow ministries. On the contrary, at the February plenum he had virtually declared war on them, warning the Central Committee that in the execution of the new agricultural policies 'we shall meet with stubborn resistance from the bureaucrats'. Among those he criticized by name was the same A. I. Kozlov, now Minister of State Farms, who had abetted Malenkov in his moves against Khrushchev during the Ukrainian crisis (see page 77). The bureaucrats, angered by Khrushchev's attitude and supported by Malenkov, certainly did resist. Gosplan (the state planning authority) declared that it could not allocate money or materials to the new scheme, and other officials argued that the virgin lands had insufficient rainfall (a plausible argument about which Khrushchev was particularly touchy). Malenkov, in the summer of 1954, seems actually to have forbidden officials in the new territories to create any more state farms.

This battle over the allocation of funds to the virgin lands damaged Khrushchev, and by the summer of 1954 he was suffering a quite evident decline. At yet another Central Committee plenum on agriculture in June his enemies, the agricultural ministers, made the reports while he did not speak at all. But already by then the feud between the two principal leaders had taken a turn that was to be fatal for Malenkov. In pursuing his consumer goods policy, Malenkov had to take great care not to offend the main dogma of Soviet economic development – the priority of heavy industry. This was something that the Party old guard, led by Molotov and Kaganovich, would not easily allow. Yet it was hard to see how a rapid expansion of light industry could be achieved without a substantial reallocation of resources. The ending of the Korean war in July 1953 had allowed the military budget to be cut, but a further reduction in defence spending was obviously tempting to anyone in Malenkov's position. The chance came in the shape of the hydrogen bomb. Malenkov had announced Soviet possession of the H-bomb in the same August 1953 speech that had contained his new consumer goods programme, and already by the end of the year there were indications that he had thought through the tangle of nuclear problems to the conclusion that the possession of this terrible weapon by both the Soviet Union and America lessened the chance of war. The H-bomb, in other words, had created a state of mutual deterrence in which war would be avoided because all knew it meant the literal destruction of both sides. If this were really so, the Soviet Union would only need the 'ultimate weapon', and the escalation of defence costs might be halted to the benefit of neglected areas in the economy.

In March 1954 Malenkov publicly suggested that a world war would destroy communism as well as capitalism: it would mean, he said, 'the destruction of world civilization'. This was the first time that a Soviet leader had queried the invincibility of communism as laid down by Marx and Lenin. Malenkov must have known he was taking a risk, but presumably he did not foresee that it was around just this issue that Khrushchev was to find a majority in the Presidium against him. The first hint of the new grouping came at a Supreme Soviet meeting in March, when Khrushchev, Bulganin, Molotov, Kaganovich and Voroshilov all declared that the Soviet army needed strengthening. The next month Malenkov had to alter his views on modern war to maintain that it would cause the collapse of capitalism only.

It is impossible to say at what point Khrushchev realized that he could destroy Malenkov by stressing the likelihood of war and the need to strengthen Soviet defence and accordingly heavy industry too. Certainly by June he was taking a line diametrically opposed to Malenkov's and in a speech at Prague talked aggressively of the Soviet H-bomb and of the great difficulty of coming to any sort of terms with the West. Although Malenkov was apparently still strong enough to keep these remarks out of the Soviet press reports of the speech, Khrushchev had nevertheless seized the initiative again, and in August he won an extremely important tactical victory – the formal recognition of the Party's superiority over the state apparatus. This was implicit in a new order of signature for Party-state decrees which from now on put the Party first. This would hardly have been done without the approval of a majority in the Presidium who believed it to their advantage to bolster Khrushchev's strength against Malenkov's. The campaign against Malenkov's policies gathered momentum from now on. He was not a member of the Soviet delegation

(Khrushchev, Bulganin, Mikoyan) that went to Peking in October to lay the foundations of a new accord with China which included increased Soviet aid. Khrushchev, by contrast, flourished. In November he published an edict on religion signed by himself as first secretary and not by the Central Committee as was usual practice. In December the secret policemen responsible for the Leningrad Affair went on trial – another obvious threat to Malenkov, who had organized it. Khrushchev delivered the *coup de grâce* himself at a meeting of the Central Committee in January 1955 when, without naming Malenkov, he attacked 'theoreticians' who believed that at a certain stage in the development of socialism light industry should be allowed to overtake heavy industry in the cause of consumer goods production. Such views, he declared, were no more than a 'belching forth of the right deviation ... of the views hostile to Leninism which in their day were preached by Rykov, Bukharin and their kind'. Khrushchev thus identified Malenkov and his supporters with men who had been executed for these sins by Stalin.* On 8 February Malenkov's resignation of the premiership was read to the Supreme Soviet. He pleaded lack of experience and acknowledged his responsibility for the poor state of agriculture, but he kept his seat on the Party Presidium.

The struggle with Malenkov displayed Khrushchev's qualities as a fly politician better than any other episode in his career. Having begun by alienating much of the Presidium through his own agricultural policies, he was quick to spot the issue which could be turned into a rallying point against Malenkov. It was of absolutely no importance to him that the ideas of Malenkov which he now criticized were close to his own way of thinking. It was a case of 'In a fight you don't stop to pick your cudgels' – apparently a favourite saying of his. As later events were to show (and indeed as his previous career indicated), Khrushchev was at core a 'consumer communist', with a strong commitment to avoiding war. Very likely Malenkov, with his more speculative

* Aleksei Rykov succeeded Lenin as head of the Soviet government on the latter's death, and the placing of him before the better-known Bukharin may have been to stress the similarity with Malenkov. Stalin accused Rykov of supporting an increase in the standard of living at the expense of economic growth. The expression 'the belching forth of the right deviation' was used by Stalin when he was out for the blood of the Rightists in the 1930s.

mind, took his ideas on the reorientation of the Soviet economy and on the repercussions of nuclear weapons on international relations further than Khrushchev could follow at the time. But in any event it is most improbable that Khrushchev felt any qualms about attacking these ideas for his own advancement, once he saw that the Soviet establishment could be excited to oppose them and any man who propagated them. Malenkov, for all his originality and daring, lacked Khrushchev's political sense of what was possible, and this was his downfall.

Khrushchev quickly saw that Malenkov's policies could be made to seem dangerous to the main Soviet interest groups. Within Malenkov's own preserve of the state and economic apparatus, there were many for whom the priority of heavy industry was as absolute a truth as the rising of the sun in the east. It was not hard to set them against the man whom they might otherwise have supported as a protector against the encroachments of the Party. Just as important, the main source of brute power in the country, the army, needed no encouragement to oppose Malenkov's idea of 'mutual nuclear deterrence' and to insist that it be given a full armoury of nuclear weapons. It was perhaps partly because these interest groups could be encouraged without any difficulty to oppose the Malenkov line that men like Molotov and Kaganovich failed to see how by removing Malenkov they would be helping Khrushchev, in whom they certainly did not have complete confidence. Even at this stage Khrushchev was not taken altogether seriously by his colleagues. His personality lacked the stone-faced dignity that had come to be expected of leading Soviet figures, and his generally acknowledged weak grasp of Marxist theory made him seem an odd candidate for supreme power in the motherland of Proletarian Revolution. He was the natural gopak dancer among Stalin's entourage, and this was scarcely how eminent Soviet figures imagined the man who might rise to supremacy amongst them. All this was greatly to Khrushchev's advantage, and served to mask his threat to the post-Stalinist collective leadership.

Chapter 12
Consensus

The campaign against Malenkov, with its beating of the war drum and hymns to the god of heavy industry, disguised the extent to which the Soviet leadership was moving towards a new strategy which enjoyed broad support among the main Soviet interest groups. A good part of the apparatus of Stalinism had already been dismantled by 1955. After Beria's death, the security forces were brought under stricter control by the new leaders. Many prisoners were released from the forced labour camps, and the economic enterprises of the MVD were returned to the ordinary ministries. There were other smaller but nonetheless significant changes. In the summer of 1955 the Kremlin, the fortress centre of Moscow which under Stalin had remained as secret and forbidding as under the most terrible Tsars, was opened for the public pleasure. During Malenkov's ascendancy there had also been a sense of promise, of gathering freedom in the cultural world. And although this so-called 'thaw' was most likely encouraged by Malenkov and accordingly suffered a setback during the manoeuvres against him, this process continued. The leadership was to tolerate an erosion of the old Stalinist cultural dogmas provided that this kept within limits (limits which were defined in Khrushchev's case, it is true, by the political demands of the moment).

These changes were symptoms of the new attitude displayed by the leadership to the problems of Soviet development. Stalin's sledgehammer was abandoned for a more self-critical approach which concentrated on the problem of efficiency. This was shown in Khrushchev's analyses of the agricultural crisis and in a detailed critique of Soviet industry made by Bulganin, Malenkov's successor as Premier, in July 1955. The modernization at which Stalin's successors aimed was impossible without more attention to the workers and peasants in their role as consumers. In this they were not so very far from Malenkov, whom they had reviled for his emphasis on consumer goods (an emphasis which anyway was never so strong as their propaganda suggested). At the same time it was clear that the attitude of suspicious isolation from almost the whole of the world that Stalin had bequeathed to them was not to the Soviet Union's advantage. For one thing, the Soviet leaders understood that the West offered the quickest route to the vast amount of technical skill and equipment now needed by the Soviet economy, an attitude akin to Lenin's view of the West in his day. More important, the growing awareness of the implications of nuclear warfare altered the whole long-term prospect of Soviet relations with the capitalist world. Malenkov had jumped the gun, but his successors agreed broadly that the prospect of a nuclear war was intolerable, although they still professed to believe that Soviet victory in such a war was inevitable. The conclusions drawn from this – that the two world systems would have to coexist and that competition between them would be centred on economic production – were to be inscribed in Marxist–Leninist writ by Khrushchev at the 20th Party Congress no more than a year after Malenkov's fall.

This redefinition of Soviet aims undertaken by Khrushchev and his colleagues was at heart the response of shrewd politicians to intractable facts. But the rough consensus reached among the leaders in this way was hidden for the next few years by a personal rivalry among them in which the initiative was taken and held throughout by Khrushchev. The reason was that Khrushchev himself could not rest easy while Malenkov and Molotov were still in the leadership. Malenkov would be a threat to him as long as he remained in active politics. Molotov's threat was of a different sort: as the most important convinced Stalinist within the leadership, he was the man most likely to object to the post-Stalin consensus. Alone of Khrushchev's opponents, Molotov retained his regard after being defeated. 'We must respect Molotov,' Khrushchev said to a foreign visitor. 'He has firm convictions and sticks to them, although I often disagree with them.' Molotov's opposition to the way Soviet policy developed in 1955 had wide significance, because it served as a rallying point for the hard core of Stalinists that still existed in the Party and government apparatus. Equally important, Malenkov and Molotov together looked likely to be able to control a majority in the

Presidium if Khrushchev should drive them into joint opposition against him.*

Khrushchev's response to this situation was to build up his own bases of power within the Soviet system and at the same time to launch himself as an international figure, so in turn strengthening his hand at home. Khrushchev set about placing men friendly to him with the greatest skill. Already by February 1955, in spite of Malenkov's grip on the Party through his associate Shatalin, the leadership of the Leningrad, Ukrainian and Georgian organizations had been changed to Khrushchev's advantage. In Leningrad Frol Kozlov, a heavy, handsome man of somewhat sinister connexions with Stalin's preparations for a final purge, had been elected Party leader in Khrushchev's presence in November 1953. Until then the powerful Leningrad organization had probably been under Malenkov's influence, and Kozlov was to prove for the next few years a Khrushchev man. In the same year the Ukrainian and Georgian Parties were taken over by Aleksei Kirichenko and Vasili Mzhvanadze respectively, both of whom had served under Khrushchev in the Ukraine. In early 1954 there was also a change in the control of the Moscow organization which probably increased Khrushchev's influence there. Malenkov's defeat in 1955 meant that Khrushchev was also soon able to remove Shatalin from the Party secretariat, and after this his control over appointments in the Party machine was more or less undisputed. The importance of Khrushchev's grip over the Party was perhaps not understood fully even by his colleagues in the Presidium. What Khrushchev was able now to do was build up a majority of his own supporters in the Central Committee, through his control over the regional Parties. Perhaps Khrushchev himself did not realize that he was thus turning the Central Committee into an instrument with which even a hostile Presidium could be subdued. But the Central Committee had already since Stalin's death recovered much of its old Leninist standing, now meeting

* In July 1955 the Ukrainian Party leader Kirichenko and the Party theoretician Mikhail Suslov joined the Presidium, bringing its strength up to eleven. As things turned out, it was only these two plus Mikoyan who were to stand by Khrushchev when the final showdown in the Presidium came.

regularly to discuss the problems facing the Soviet Union, and so control over it was desirable in itself.

Khrushchev was not content, however, just to build up his position in the Party organization. In the spring of 1954 the security police were taken from the control of the MVD and put under a newly created State Security Committee (KGB). The head of the new committee was Ivan Serov, who had worked in the Ukraine with Khrushchev before the war. Serov was presumably judged acceptable by the whole Presidium, but he apparently performed his work to Khrushchev's particular satisfaction. More important was Khrushchev's assault on the affections of the military leaders. There were others in the Presidium traditionally far closer to the army than he, such as Molotov, Bulganin and Voroshilov, but Khrushchev won an *entrée* by his support of the military's objections to Malenkov's policies. Immediately after Malenkov's removal from the premiership there were large-scale military promotions, and among the newly created marshals a majority had been closely associated with Khrushchev during the war or later in the Ukraine. Again, though Khrushchev can scarcely have foreseen this in 1955, the army was to play a decisive role in Khrushchev's coming battle with the Presidium. Khrushchev even extended his influence into the government apparatus. Although events were to prove the new premier Nikolai Bulganin not entirely reliable, there was no doubt that Khrushchev was personally able to dominate him. He was also able to remove his old enemy A. I. Kozlov from the State Farms Ministry, an important step in promoting his own ideas of agriculture.

In such ways did Khrushchev with great skill increase the number of men well disposed to, or dependent on, him throughout the main Soviet power groups. But it was not so much this prowess as a political manipulator that drew attention to him in 1955 as his emergence in the role of an international statesman. Soviet foreign policy was waiting for a bold executant able to show the world that it was now operating from revised premises. The Soviet Union now wanted a *détente* with the West, although she considered that self-defence also demanded rapid development of her own nuclear strength. At the same time the Soviet leaders were prepared to abandon positions that did not materially affect

Soviet security, such as the Soviet occupation zone in Austria and the Soviet base in Finland (both were given up in 1955). Equally dramatic was the reassessment of the part to be played by the uncommitted world in the struggle – now foreseen as a long and mostly peaceful one – with capitalism. This came not a moment too soon, because with the collapse in Africa and Asia of the old European colonial systems and the proliferation of new nation states, the uncommitted world was growing more influential and clamorous. One of Russia's first problems was simply to break down the austere, not to say repugnant, image that she had presented under Stalin to almost all but loyal communists abroad. This image was personified in Vyacheslav Molotov, who with only a short break had been Foreign Minister since 1939. Of his ability in foreign affairs there was no doubt. Winston Churchill had said that Mazarin, Talleyrand and Metternich would welcome Molotov to their company. But Churchill had also nicknamed him 'old stone-bottom', and this alas was nearer to the common view of him outside the Soviet Union. In Khrushchev, on the other hand, the Soviet Union found a natural salesman for her new foreign policy. When Khrushchev made his first trips abroad in 1955, the world saw a Soviet leader astonishingly forthcoming and spontaneous in public. Even the ugly conventions of Soviet official dress, which he still observed at this time, could not disguise that here was a quite different sort of Soviet leader. Perhaps there is something inevitably attractive about a short, stout man of great energy who is not afraid to admit the indignity of his appearance and even increase it at times by his behaviour.

The three journeys abroad that Khrushchev and Bulganin made in 1955 did not just show to the world the new course of Soviet foreign policy in action. They also indicated the extent to which Khrushchev would manage to make that policy seem his own because of the extremely personal way he set about executing it. The first trip – to Yugoslavia – certainly demanded all the skill he could command. Stalin had excommunicated Marshal Tito from the true communist brotherhood after Yugoslavia's refusal to take orders from Moscow, in the belief, according to Khrushchev, that he only had to shake his little finger for Tito to fall. Yugoslavia, however, had not fallen. On the contrary she had gone from strength to strength and by 1955 considerably threatened the already shaky East European stability by the independence of her ways. More than that, the existence of a communist country that did not acknowledge Moscow as the Rome of all Marxists severely damaged Soviet pretensions to authority. Tito for his part was ready for closer government relations with Russia but he was very chary about a reconciliation with the Soviet Party, fearing that Moscow could never tolerate the Yugoslav insistence on independence, however much it might protest that everything had changed since Stalin's death.

Khrushchev, on the other hand, was very keen to renew relations with the Yugoslav Party and typically, although he knew of Tito's objections, brashly pursued this aim from the moment that he, Bulganin and Mikoyan arrived at Belgrade in May. Yugoslavia then and later brought out one element in Khrushchev's character above all others: an insensitiveness to subtleties of feeling and atmosphere in other countries, perhaps particularly small countries. This was not just a matter of any great nation's inclination to bully. Khrushchev shared something of the old Russian feeling that no part of the world is as real as Russia, and had given this a modern gloss by his own simple belief in Marxist dogma which affirmed the primacy of Russia as the first socialist state. At the same time Khrushchev had as yet little personal experience of the outside world, and for a man of his temperament it was personal experience that mattered most of all. His only trip outside the Soviet Union apart from Eastern Europe had been to the Soviet occupied zone of Austria after the war's end. Yet he approached the outside world with all the confidence of a man who had held senior posts in his country for close on twenty years and who had taken a direct part in the destruction of that one-time wonder of the world, Hitler's Germany. This confidence in himself, his country and his beliefs clashed with the limited awareness of his ignorance and was largely responsible for the unattractive bragging and bullying of which he was sometimes guilty abroad.

Khrushchev had, of course, cursed Tito like every other Soviet politician had done when Stalin was alive, and in similar circumstances few men would have shown such bounce the minute they landed on Yugoslav soil. But Khrushchev, undaunted by Tito's splendid uniform and magnificent Rolls-Royce, not only made his interest in resuming Party relations clear in his speech at Belgrade airport but put all the blame for the trouble between the two countries in the past on Beria. The Yugoslavs had already indicated that this face-saving explanation was unacceptable to them, and Khrushchev can hardly have been surprised at Tito's open annoyance when he came out with it. A man with greater awareness of Yugoslav pride and less passionately intent on a practical solution that ignored responsibility for the troubles of the past would have used a more subtle approach. Khrushchev's point was well made by the time the visit was over, but he was never to succeed in winning the Yugoslavs round to a complete acceptance of it, and his style of diplomacy was doubtless partly to blame for this.

Most startling to the general eye was Khrushchev's uninhibited behaviour in public during the Yugoslav visit. Under Stalin the Soviet leaders had been remarkable enough for their heavy eating and drinking, but this had been done in the privacy of their country dachas or the Kremlin. In Belgrade Khrushchev behaved on one notable occasion as though the world press, which had no qualms about making him look ridiculous, simply did not exist. At a big reception the Soviet and Yugoslav leaders had spent a considerable time in a private room. Then, in the words of one American journalist:

> The dignitaries . . . tottered out behind a hefty Soviet general and an immense Yugoslav: Khrushchev, clearly boiled in slivovica . . .; Bulganin, red-eyed and red-faced; and Tito, seemingly peering through a slight mist. When Khrushchev's gallant instincts got the better of him and he sought to embrace the ladies in a clumsy fashion, two of his plain-clothes agents hefted him up by the elbows, pushed him into a large, armoured limousine, slammed the door and sent him home.

Khrushchev, wearing 'an incredibly badly cut Soviet sack suit that looked as if it hadn't ever been pressed' reminded the American of a 'little gypsy dancing bear' – a description that in its mixture of scorn and apprehension was typical of much Western reaction to Khrushchev. But from this moment on there was never any doubt of his ability to capture people's attention. Greater experience of the pitfalls in foreign travel and pressure from his colleagues would eventually force Khrushchev to modify some of his more uninhibited ways, but this did not affect his ability to draw attention to himself. This gift for self-publicity was to contribute powerfully to the popular belief that Khrushchev was pursuing personal policies, when in fact they had usually been reached in agreement with his colleagues.

It was not until the Big Four summit meeting at Geneva the same summer, which Khrushchev attended with Bulganin and Molotov, that the extent of his power was understood by the West. Both President Eisenhower and Anthony Eden noted Khrushchev's dominant role at Geneva. 'Mr Khrushchev,' Eden wrote in his memoirs, 'was vigorous, downright and stubborn, but prepared to laugh. A forceful personality, always ready to go over to the attack....' Although Bulganin, as Prime Minister, did most of the talking at the conference table, 'The authority of Khrushchev could always be felt when the two men were together. He is perceptive and a man who knows his power; he could even overestimate it.' The authority that the Western leaders sensed in Khrushchev at Geneva was partly the result of the victory he had just achieved over Molotov's opposition to the new course of Soviet foreign policy. At a Central Committee plenum a matter of days before the summit conference Molotov, who particularly disliked Khrushchev's attempt to restore Party links with Yugoslavia, was beaten into an admission of his errors, quite possibly fearing that unless he capitulated Khrushchev might manage to remove him. With Malenkov disposed of, and Molotov on the decline, Khrushchev was free to abandon his past alarming talk of the dangers of war and exploit the spirit of Geneva to the full (Khrushchev's view of the international situation was often tailored to fit his domestic political needs). Although many people in the West were disappointed by the inability of the Geneva meeting to produce results, Khrushchev and his colleagues were probably better pleased. While not budging on German reunification, and committing themselves to no disarmament proposals which might hinder Soviet development of a nuclear arsenal (both areas where the West, misguidedly, had hoped for progress), Khrushchev and Bulganin managed to convey the Soviet commitment to coexistence. As Eden put it, 'Each country present learnt that no country attending wanted war and each understood why.' The reason, of course, was that all present had been initiated into the facts of nuclear life.

The implementation of the new Soviet foreign policy was continued in the most dramatic way possible by Khrushchev and Bulganin's tour of the Indian sub-continent in the winter of 1955. Nothing was better calculated to symbolize the Soviet change of heart towards the 'third world' since Stalin's death. The trip also showed for the first time the full range of Khrushchev's gifts as Soviet ambassador to the world at large. He was always to be slightly restrained when talking to purely communist or capitalist gatherings as in Yugoslavia and Geneva, but by contrast a large audience which he believed could be persuaded to share his own communist beliefs saw him at his most persuasive and frank. Above all in India Khrushchev was able to convey a powerful sense of friendliness, which did much to convince people that the changes in the Soviet Union were genuine. Amid vast crowds Khrushchev and Bulganin behaved as though they had spent their whole lives surrounded by hundreds of thousands of people. They wore garlands and Gandhi caps ('regardless of the fact that the Gandhi cap is the emblem of the Congress Party which has given no quarter to communists in India', noted the Indian ambassador to Moscow). When their car broke down in the middle of a three million crowd in Calcutta and they had to be whisked to safety in a police van, the two men took the incident easily in their stride.

At the same time, Khrushchev expounded Soviet thinking on India and other neutral countries with great forcefulness. He gave his support to India's policy of neutrality and praised Mr Nehru as a 'remarkable leader'. He took considerable trouble to show that Western, and particularly British, interest in India had not been benevolent in the past and could not be so in the future. The British in India had been 'robbers in the full sense of the word', and not even sounds of indignation from Britain, which he had an invitation to visit in the following year, made him moderate this tone. By contrast he announced to the whole third world that the attitude of the Soviet Union was quite different. After explaining how the Soviet Union had developed since the Revolution, he would say:

I am speaking of this not because I want to impose on you the Soviet path of development, but to give you a fuller idea of the different path travelled by our own people. . . . We have accumulated great experience during these years, and should you want to use to some extent our experience . . . we will readily . . . share it with you.

Khrushchev was a good salesman because he believed in what he was selling and was as impressed by the development of his country as he hoped others would be. The Soviet decision to avoid alarming neutralist leaders by making little mention of communism as an ideology and by completely ignoring local communist parties suited Khrushchev perfectly, because he believed that other people, like himself, would be more swayed by Soviet achievements than by Soviet ideas, however noble they might be.

The full extent of Khrushchev's skill in his new-found role of diplomat-extraordinary was still partly hidden by the presence of Bulganin, and when the two men returned to Moscow in December 1955 both of them reported to the Supreme Soviet on their visit. It was also as a member of a team that Khrushchev made his report to the 20th Party Congress in the following February, albeit as an increasingly important member. In it Khrushchev summed up the new points in Soviet policy on which the leaders had been able to reach general agreement. The report contained the guide-lines from which Khrushchev himself was to work when he had won political supremacy and is perhaps the best evidence of the extent to which the man who seemed so to dominate Soviet politics was in fact not forcing a policy of his own on the country, but was basically acting as the servant of a consensus. Khrushchev first dealt with foreign affairs, stressing three things above all: first, that peaceful coexistence between East and West was possible; second, that it was now possible to avoid war; and last, that there was no one pattern which all countries had to follow so as to become socialist. Khrushchev chose his words with particular care on the second point, the question of the inevitability of war. He said that as long as imperialism existed, Lenin's theory that the economic conditions for war also existed, still held good, but that nevertheless there was no longer 'a fatal inevitability of war'. The tautology only barely hid the slenderness of agreement within the leadership on this cardinal point. Both Molotov and Kaganovich took a far harder line in their speeches at the Congress. Molotov said pointedly:

We should not minimize the danger of war nor surrender to the illusion that peace and a quiet life are assured in all circumstances.... We should not surrender to complacency as if it were possible to convince the imperialists with nice speeches and pacific plans.

Similarly Khrushchev's third point – that there could be different ways of achieving socialism – raised a controversial issue because he explicitly included the possibility that some countries might become socialist by peaceful and parliamentary means. The Soviet example, in other words, was no longer obligatory for all.

This restatement of the Soviet Union's relations with the rest of the world affected everything that followed in Khrushchev's report, and above all it gave the section on the country's economy an altogether different emphasis. Khrushchev announced that Soviet development was still based on the 'preferential growth' of heavy industry, and that its other aims were to increase defence capacity and improve the standard of living. But this order of priorities, which apparently placed the consumer last, did not look so gloomy in the light of the new foreign policy principles. If there was to be coexistence with the West, and a good chance that war could be avoided, then this obviously meant that the final victory of communism could only be won if the Soviet Union achieved greater economic production than the West and so proved the superiority of her system for all the world to see. Although this certainly demanded considerable investment in heavy industry, proof of communism's superiority in the long run would have to be a higher standard of living (of this Khrushchev, at any rate, had no doubt). And Khrushchev did in fact devote a section of his report to this question, admitting that there was a great deal to be put right. But it was not so much what he said as the long-term conclusions to be drawn from the main theme of the speech that justified the Soviet citizen in expecting more from the future than would have seemed remotely possible three years earlier. The Soviet citizen might have been even more hopeful had he realized the extent to which the development of nuclear weapons had deprived his leaders of the chance to pursue a more aggressive strategy. And he would perhaps have been more confident about the future still had he known that the new policy gave Khrushchev just the scope he needed to make full use of his abilities and at the same time satisfy his own political desires.

Chapter 13
Khrushchev versus Stalin

Many speakers at the 20th Party Congress, Khrushchev included, showed a marked reluctance to make any but the briefest laudatory references to Stalin. This was in keeping with the practice established by the Soviet leaders after Stalin's death of removing the old dictator wherever possible from the public mind, while at the same time discreetly abandoning many of the most unpleasant features of the Stalinist system. But by 1956 the pressures for a more open approach to the Soviet past had become strong. Naturally it was the writers who had first felt compelled to discuss, albeit in cryptic terms, the meaning of the terrible experiences that their country had undergone. But there were other important groups throughout Soviet society which had a personal interest in some acknowledgement of the injustices they had suffered under Stalin. There was the whole academic community, so much of whose work had been shamefully perverted by the demands of Stalinist pseudo-science and many of whose members had been killed or imprisoned. There were the armed forces whose honour had been impugned by the execution of Marshal Tukhachevsky and his colleagues, and whose present leader, the Defence Minister Marshal Zhukov, had been personally humiliated by Stalin. The powerful state bureaucracy had its martyrs too in men like the brilliant planner Nikolai Voznesensky, who was shot on a trumped-up charge in 1950. Even within the Party a man who had been as close to Stalin as Anastas Mikoyan clearly felt the time had come to make some amends for the damage that Stalin had also inflicted on the Party. Given the existence of these pressures, the act of holding a Party Congress was bound in itself to seem an argument for some discussion of Stalin. According to Khrushchev, some Presidium members argued that it was precisely because this was the first Congress to be held since Stalin's death that the issue had to be discussed now: a postponement of discussion to a later Congress might not have been – as Khrushchev put it – 'understood'.

There is no evidence that it was Khrushchev who first suggested to the Presidium that some criticism of Stalin would now have to be made. On the contrary there were signs in 1955 that Khrushchev felt his hand could best be strengthened by identifying himself with Stalin and by claiming the leadership of the Presidium on his authority as first secretary of the Party – a move that would have had much in common with the way Stalin gained power in the 1920s as the Party's General Secretary. It has even been suggested that the Stalin issue was raised (possibly by Mikoyan) to stop such a dangerous manoeuvre by Khrushchev. Whatever the truth of the matter, there is no doubt that the Presidium was plunged into an extremely uncomfortable debate once the question had been broached. Khrushchev and his colleagues must have understood the great danger involved not only to the authority of the Soviet system but also to their personal standing as the men who had been Stalin's lieutenants. At the same time Khrushchev's political sense must have warned him that if an agreement was reached to reveal some of the truth about Stalin, he could not afford to allow anyone else to take the initiative. Whatever his original reaction to the idea, Khrushchev at some point came to see that the man who could saddle Stalin with the blame for the past while at the same time keeping the authority of the Party intact would be in a very strong position. He would have wide popularity and he would also have power. A sense of moral compulsion to make amends for the past probably affected Khrushchev's decision little if at all. He certainly had come to believe that Stalin's methods were wrong, at least in the last years of his rule, but it was quite another matter to say so publicly. Had silence still been possible in 1956, Khrushchev would have chosen silence.

The discussions in the Presidium turned (in Khrushchev's own words) into a 'very intense struggle', and a final decision may not even have been reached by the time the Congress began. The first sign that something was up came in Mikoyan's speech two days after Khrushchev had opened the proceedings. Mikoyan spoke ostensibly about the failings of Soviet ideological work, but in effect he was attacking the historical and economic theories that had been constructed to fit the Stalinist system and so by implication the system itself. The speech caused a sensation. According to the correspondent of the Italian communist paper *L'Unità*, who attended the Congress, after Mikoyan had spoken 'with passion, rapidly, half swallowing his words, as if fearful he would not have enough time to say everything ... the hall burst into animation; the delegates were exchanging opinions noisily. The succeeding orator was heard by no one.' Was Mikoyan the spokesman for a group which was trying to push a Khrushchev still uncommitted at this late stage into an attack on Stalin, or was he just testing what the reaction of the Congress might be to further and more damaging revelations? There is no way of telling for sure. But it is certain that Mikoyan's speech made a further pronouncement on the matter inevitable, because its implications were far too dangerous to be left unqualified. It was presumably with such considerations in mind that the Presidium decided to go ahead with an open attack on Stalin.

It was perhaps natural that Khrushchev should have been chosen to deliver the speech (irrespective of his own wishes in the matter) because he was, as first secretary, the Party leader, and it was clearly decided to limit the revelations as much as possible to Stalin's crimes against the Party. But there were probably other reasons, too, for the choice. We have Khrushchev's word for it that the Presidium was by no means sure of the effect the speech would have on the Congress, let alone the Party or the country, and the man who made it was almost certainly taking a considerable risk. Indeed Molotov and Malenkov most likely thought that Khrushchev would do himself more harm than good by the speech: if so, they were very nearly proved right. This would also explain why they allowed Khrushchev to make the speech that he did. All the senior members of the Presidium, Khrushchev excluded, were implicated by it in varying degrees as Stalin's accomplices. Molotov and Kaganovich were described as receiving Stalin's orders for the final great purge of 1936–8. Malenkov was shown as particularly close to Stalin. The Leningrad affair, in which Malenkov had been involved, was dealt with at length. Khrushchev on the other hand appeared only in the rosiest of lights. So very noticeably did Marshal Zhukov, who was shown as the victim of Stalin's vanity. It was not possible for Khrushchev to force the Presidium to accept this sort of speech. Otherwise he would also have had the power to bring about a re-shuffle in the leadership. What is more likely is that Khrushchev for his part saw, with his daring as usual bordering on rashness, that the speech could be an invaluable political weapon for him. His colleagues on the other hand were quite happy not to associate themselves at all closely with such a potentially dangerous enterprise. In this way Khrushchev was given freedom to give his own gloss to what must have been otherwise a broadly agreed outline for the speech. He was thus able to 'neutralize' incidents that were most embarrassing for himself, like the destruction of the Ukrainian leadership in 1937, while at the same time dramatizing his own conflicts with Stalin during the war to show that he at least had stood up to the dictator. Throughout the speech Khrushchev made points from his own personal experience – some of them may even have been impromptu – which also added considerably to the impression that it was above all Khrushchev who was locked in combat with the ghost of Stalin.

Khrushchev's exploitation of the speech for his own political ends was nevertheless substantially limited by his own interest in seeing that the attack on Stalin did not develop into an attack on the Soviet system itself. While he was keen to imply that men like Molotov and Kaganovich were guilty of abetting Stalin, it was necessary both for his own safety and for the preservation of the leadership's authority also to show that Stalin's colleagues were powerless to prevent the crimes. So Khrushchev described how even Politburo members went in fear of their lives:

> In the situation which then prevailed, I often talked with Nikolai Aleksandrovich Bulganin; once when we were travelling in a car, he said, 'It has happened sometimes that a man goes to Stalin on his invitation as a friend. And when he sits with Stalin, he does not know where he will be sent next, home or to gaol.'

Such a state of affairs, Khrushchev said, 'put every member of the Political Bureau into a very difficult situation,' and if Stalin's refusal to hold regular meetings of even the Politburo was taken into account too, then 'we will understand how difficult it was for any member of the Political Bureau to take a stand against one or another unjust or improper procedure....' But the core of Khrushchev's personal apologia as well as his defence of the whole Soviet system was not this unconvincing plea of helplessness, but the claim that all the terrible mistakes had been the result alone of defects in Stalin's character. All would have been well in the Soviet Union, the argument ran, had it not been for the cult of Stalin's personality. This was something alien to the Soviet system, imposed on it from outside, and all it was now necessary to do in order to restore the system to perfection was to expose the cult. Khrushchev was also very careful to date the beginning of Stalin's personality cult, lest anyone should be so misguided as to imagine that such episodes as Stalin's destruction of open political opposition, collectivization and the terrorization of the old intelligentsia could now be attacked as part of the personality cult. Khrushchev claimed that at first Stalin had been a true heir of Lenin. He presided over the great achievements of the industrial, agricultural and cultural revolutions for which he gained 'great popularity, sympathy and support'. It was necessary, too, to fight the 'Trotskyites, Zinovyevites and Rightists, and Bourgeois Nationalists' who had tried 'to lead the country away from the correct Leninist path'. But, Khrushchev went on, 'Later ... Stalin, abusing his power more and more, began to fight eminent Party and Government leaders and to use terroristic methods against honest Soviet people.'

The face-saving purpose behind this explanation was so plain that in the eyes of many communists, particularly outside Russia, it almost did more harm than good. Soon after the Party Congress the Italian communist leader Palmiro Togliatti expressed what a lot of people even in the Soviet Union must have thought to themselves:

> Previously all the good was due to the superhuman qualities of one man; now all the evil is attributed to his equally exceptional and shocking defects.... The real problems are skipped over – how and why Soviet society ... could and did depart from the self-chosen path of democracy and legality to the point of degeneration.

The problem that tortured Togliatti and many other communists was how Stalinism had developed out of the system created by Lenin. Was there something essentially wrong in the Leninist system which made the Stalinist perversion likely from the very start? It is most improbable that Khrushchev was able to grasp the fundamental importance of this line of questioning. It is therefore quite wrong to explain the inadequacies of the secret speech just by the fear of the new Soviet leadership that a more objective analysis of the past would reveal their own responsibility and by their anxiety to find a scapegoat (although, as his use of Beria to explain the troubles in Soviet–Yugoslav relations showed, Khrushchev had no objection to using such a contrivance). Khrushchev could not grasp Togliatti's point for two reasons. The first was that he could not acknowledge that Stalinism was more than the work of one man without admitting to himself that the very core of his own beliefs and work had also been tainted. But looking back over his own life Khrushchev believed that he saw there justification for his own rather crude belief in communism. His practical mind demanded only the most obvious sort of evidence of success and found it above all else in the fantastic material growth of the Soviet Union. Uninfluenced, as were Western communists such as Togliatti, by the more gentle climate of West European democracy, Khrushchev was ready to accept much of the suffering endured in Soviet Russia as necessary. Where he differed from a more logical, less humane man like Molotov was in his later refusal to accept all Stalin's victims as 'painful revolutionary necessities' (a phrase Molotov is said to have used in the Presidium debates when arguing against the rehabilitation of Stalin's victims). This was because Khrushchev's confidence in Stalin had been shaken before 1953, and it was then that Khrushchev's explanation of the unpleasant aspects of Stalinism by Stalin's personal faults must have been born. Khrushchev's inability to offer a deeper explanation of the horrors under Stalin's rule involved self-preservation of a far more fundamental sort than the merely careerist.

The second reason why Khrushchev could not satisfy communists like Togliatti was that he was in one very important sense a Stalinist himself. Stalin had developed Lenin's idea of a guiding Communist Party into a system that justified his absolute control over all aspects of Soviet life. And Khrushchev, too, believed that the Party should have as absolute a control over Soviet life as Stalin had exercised in his own person. He certainly held that the Party's control should be much less arbitrary than Stalin's, but none the less thorough for that. Accordingly in the secret speech one of Khrushchev's main concerns was to see that, despite the admission of past errors, nothing should be done to damage the

Party's claim to authority. It was with thoughts like these in mind that Khrushchev had already advised the Hungarian leadership in 1953 and 1954 to rehabilitate some of its victims in order to *increase* its authority, and at the same time made it clear that even the Hungarian leader Rakosi would have to be sacrificed if the maintenance of the Party's authority demanded it. Khrushchev expressed the same idea when justifying the secret speech to a Hungarian audience in 1959 – that is, after the disturbances in Eastern Europe touched off by its revelations were over:

> Following the 20th Congress ... some Parties, including our own, experienced certain difficulties, something like a fever.... Some people have said that certain complications in public life of the socialist countries stem from the 20th Congress of our Party, that the question should not have been raised so sharply.
>
> No, comrades, it had to be done.... Just as an artist sometimes has to remove the grime of time on a painting to restore its colours, so we had to clean up some things to show the real face of creative Marxism-Leninism.

Khrushchev's long-term interest in the secret speech – that it should strengthen the authority of the Party – was in fact dangerously at variance with his short-term political aim of using it to damage his rivals. From now on Khrushchev was to be continually tempted to brand men as different as Molotov and Malenkov as Stalinists. This was at times to prove very effective, but it also gave encouragement to more thorough-going critics of Stalin than Khrushchev was both in the Soviet Union and Eastern Europe.

The immediate effect of the speech was to throw the whole country into – as Khrushchev put it – a 'fever'. Rumours about the speech began to flash around Moscow within twenty-four hours, and within days they were confirmed at special Party meetings throughout the country at which a version of the speech was read. Eventually there can have been few Soviet citizens who did not have some idea of what had been said, in spite of the fact that not a word of the speech was published in the press. The effect, particularly on young intellectuals and students, was shattering, for the greater part of what they had been taught at school and university was now revealed as untrue. The more adventurous among them believed that they now had semi-official encouragement to think along new lines, and as the year went on Soviet writers produced a series of works that expressed a longing for radical, democratic reforms of the system. At first this mood was greatly to Khrushchev's advantage. Popular government measures were enacted to end the strict labour discipline regulations imposed by Stalin and to increase pensions and minimum wages. The conservatives in the leadership were undoubtedly weakened, and in early June Molotov and Kaganovich lost their important governmental posts. Molotov was replaced as Foreign Minister by Dmitri Shepilov, an intellectual who had aided Khrushchev in his fight with Malenkov in 1954–5. Molotov's demotion came significantly just before Marshal Tito arrived on an extended visit to the Soviet Union. The Tito visit, together with the earlier dissolution of the Cominform – the organization through which Stalin had dominated the world communist movement – was taken as a sure sign that the Soviet Union was now committed to tolerating considerable variety in the communist world and so by implication was also ready to admit sizeable flaws in her own system.

The Polish communist leader Edvard Ochab is said to have asked Khrushchev shortly after the 20th Party Congress what his policy should be. 'Make yourself popular,' Khrushchev replied. In the months after the Congress Khrushchev certainly tried to follow his own advice, and this disguised the fact that he wanted popularity on his own terms. When a workers' strike turned into a revolt at the Polish town of Poznan on 28 June, and the Polish and Yugoslav Parties actually gave public sympathy to the workers' complaints, Khrushchev abandoned his search for popularity quickly enough. The Soviet press published within days articles which laid down firm limits to de-Stalinization. Given the balance of power within the Presidium, Khrushchev can have had little doubt about the desirability of changing course once Poznan had shown where de-Stalinization might lead. As the author of the secret speech he was now in an extremely vulnerable position, and one from which he could escape only by showing himself as firm as his most conservative colleagues in stopping the rot. At the same time he almost certainly did not realize until Poznan just how destructive of that Stalinist system which he had no wish to challenge the secret speech would be, once it took effect in the very different world of Eastern Europe. Khrushchev had failed to see that in countries like Poland and Hungary, where there was strong national resentment at Russian, and not just communist, domination, and in which communism had barely a decade of existence, the secret speech would light a fuse to a stack of dynamite. For the next year Khrushchev would have to wage the greatest of all his fights to save not only Soviet authority but himself from being destroyed by the explosion that followed.

Chapter 14
The Anti-Party Group

The irony of the revolts in Poland and Hungary in the autumn and winter of 1956 was that eventually they were to make communism more secure in those traditionally turbulent countries than all the preceding ten years of Stalinist-type rule had managed. It was perhaps a measure of the state of near-panic which possessed Khrushchev after the Poznan riots that he at first failed to see in Vladislaw Gomulka, who was brought to power by the Polish troubles, a communist of very much the same convictions as himself. Khrushchev's panic was understandable enough. Poznan after all seemed proof that his enemies had calculated correctly that he would do himself more harm than good by the secret speech. It was now inevitable that Molotov and Kaganovich would regain much of the influence they had lost. Most men in Khrushchev's position would probably have played safe. They would have swung with the prevailing political wind and taken care not to draw attention to themselves by any display of idiosyncrasy. But the most fascinating part of Khrushchev's political technique was always his aggressiveness under attack. Of course he was now to swing to some extent with the new wind, but at the same time in the months that followed Poznan he was to give the most dazzling display ever of his peculiar political skills and tricks.

His first significant move was to try to gain the support of Marshal Tito and the Yugoslavs in the struggle with his colleagues in Moscow. By September it seemed that perhaps the only way to calm down Eastern Europe, and particularly Poland and Hungary, was to get Yugoslav blessing for the régimes there, which the Russians were now ready to change somewhat. To this end Khrushchev spent the second half of September in Yugoslavia, unaccompanied by any of his senior Soviet colleagues. Khrushchev tried to persuade Tito to help the Russians on the grounds that otherwise a Stalinist faction would get the upper hand in Moscow, and when Khrushchev took Tito back to the Soviet Union with him for a brief Black Sea 'holiday', the argument was no doubt repeated by the galaxy of young Khrushchev stars who also happened to be having a holiday there. Taking part in this, the first clear Khrushchev group action, were Aleksei Kirichenko; two new candidate members of the Presidium, Leonid Brezhnev (from Khrushchev's Ukrainian apparatus and one of the first men to be entrusted with the supervision of Khrushchev's precious virgin lands programme) and the blonde and handsome Yekaterina Furtseva (whom Khrushchev had spotted in the Moscow apparatus)*; and significantly the KGB chief Ivan Serov and a 'Khrushchev soldier', Marshal Grechko. Just what Khrushchev and his men said to Tito was clear enough from a speech made later that year by the Marshal. The Soviet attitude on Eastern Europe, Tito said, was wrong but it had been 'imposed by those people who took up and today still take up a fairly strong Stalinist stand. . . .' Nevertheless

> there are still possibilities that those elements will be victorious in an internal evolution of the leadership of the Soviet Union which support a stronger and faster development in the direction of democratization, the abandonment of all Stalinist methods and the establishment of new relations among socialist states.

At this and other meetings with Tito, Khrushchev almost certainly made himself out to be considerably more of a 'democratizer' than he actually was in order to win the Yugoslav's support. Tito for his part probably never took Khrushchev's words at their face value but often pretended to, believing that in this way he could push Khrushchev more easily in the direction he wanted him to go. But within two weeks of Tito's return home, news from Poland was to make these subtleties of communist diplomacy so much wasted effort. In mid-October the Soviet leaders were horrified to hear that the Polish Politburo now proposed to appoint Vladislaw Gomulka, a 'nationalist' communist whom Stalin had had imprisoned, as first secretary. The Khrushchev group were in favour of rehabilitating men like Gomulka, but certainly not of giving them the leadership. Molotov and Kaganovich were opposed even to their rehabilitation. Worse perhaps, the Poles proposed to remove the Soviet

* Furtseva was conveniently married to the then Soviet ambassador to Yugoslavia.

Marshal Rokossovsky, who had been Poland's Defence Minister since 1949. For Khrushchev, who had above all to show that the process of change in Eastern Europe touched off by de-Stalinization could be controlled without damage to vital Soviet interests, the news from Warsaw came as the worst possible blow. It was not surprising, therefore, when the Soviet leaders decided that only their immediate and personal intervention could stop disaster in Poland, that both Molotov and Kaganovich should have been included together with Khrushchev and Mikoyan in the delegation that left at once for Warsaw.

The Soviet leaders arrived uninvited in the Polish capital on the morning of 19 October, the day a plenum of the Polish Central Committee was due to begin. According to the rumours of what took place at the confrontation between the Soviet and Polish leaderships, it was Khrushchev, aided by Mikoyan, who took the initiative on the Soviet side. If Khrushchev was to forestall Molotov's manoeuvres against him, this was the way it had to be. Typically, Khrushchev set the tone the moment he set foot on Warsaw airport, according to one version, shouting at the hastily assembled Polish leaders:

> We have shed our blood to liberate this country, and now you want to hand it over to the Americans, but in this you will not succeed, this will not happen!

There then followed an unpleasant exchange with Gomulka, who is said to have reminded Khrushchev, in Polish, who he was and that he had suffered imprisonment at Russian hands. The discussions proper were held in the incongruously elegant Belvedere Palace. Khrushchev was still in a considerable rage and indulged in a good deal of finger wagging which by all reports left Gomulka completely unmoved. Khrushchev and Mikoyan appear to have argued that Poland was slipping into anarchy. The Polish press, which had been outspoken in its criticism of the Soviet Union and of communism, must be controlled and all opposition crushed. It was all right for Gomulka to join the Politburo, but the friends of the Soviet Union in the Polish leadership and in particular Marshal Rokossovsky (who was a Soviet citizen) must remain. Their departure would signal that Poland was about to leave the Soviet bloc, and Moscow would use force to prevent this.

If this is a fair summary of the arguments that Khrushchev used, it suggests that on that grey and rainy day in Warsaw he was a rattled man indeed. The need to talk tough so as to impress Molotov as much as the Poles, combined with a situation in Poland itself that he came nowhere near to understanding, made him exaggerate the dangers. Even though, as he was to learn that day, the Polish army and security forces were ready to fight against Soviet troops, this could have done no possible good in a country that was surrounded by other communist states. For simple geopolitical reasons, there was never any serious chance that Poland would leave the Soviet bloc. It was also a comment on Khrushchev's inability to understand the state of affairs in Eastern Europe and the extent of the 'Stalinist' traces in his own thinking that he could not accept the Polish leaders' arguments that only if they were left to cope with the crisis themselves could an explosion be prevented. The Soviet leaders flew back to Moscow early the next day without having won a single concession, and very likely still planning to bring the Poles to heel by force. Any such plans were abandoned, however, when on 23 October there broke out in Hungary a revolution which really did threaten to take that country out of the socialist bloc. (It is also likely that the Chinese advised Moscow to accept the Polish terms while at the same time recommending force to keep Hungary communist.)*

The Hungarian rising was even more dangerous for Khrushchev because he and his men had already worked hard to produce a cautiously de-Stalinized régime there. Mikoyan had gone to Budapest in the summer to sack the incorrigible Stalinist Rakosi. Khrushchev had stage-managed a meeting between the new Hungarian leader Gero and Tito when the latter visited the Black Sea in early October, hoping that a Yugoslav blessing would make the new leadership more tolerable in Hungarian eyes. It may well be, as Khrushchev later hinted, that his faction in the Presidium was at first against the use of force in Hungary, but this was perhaps not so much because of soft-heartedness as his own underestimation of the momentum that the revolt had already gathered.

* Some sources have it that Khrushchev telephoned to Warsaw on 23 October to announce that Moscow was now prepared to go along with the Polish solution.

It is probable that Khrushchev simply could not understand that this was more than an insurrection provoked by 'counter-revolutionaries' and so failed to see how any Hungarian leadership could not hope to stop it on its own. But once the 'rebel' government of Imre Nagy at the start of November announced that Hungary was to leave the Warsaw Pact (the East European equivalent of NATO) Khrushchev certainly accepted the necessity for Soviet military action quite as wholeheartedly as Molotov or anyone else. To call Khrushchev a butcher for his part in suppressing the Hungarian revolution, as so many people in the West have done, is to miss the point. Khrushchev was not a man who revelled in bloodshed or cruelty: on the contrary, by 1956 he had come to believe that communism had to win people by its example, not its brute strength. But as a Soviet statesman he was bound to prevent the disintegration of the Soviet system in Eastern Europe, and the decision of the Western governments not to intervene in Hungary was a tacit recognition of this. Khrushchev would have behaved in exactly the same way in November 1956 had he been all powerful in the Soviet Presidium and not, as was the case, living through a moment of extreme crisis in his political career.

The best comment on the weakening of Khrushchev's political position in the autumn of 1956 was the return of Molotov and Kaganovich to powerful government positions. Molotov's appointment, a couple of weeks after the suppression of the Hungarian revolution, as Minister of State Control, not only gave him considerable supervisory power over the whole state apparatus but suggested that the government's importance was once more increasing at the expense of the Party's. This, as usual, was a sure sign that Khrushchev was losing ground. The growing importance of the state apparatus was made even plainer at a Central Committee plenum in December 1956. This created a powerful new state body – the State Economic Commission – to supervise the running of the whole economy. Khrushchev did not speak at the plenum, and its decisions were obviously not to his liking. He was being pushed further and further away from the crucial control of the economy, and it is not surprising that in these circumstances he should once again have decided to hit back. The counter-attack that Khrushchev was now to launch united the Presidium against him as it had never been united before. Did Khrushchev realize that this must be so? The answer must be no: even so rash a politician as Khrushchev would scarcely have done anything consciously to help his opponents annihilate him, which was what they were very nearly to do in a few months time. The other important question is whether Khrushchev had decided that the time had come for him to replace collective leadership with his own. There was, as we have seen, already a sign that he was thinking along these lines before the 20th Party Congress. The confusion caused by the secret speech had certainly destroyed the basis of the consensus reached after the removal of Malenkov from the premiership in early 1955. The odds are that Khrushchev now believed the leadership could no longer contain himself, Molotov and Kaganovich together, just as after Stalin's death he had known he could not survive with Malenkov holding the dominant position.

Khrushchev's first move to regain the ground that he had lost at the December 1956 plenum marked out the main battlefield and divided up the armies for the approaching war. After some extremely vigorous work in the provinces and aided by his supporters in the Party apparatus, Khrushchev was able to call another Central Committee plenum in February 1957 which went completely against the decisions taken two months earlier. Khrushchev announced sweeping plans to decentralize the control of the economy, abolish many of the powerful ministries in Moscow, and set up instead a multitude of local economic authorities. At the same time Khrushchev managed to get the powers of the State Economic Commission cut and Molotov's State Control Committees publicly criticized. The reorganization plan was put up for so-called public discussion six weeks later, but not one Presidium member took part in it. The silence of Molotov, Malenkov, Kaganovich, Mikoyan, Bulganin, Pervukhin and Saburov was all the more noticeable because they also constituted the Council of Ministers – the government – and were therefore most directly concerned in any reorganization. At a meeting of the Supreme Soviet in May, Khrushchev's Ukrainian protégé Aleksei Kirichenko alone of the Presidium spoke in favour of the plan. Economic officials and planners were on the whole as silent as Molotov and his men.

The Khrushchev reorganization plan was largely a matter of power politics, and its timing probably altogether so. With it Khrushchev was hoping to weaken his enemies' power base (the state apparatus) and to a large extent replace it by his own (the Party) in the supervision of the Soviet economy. At the same time enough has already been said about Khrushchev's attitude to the Party's participation in economic work, and his own near-obsession with it, for it to be clear that he was championing the reorganization not just out of political expediency but because it in any event made sense to him. There was, too, a case to be made for decreasing the amount of centralization in the Soviet economy with the vast Moscow ministries stretching their tentacles into the minutest details of factory life. But the way Khrushchev rushed the scheme on his unenthusiastic colleagues and blithely announced that it could be carried through in a matter of weeks was in itself unlikely to encourage a calm consideration of its merits.* And with the advantage of hindsight, it is clear that from the moment that Khrushchev launched his scheme, the birth of the anti-Party group and its attempt to remove Khrushchev from power became inevitable.

The core of the anti-Party group (Khrushchev's own, and perhaps unintentionally expressive name for the conspirators) was the alliance between Malenkov on the one hand and Molotov and Kaganovich on the other. Events since Stalin's death had shown that these men had little in common, but now Khrushchev's plan not only threatened them personally but also, recklessly it seemed to them, the structure of the Soviet state. According to Bulganin they believed that the reorganization would cause 'anarchy in the direction of industry and construction', and into the bargain flouted Lenin's precepts on the division of powers between the central and local authorities (such questions of

* The scheme as presented in 1957 provided for the creation of Councils of National Economy (called by the Soviet abbreviation Sovnarkhoz) which covered an area roughly that of the administrative region in size. These, not surprisingly, were found to be far too small, and later enlarged sovnarkhozes were created. After Khrushchev's fall the ministerial system was re-established. It seems that, whatever the disadvantages of centralization in so vast a country as the Soviet Union, Khrushchev's successors, who had experienced both systems, considered them less than those of the decentralized sovnarkhozes.

Marxist-Leninist dogma did genuinely concern Soviet leaders of Molotov's intellectual bent, however much he may have also found them useful as political weapons). It was inevitable, given the resistance of this powerful trio on this issue, that Pervukhin and Saburov, both state economic administrators by background, would also be tempted to oppose Khrushchev. Pervukhin in particular had a grudge, because the State Economic Commission which he had headed was dissolved in April, and the chief coordinating economic body now left, the Gosplan, had been placed under a relatively obscure pro-Khrushchev Party official.

The reorganization went through the Supreme Soviet in early May, and one might have expected Khrushchev to set about a careful consolidation of his victory. Quite the reverse: speaking to an agricultural conference in Leningrad on 22 May, he now made as provocative a speech as any he had ever delivered. The time had come, he said, to catch up with the United States in the production per head of meat, milk and butter. He implied that the target date for milk should be 1958 and for meat 1960 or 1961. This meant producing 70 million tons of milk and 21 million tons of meat; 1956 production figures were 49·1 million tons of milk and 6·6 million tons of meat. Can Khrushchev have possibly believed such an increase possible? Specialists advised him that it was not, and they were eventually proved right. Or did he calculate that to pose as the prophet of more milk, meat and butter would improve his political standing? One thing was certain: the speech greatly annoyed his Presidium colleagues and particularly Bulganin. When Khrushchev made the same pledge a few days later in Moscow, Bulganin led some of his colleagues in a walk-out. Such a public display of political passions was unprecedented in Kremlin politics. The speech simply brought to a head all the disagreements and irritations that Khrushchev's flamboyant handling of agriculture had already provoked, beginning above all with the virgin lands, but by now including a whole range of measures affecting all aspects of agriculture.

By the beginning of June the different grudges that the Presidium members almost without exception bore against Khrushchev had turned into a willingness to conspire for his removal.

Although there was a wide difference of opinion among the opposition about what part of Khrushchev's activities was most distasteful, there seems to have been a growing awareness that something was very much wrong with his basic style of work. Khrushchev had elaborated on this in the section on Party work in his report to the 20th Party Congress, where he laid down almost as holy writ the connexion between Party and economic work which formed the nub of his ideas on the functioning of the Soviet system. Lenin, he said, had always 'connected Party work with economic activity'; but unfortunately 'over the course of many years our Party cadres have been insufficiently educated in the spirit of high responsibility for the solution of practical questions of economic construction', and a 'stupid setting-off of party-political against economic activity is tolerated'. Khrushchev then laid down the quite new principle that 'The activity of a leading Party worker must be judged in the first place by the results achieved in the development of the economy' and even proposed that Party workers' salaries should be related to production. As Khrushchev's earlier career had shown, these ideas were decidedly controversial, and when they found practical expression in the industrial reorganization scheme, more traditionally minded people, both in the Party apparatus and elsewhere, were alarmed. It was Khrushchev's attitude of 'let's get down to the main job of increasing production' that led the anti-Party group to accuse him of the sin of 'practicism, of being carried away with problems of economic construction'. They opposed the industrial reorganization simply as a wrong measure: but Khrushchev's 'practicism' in their eyes was a serious political complaint that had far wider implications. The drift of their argument was that it was wrong to make hand-to-mouth decisions unrelated to any set of principles. It is not an exaggeration to say that for a man like Molotov the decision to build, say, either nuclear or conventional power stations was as much related to basic principles as the Russian Church's decision to use two or three fingers in making the sign of the cross. In a society where a group of men claim to possess the knowledge of absolutes, everything must ultimately be related to those absolutes. Khrushchev was brought up in such a society, but this way of looking at things was by nature utterly alien to him. Molotov, as in his defence of Stalin, was again being more logical, and Khrushchev, once again, more practical.

The plan to remove Khrushchev was put into action at a meeting of the Presidium on 18 June. Malenkov, Molotov and Kaganovich knew that they could count on a majority among its eleven members, including Bulganin (whose house and Kremlin office had served as a meeting place for the conspirators), Pervukhin, Saburov and Voroshilov (who played only a rather passive part in the whole affair). Khrushchev, they knew, could only count on Kirichenko and Mikoyan, the latter's distaste for the Stalinist elements in the anti-Party group apparently counting for more than his scepticism towards some of Khrushchev's own policies. Even if Suslov, the ideological expert, went to Khrushchev, the conspirators could count on a majority of seven to four. The pretext for the attack was a proposed visit by Party leaders for some planned festivity in Leningrad. Malenkov is believed to have led off by saying that such a 'grotesque figure' as Khrushchev could not possibly go to Leningrad and went on to make a full-scale attack on Khrushchev and his policies.

The conspirators hoped to force a vote in the Presidium and replace Khrushchev by their own representatives – probably Molotov as first secretary and Malenkov as Prime Minister. The changes would be immediately broadcast, and Shepilov, who had abandoned Khrushchev, was to draft a statement for the press. All this seems to have taken Khrushchev completely by surprise, and had the conspirators prepared the base of their coup better, he would have had no choice but to surrender. Yet whatever contact Malenkov and Molotov had with the army and the security forces, it did not extend to arranging for their victory in the Presidium to be backed up by a show of force. Perhaps they had not dared do more than make preliminary soundings. Perhaps they believed it would not be necessary. Either way, it looks as though once again they had simply underestimated Khrushchev's resourcefulness, because at some stage during the wrangle in the Presidium he realized that he could save himself by appealing to the Central Committee. His control over the Party apparatus meant that many of the jobs that carried Central Committee status were virtually his own appointments, and by mid-

1957 he could count on a comfortable majority of supporters among its members. It is most unlikely that Khrushchev ever imagined using the Central Committee to back him up against the rest of the Presidium in this way, and so unprecedented was it to refer matters from the Presidium to the committee that Molotov and Malenkov also can scarcely have thought of it as a possible escape route. Khrushchev's demand that the Committee be called was met with a refusal, but after the Soviet leaders had been arguing for two days a group of Khrushchev's closest supporters in the Party, who had somehow been informed of what was going on, sent a letter demanding that a plenum be called. The letter was followed by a group of Khrushchev stalwarts who arrived in person at the room in the Kremlin where the Presidium had been in constant session, despite the guards placed to stop any Central Committee members. This was the beginning of the end for the conspirators, and as soon as they saw among the group none other than the Defence Minister, Marshal Zhukov, they must have known it.

Military planes, on the orders of Zhukov, had already begun ferrying Central Committee members to Moscow from all over the Soviet Union. The plenum – some three hundred people in all – finally began on 22 June. It was a mammoth meeting, lasting a week. The first session is said to have gone on for thirty-five hours, during which Molotov and his allies were still on the offensive, and Khrushchev made a three-hour speech in his own defence. In all sixty of the most powerful men in the country spoke. At some stage during the proceedings, Khrushchev's enemies seem to have realized that they could not swing the Central Committee, and, with the exception of the magnificently stubborn Molotov, admitted that it was they who had been in the wrong. On 4 July, *Pravda* announced that Molotov, Malenkov, Kaganovich and Shepilov had been removed from their posts and expelled from the Central Committee.*

The fight had left Khrushchev stronger than ever: the new

* The part of Bulganin, Voroshilov, Pervukhin and Saburov in the anti-Party group's plot was not admitted till later, presumably because it was felt better not to admit that Khrushchev had been opposed by a majority of his colleagues in the Presidium. Bulganin accordingly remained Prime Minister and Voroshilov Soviet Head of State.

members elected to the Presidium to replace Molotov and his co-plotters included Khrushchev supporters from the Party secretariat, and this gave him for the first time a chance to dominate the country's ruling body; his enemies looked most unlikely ever to recover from the blow they had just been dealt. The man who had been so consistently underestimated by his opponents had now achieved a more powerful position than any other Soviet politician since the death of Stalin.

Chapter 15
Khrushchevism

In March 1959, a little less than two years after his defeat of the anti-Party group, Khrushchev took over the premiership from Bulganin. The new appointment was a formal expression of the growth of Khrushchev's power since the intrigues of June 1957. Was this power enough to give him real domination (of a kind, say, similar to that of Lenin or Stalin) over the Soviet Union and to allow him to execute policies of his own choosing?

In 1955 Khrushchev said to Dr Subandrio, the Indonesian Foreign Minister, that 'Stalin was a god; he could make and unmake men and things; we can't.' Some time later – after his criticism of Stalin in the secret speech – Khrushchev remarked in similar spirit to another foreigner, 'If you put fifteen of us end to end it would not make Stalin.' Khrushchev never believed that he could aspire to the greatness, terrible or otherwise, that Stalin achieved. Even the secret speech was in its way a tribute to Stalin, because however much Khrushchev reviled him, he knew he could never destroy the dead dictator's hold over his own and other Russians' imagination. Stalin had had no doubts about his ability to fill the vacuum caused in the Soviet Union by the death of Lenin, the genius of the Revolution. Khrushchev's recognition that in the final analysis he could not measure up to Stalin acted as a self-imposed limit to the extension of his own power and from the start made a direct comparison between the two men's authorities unprofitable. Nevertheless, within this limit Khrushchev amassed a very considerable amount of power. It was based on his holding of four posts which together gave him an unrivalled grip on all aspects of the country's life: his seat in the Presidium; the premiership; and his leadership both of the Central Committee secretariat and the Party bureau of the Russian republic, a new body he had created at the 20th Party Congress and through which he controlled Party activities in the largest republic of the Union. None of Khrushchev's colleagues had places in more than two of these bodies, for example combining the Presidium with a seat in the Council of Ministers or with membership of the secretariat. This meant that Khrushchev received more information about what was going on than anyone else and was to a considerable extent able to control the supply of information available to his colleagues. At the same time, through his dominance of the Party machine, which was of course the basis of his power, he was able to control the execution of policies.

Khrushchev's power also depended on having men of his own choosing placed strategically throughout the country's main centres of power. An example of the thoroughness with which he set about this is the number of key appointments held for all or much of the period from 1959 onwards by men with whom Khrushchev had worked during his long rule over the Ukraine. Khrushchev 'Ukrainians' headed the key Central Committee departments which controlled Party appointments and supervised the security and police forces and heavy industry. 'Ukrainians' inevitably held command posts in the agricultural ministries. And Khrushchev also chose 'Ukrainians' to control the most important power centres independent of the Party – the security forces and the army. By 1962 the Procuracy-General, the KGB and the army's political department were all headed by men who had begun their careers in Khrushchev's Ukraine. After the removal of Marshal Zhukov in late 1957, the Defence Ministry was given to Marshal Malinovsky, who had fought with Khrushchev at Stalingrad and in the Ukraine. Similarly after the 22nd Party Congress in 1961, the number of military members of the Central Committee who had similar wartime connexions with Khrushchev increased to ten compared with only three before 1956.

At the same time Khrushchev developed his own private secretariat, which came to work very closely with the Soviet publicity media in a way quite revolutionary for the Soviet Union. The private secretariat gave Khrushchev an information service that was independent of the Party and all other Soviet bodies. It could also provide him with the arguments needed to bolster up any controversial policy which he wished to force on his colleagues (his personal agricultural expert, also a Ukrainian, was particularly useful in this). Working with the press and radio, whose main organs were also controlled by Khrushchev associates, the secretariat created a degree of personal publicity for him that at times reached almost Stalinist proportions. Particular attention was paid to building up the image of Khrushchev as a world statesman. Collections of his speeches on foreign policy were brought out regularly, and long, triumphant accounts of his foreign tours (notably the American trip in 1959) were written by teams of leading Soviet journalists and Khrushchev's personal assistants. Khrushchev also took to making television speeches on his return from abroad. At the same time his war record was given a burnish in articles, scholarly books and films, usually by the simple process of omitting to mention the contribution made by others. A film biography of Khrushchev, made with the cosily sympathetic title of *Our Nikita Sergeyevich*, was widely shown and subsequently put on television. It became a matter of course that weighty articles in the press should begin and end with quotations from a Khrushchev speech. And with the launching of the first sputnik in 1957, great care was taken to see that Khrushchev was linked as closely as possible with Soviet space successes, to the extent finally of turning him into an uncle-figure of the enormously popular cosmonauts.

It would be wrong, however, to see this build-up of Khrushchev as just a personal enterprise. It was partly the result of the Soviet leadership's understanding that de-Stalinization had left a dangerous void in the political feelings of ordinary people. Very largely because of the war, Russians had come near to worshipping Stalin in spite of all the suffering he inflicted on them. Every nation has a desire, more or less well controlled, for a hero-leader, and Stalin had satisfied the Russian desire to the full. After de-Stalinization had begun, the Kremlin did their best to find a substitute in a vigorous Lenin cult, in particular using the image of a wise and good Lenin as a source of moral guidance in education. But although Lenin might often be spoken of as if he were still alive, a living leader was obviously necessary too. The Khrushchev build-up was at its height in the years between the defeat of the anti-Party group and the 22nd Party Congress in the winter of 1961, when the need to demonstrate the stability of the new leadership to the Soviet people and the world at large was greatest. The Khrushchev cult therefore excited less antagonism than it might have done, even though it gave Khrushchev a valuable edge over his colleagues which he did not scruple to use when faced with opposition to one of his pet projects.

Mikoyan once remarked in Khrushchev's presence: 'Nikita can't send me to Siberia any more. He's too late. That sort of thing is ended.' The agreement among Stalin's successors to abandon terror as a political tool was the most obvious limitation placed on Khrushchev's exercise of power. Khrushchev was able to scare an errant young writer, but he could not inspire fear among his colleagues as Stalin had done. For all his care to have a man well known to himself in charge of the KGB, there was never any sign that Khrushchev planned to revive the security services as an instrument of personal power. Only in this way could Khrushchev have broken away from the consensus that had developed within the leadership after 1953 and whose existence was in fact the strongest restriction of all on any wilful exercise of power on his part. Khrushchev dominated his colleagues in the execution of that consensus because of his vastly greater resourcefulness, energy and initiative. But he had no claim to the sort of dominance that both Lenin and Stalin had enjoyed as philosopher-kings. Few people, and least of all his colleagues, were ready to accept a pronouncement by Khrushchev as absolutely authoritative, derived from an exceptional closeness to the true spirit of Marxism. His colleagues knew well enough that Khrushchev had not invented the consensus, whereas Lenin and Stalin in their day had produced their strategy for the country, and either persuaded or forced others to accept it. And in a communist country, where it is a matter of public belief that there exists an ascertainable truth on all matters, a man who wishes to be a dictator must show himself to be in unique possession of that truth. Lenin and Stalin, each by his particular genius, had persuaded people that they possessed the truth. Khrushchev could never make such a claim. After Stalin the Soviet leaders could only claim that they knew the truth collectively.

Khrushchev moreover showed a genuine anxiety that the country be run according to 'constitutional' methods. As far as it is possible to know such things, the Presidium under Khrushchev met regularly, probably at least once a week. He did not, like Stalin, try to split up the Presidium so as to confine its members to limited functions. Because all matters of any importance were discussed in the Presidium, it meant that at the top of the Soviet hierarchy there were a dozen or so men well briefed on much of the details of home and foreign affairs. The even spreading of such knowledge was a considerable barrier in the path of any would-be autocrat. At the same time the rules governing the regular calling of Party Congresses and Central Committee plenums were usually observed. Khrushchev himself had given the Central Committee quite unprecedented importance by asserting its right to overrule the Presidium during his showdown with the anti-Party group. In the years that followed he was to show a preference for enlarged plenums, attended by officials and experts as well as by the Central Committee members proper. This may have been partly intended to prevent the Central Committee from developing into a well-knit group conscious of its strength, but Khrushchev had shown a liking for such enlarged plenums in his Ukrainian days, when he had used them as seminars on current economic problems, and very likely this was one purpose behind the plenums that he now organized as leader of the Soviet Party.

Later events were to suggest that for all Khrushchev's authority, neither the Presidium nor the Central Committee were afraid to oppose him, particularly when his schemes threatened to damage one of the power groups whose cooperation was necessary in working the post-Stalin consensus. In particular Khrushchev could always expect difficulties when his ambitious ideas on economic development clashed with defence interests (this is discussed in more detail in Chapter 18). At the same time he always had to take into account the danger that defeated opponents like Molotov might provide a rallying point for malcontents. Molotov himself, though sent in diplomatic banishment first to Outer Mongolia and then to Vienna, continued to criticize Khrushchev, and just before the 22nd Party Congress sent a letter to the Central Committee not only attacking him personally but dubbing the new Party programme 'pacifist and revisionist'. Molotov's main threat to Khrushchev was that he was putting forward arguments against the whole trend of post-Stalin Soviet policy from very much the same point of view as the Chinese, whose own disillusionment with Khrushchev was complete by the time that the 22nd Party Congress met. Khrushchev tried to discredit the Molotov line by writing off the whole anti-Party group as conservatives stuck in the old Stalinist ways, while posing himself as the champion of the new and the young, a by no means accurate picture of the real state of affairs. But the existence of Molotov supporters inside the Soviet Union, encouraged increasingly by Chinese pressure from without, put a very real brake on Khrushchev and in particular forced him to be more cautious than he might otherwise have been in the conduct of defence and foreign policy.

In the first years after the defeat of the anti-Party group, Khrushchev was largely able to satisfy his ambitions within the scope of the consensus. The twin aims of rapid construction at home and peaceful coexistence abroad needed the dramatic gestures that he was so adept at making. Above all his daring seems still to have been a matter for admiration and not, as it was to become later, of concern. Khrushchev himself provided the explanation of why this was so in an impromptu parable he told shortly before the dismissal of Marshal Zhukov in October 1957. The story concerned three prisoners: a social democrat, an anarchist, and a little Jew with scarcely any education called Pinya. The latter was elected their chief to supervise the distribution of food and tobacco. All went well until they decided to escape through a tunnel. They knew that the first man through the tunnel would have to risk being shot at by the sentries and so they turned to the anarchist, who was the biggest and strongest of the three. But he was afraid. Then little Pinya got up and said that since he had been elected chief, he would go first. The moral of the tale, said Khrushchev, was that 'however modest a man's beginnings may be, he will always reach the heights to which he is destined.' And then he added, 'I am little Pinya.' Although Khrushchev seems to have meant the story to relate to his quarrel with Zhukov (the anarchist), it also suggests that Khrushchev prided himself on being more ready than others to risk his neck for the good of the cause. It was after all his neck that the anti-Party group nearly broke in 1957. His willingness to assume responsibility and stand in the glare of publicity (something which Soviet politicians find particularly distasteful) did much to persuade his colleagues to accept his dominance.

If Khrushchev had no right to claim personal authorship of the strategy followed by the Soviet Union under his leadership, there were certain important areas where he was more or less free to do as he liked. Above all he enjoyed, if that is the appropriate word, this freedom in agriculture. Only a man of great daring would have chanced his reputation on solving the Soviet farm problem; but Khrushchev, quite apart from the political advantage he calculated that success would bring, had since his days in the Ukraine been captivated by the prospect of agricultural abundance. All the radical measures designed to improve agriculture since Stalin's death, from the virgin lands scheme to the abolition of the Machine Tractor Stations and the massive use of chemicals, were Khrushchev's brain children. He expounded them in hundreds of speeches (his agricultural pronouncements were eventually published in an eight-volume collection) and he travelled thousands of miles round the country checking on their progress. The amount of work he put into agricultural matters alone would have consumed the energies of most normal men. At first Khrushchev seemed to be succeeding. The total grain harvest increased from 82·5 million tons in 1953 to 141·2 million tons in 1958. Even more important from Khrushchev's own point of view, bumper harvests were gathered from the virgin lands in 1956 and 1958. In spite of far less satisfactory figures for the expansion of meat and animal products, which on close examination made the boast about overtaking America dangerously absurd, the good harvests disguised to a considerable extent Khrushchev's hastiness. Even his vision of prosperous rural life along the lines of the model village which he had constructed in his native Kalinovka (the plans bore a strong resemblance to the old agrotown scheme) did not seem so very far-fetched.

Khrushchev also had his way in a variety of lesser matters, ranging from the protection of the Stalinist biologist Lysenko from the wrath of the respectable Soviet academic world – Khrushchev apparently found Lysenko a good companion to talk farming with – to the decision that Russia was not to go in for the mass manufacture of motor cars. Education reforms which introduced a large measure of practical work into secondary schools and universities, together with an increasingly tough attitude by the authorities towards people who offended against communist morality, also reflected Khrushchev's essentially simple and proletarian convictions. But although Khrushchev's prejudices were to come more to the front as the years went by, his unique contribution – what with justice may be called Khrushchevism – lay in the speed and the style with which he chose to execute the policies of the consensus.

Khrushchev was by nature an impatient and impulsive man. Particularly after his visit to America in 1959, he came to be more and more obsessed by the time that it would take for the Soviet Union to match the achievements of the United States. The reason for this concern was Khrushchev's completely matter-of-fact approach to communism. Personally convinced of the moral superiority of the Soviet system, he was not the sort of man who could live through the grim times of industrialization, the horror of the war and the patient reconstruction afterwards, and still demand of people that they comfort themselves with moral perfection alone. Some time after the war, very possibly in part because of his experiences in the Ukraine where many people were hostile to the Soviet régime, Khrushchev evidently convinced himself that only results could be relied upon to win people over to communism. This was of course one of the underlying reasons for his interest in agriculture, which held the key to any increase in the Soviet standard of living. Soon after Stalin's death Khrushchev was telling people that they were right to demand a better life. He told an agricultural conference in early 1954:

> We must produce more grain. The more grain there is, the more meat, lard and fruit there'll be. Our tables will be better covered. And if there is sausage and fruit, then people will say: give us grapes, and with grapes one must have wine and all sorts of other things. And these are legitimate demands.

The following month he coined the phrase that might be taken as his political motto – 'And what sort of communist society is it that has no sausage?' It was this crude interpretation of the goals which the Soviet Union should hold before her in her competition with the capitalist world that was at the root of Molotov's criticism of him as a 'practicist'. The Yugoslavs too, after the collapse of Yugoslav–Soviet relations that followed the suppression of the Hungarian revolt, called Khrushchev a practicist ignorant of Marxist theory. Khrushchev knew quite well what they meant. In an interview he gave to the Indian ambassador in Moscow in the summer of 1958, he remarked that he was proud to be a 'practicist'.

I do believe that what counts more than anything else is practice. Marxist theory helped us to win power and consolidate it. Having done this we must help the people to eat well, dress well and live well. You cannot put theory into your soup or Marxism into your clothes. If, after forty years of Communism, a person cannot have a glass of milk or a pair of shoes, he will not believe that Communism is a good thing, no matter what you tell him.

In 1958 it was by no means possible to get a glass of milk everywhere in the Soviet Union, nor was it a simple matter to buy a pair of new shoes. To Khrushchev's practical and far from complicated mind, the problems facing the Soviet Union could honestly be summed up in the question 'What sort of a communist society is it that has no sausage?' To an intellectual communist of Molotov's calibre and equally to the 'progressive' Yugoslavs who were so proud of their innovations in Marxist–Leninist theory, however, this approach was embarrassingly crude. It produced much the same sort of effect on 'serious' communists as Mr Macmillan's cry of 'You never had it so good' among the puritan and idealistic in Britain.

Khrushchev's confidence that his vision of a Soviet Union in which every house had a well-covered table could, within a reasonable period of time, be turned into fact, was at its highest when the 21st Party Congress met in January 1959. The years since Stalin died had recorded economic growth of impressive rapidity. The 1958 harvest was an all-time record. Against this encouraging background, Khrushchev did not make a simple report to the Congress: he introduced the seven-year plan which promised an equally splendid performance for the economy up to 1965. The plan was impressive throughout, but most striking were the promises that Khrushchev made to the Soviet consumer. By 1965 *per capita* real income was to increase by forty per cent. The minimum wage would be doubled. 1962 would see the introduction of a forty-hour working week, with a thirty-five-hour week promised soon after. The Soviet Union would then have the world's shortest working day and the shortest working week. Particularly startling to Western ears was the promise that by 1965 income tax would be abolished (in fact income tax is relatively insignificant in the Soviet system of taxation). Khrushchev also looked further into the future, to 1970, when he prophesied that Soviet agriculture and industry would be producing more than their American counterparts both *per capita* and in total output. The new plan, Khrushchev said, was the start of a new stage in the history of the Soviet Union – the 'full-scale construction of communist society'. In other words the Soviet Union's ultimate goal of communism was appreciably nearer. Khrushchev left no doubt as to why he was so interested in speed:

> The root problem of the coming seven years is the problem of the maximum gaining of time in the peaceful economic competition of socialism with capitalism.

Khrushchev's account of the prosperous future ahead was very good for his political standing, and the 21st Party Congress was undoubtedly one of the most triumphant moments in his career. The insistence on speed must have seemed dangerous then only to the far-sighted. After all, Soviet industrial and agricultural production had risen by fifty per cent between 1954 and 1958, even according to the estimates of critical experts in the West. The Western world, already shocked by the Soviet Union's headstart in space (the first Soviet sputnik was launched in 1957), was now inclined to regard the Soviet economy as no less brilliant a piece of machinery than the sputniks and capable of sustaining a growth rate far above that of any capitalist country. Unfortunately for Khrushchev, however, the Soviet economy was to experience mounting difficulties almost from the moment that he announced his magnificent plan. Many of the promises he made to the ordinary Soviet citizen were in the event not kept. It was in these circumstances (which are discussed more fully in the final chapter) that Khrushchev's speed mania was to lead him into serious disagreement with influential parts of the Soviet establishment and his colleagues, and that Khrushchevism came to seem very much more like boasting and bravado than sound policy.

The second element in Khrushchevism – the man's style of leadership – was first and foremost a matter of Khrushchev's use of the Party. We have seen how his conviction of the Party's supreme usefulness as an economic tool had developed over many years and how, too, after Stalin's death, he had used the Party with considerable skill as his own political agent. But now that Khrushchev's concern was with the whole of the Soviet Union, he came to rely more and more on the Party as a sort of personal extension, to ensure that everything that ought to be done was being done. It has always been the case in so vast a country as Russia that an energetic ruler must become obsessed with seeing that his orders are obeyed. Averell Harriman once expressed surprise when Khrushchev told him that people had ignored an order of his, remarking that he had always thought Khrushchev's word was law in the Soviet Union. 'It is,' Khrushchev said coolly, 'but there's always a way of getting round the law.' He might well have added that there are even more ways than usual in a country the size of the Soviet Union. After 1959, when Khrushchev doubled the jobs of Party first secretary and Prime Minister, and the demands on his time by foreign affairs were extremely heavy, he still travelled about the Soviet Union as much as he could, seeing things for himself and checking on what had been done and what left undone. After his exhausting visit to America in September 1959, which he rounded off by a dash to pacify the Chinese in Peking, he found the time and energy to spend a week touring Siberia on his way back to Moscow. Whenever he went on his regular Black Sea holiday, he would always stop off to inspect places both on the way there and back. And of course where agriculture was concerned there was no limit to the distance he was ready to travel or to the number of details he was prepared personally to check.

Khrushchev had given the most detailed expression of his ideas on the relationship of the Party to economic work at the 20th Party Congress in 1956, and it has already been pointed out that they were one of the reasons for the growing mistrust of Molotov and others towards him. Khrushchev made sure that his ideas on the subject should be more than pious hopes by also suggesting at the Congress that the training given in Party schools (roughly technical colleges for young Party careerists) should be reorientated along economic lines. This was done in the following year, when the average training period was lengthened from two to four years. Out of 3,200 hours of teaching, only 1,400 were now to be spent on political and ideological subjects, whereas 1,800 were to be devoted to practical economic matters, including 100 on livestock farming. Khrushchev's interpretation of the Party's proper role not only worried those in other parts of the

Soviet system who found the Party interfering more and more in their work. There were also Party workers who disliked the new ideas. Khrushchev had had to battle with them from the very start, and although his position enabled him to remove many who disagreed with him, he felt obliged again and again to remind Party officials of their economic duties. An incident in January 1961 in the celebrated grain-growing region of Krasnodar in southern Russia illustrates his increasing impatience with the dilatoriness which some officials still showed in putting his theories into practice. Confronted with an unsatisfactory performance in maize growing, Khrushchev in public told the region's Party secretary, an important and powerful man in the Soviet hierarchy, that he should take lessons from a woman farmer who had recorded maize crops to her credit: 'Don't be embarrassed, don't think the leaders should teach everyone else but refuse to be taught themselves.' He then suggested that the successful farm girl might be elected Party secretary: 'What did you expect? Do you think all of us are immortal? The time is past when the leadership was hereditary. Now, work well and you'll be praised, work badly and you'll be replaced.'

Khrushchev's ideas about the economic role of the Party together with his uneasiness that his orders were not being properly carried out resulted in a series of measures which in the end completely altered the structure of Soviet administration. The reorganization of industrial management in 1957 which had so angered Molotov and Malenkov was only the first stage in the Party's growing power at the expense of the state officials and industrial managers. In 1959 Khrushchev decided to create Party control commissions in factories, shops and offices. These were to check on the prompt fulfilment of plans and had the power to make complaints about any misbehaviour in the enterprise under their control to a higher authority. At the 22nd Party Congress in 1961 the economic role of the Party was written into the new Party programme, which declared that the construction of the 'material and technical base for communism' was to be 'the cornerstone' of the Party's 'general line'. In March of the next year Khrushchev made a first step towards altering the Party's organization to suit better its economic function. The administration of farms at the lowest territorial level was altered to increase the amount of outside control over farm production, and in the exercise of this control it was the Party officials who were meant to predominate. This development was carried to its logical conclusion at a Central Committee plenum held in the following November. Khrushchev now announced that the Party was virtually to be split into two, with one half supervising agricultural, and the other industrial, production. And the split was to extend from the lowest to the highest Party level, culminating in separate agricultural and industrial bureaux in the Central Committee at Moscow.

This was the most radical measure for which Khrushchev was personally responsible (the state apparatus was also to be split in two, along with the Party), and at the same time it summed up all that he had come to feel most deeply about his work. Typically the traditional concerns of the Party such as organizational and ideological matters were pushed into the background, so much so indeed that at first there was even confusion about just how they would be fitted into the new system. Khrushchev produced his scheme against the background of an extremely discouraging economic situations. The loud promises he had made were increasingly a source of embarrassment. Above all, he was losing the battle with time. The impulsiveness which had led him to demand that everything be done at top speed had now forced him to reconstruct the Party literally in his own image. It was to dominate what counted for him above all else – the production of iron and steel, of plastics and textiles, of grain and meat. Just as Khrushchev had always had confidence that his own personal supervision could clear away all obstacles, so now he believed that only if the Party could be everywhere, making sure that every tractor was repaired on time, every factory prompt in its delivery dates, would the material abundance he had promised be rapidly achieved. It could now be said, not altogether unfairly, that he had at last managed to turn the Party of Lenin and Stalin into a Party of sausage makers.

Chapter 16
America

On 14 September 1959 the Soviet Union became the first country in the world to land a rocket on the moon. The next day, shortly after noon, Nikita Khrushchev arrived at Andrews Air Force Base near Washington in a giant TU 114 airliner. The timing of the two events added considerably to the tension of what was anyhow bound to be a difficult occasion. The American officials waiting to greet Khrushchev looked grim. The crowds on the route to Washington were quiet. Khrushchev, too, seemed unsure of himself. In appearance he was a very different person from the baggy-suited man who had made such a display of himself at Belgrade in 1955. *The New York Times* noted his black, three-button suit of light-weight worsted; his hand-made Italian style black shoes; gold cuff-links; and white silk tie with a light blue centre-stripe. In spite of this new-found elegance, Khrushchev fiddled uneasily with his hat while President Eisenhower read a short speech of welcome, uncertain whether it was proper for him to put it on to protect himself from the hot sun. When Khrushchev mentioned the Soviet moon shot in his speech, the Americans froze at such a lack of tact.

Many Americans looked on Khrushchev's arrival with about as much horror as their Puritan ancestors would have greeted a visit by the Pope of Rome. It was not just that he was called the butcher of Hungary – the Hungarian tragedy was barely two years old in September 1959 – and generally believed to be a man of blood. The almost unanimous hostility of the American press towards him reflected the terrifyingly wide gulf that had come to separate the communist from the Western world, a gulf in which mutual fear based very largely on ignorance had flourished above all else. And so, although it was partly as a sort of Columbus that he came to the United States, Khrushchev at the same time knew very well that the success of the visit depended not so much on what he discovered in America as on what the American people discovered in him. Another Soviet leader would very likely have been content to carry out the *détente* with the West that

Stalin's successors had decided upon by the more impersonal means of traditional diplomacy. But perhaps nowhere was Khrushchev's contribution to the execution of Soviet strategy more valuable than in his decision to try to sell the *détente* personally to the Americans. *Time* magazine, with its usual verbal exuberance, described the trip as 'a historic and tireless one-man campaign to cajole, flatter, wheedle, shame, threaten and defy the US into changing its way of looking at the world'. Perhaps it would be more accurate to say that Khrushchev tried to change the American way of looking at the Soviet Union, and in spite of the Berlin, Cuba and other crises that followed the visit, in the long run he did manage to do just this.

The reasons for the change in Soviet policy towards the West after Stalin's death have already been touched on. The strategy of Stalin's successors had two bases: first, that nuclear warfare had made coexistence between the great powers obligatory; second, that the victory over capitalism promised by Marx would be achieved by superior economic production. Khrushchev was tempted as time went by to simplify this latter aim into the crude proposition that communism could only prove its superiority by offering more material goods than any other system. And for the former, he was also inclined to take his interpretation farther and faster than were his more cautious colleagues. Khrushchev's gift for seizing the raw truth in a complicated situation pushed him towards the idea of a Soviet–American understanding which would guarantee world peace. Just before he set off on his American trip, he announced that if America and the Soviet Union, 'the two biggest countries in the world', could develop friendly relations, 'peace on earth will be more stable and durable'. A couple of months earlier he had said: 'If other countries fight among themselves, they can be separated; but if war breaks out between America and our country, no one will be able to stop it. It will be a catastrophe on a colossal scale.' Khrushchev believed that if America and the Soviet Union could agree on rules to prevent war between themselves, they would also be able to prevent conflicts in other parts of the world from developing into a threat to world peace. This was perilously close to saying that America and Russia should act as the world's policemen to impose a *Pax Sovietica–Americana* – a hard thing for many Soviet communists to accept and an obscenity to the Chinese and other revolutionary communists. The vigour of official Soviet denials that Khrushchev had proposed a deal with America on 'the division of the world' after he had given interviews at various times to Western journalists and statesmen showed how sensitive Moscow was on this matter. But for all the ups and downs in Soviet–American relations, Khrushchev never lost his awareness of the direction in which his responsibilities as the leader of a nuclear power compelled him to move. Ironically it was in July 1962, not long before the Cuban crisis, that he spoke again about Soviet and American responsibilities in plainer terms than usual to a group of visiting American newspaper editors:

> If some unintelligent statesman of some small state goes mad, this harms no one.... But if lack of intelligence is shown on the part of leaders of such states as the United States of America and the Soviet Union, then it would not only be a calamity for the people of our countries, but for the people of the whole world. A great deal depends on the mutual understanding between our two states.

Even for Khrushchev himself, however, there were two sizeable obstacles in the way of a firm Soviet–American understanding: the difference between Khrushchev's and successive American presidents' understanding of the rules of peaceful coexistence; and Khrushchev's own attitude to America. Khrushchev put his objections to the Western idea of coexistence very simply on Soviet television after his return from the 1961 meeting with President Kennedy in Vienna.

> Our conversations with President Kennedy revealed that we have different conceptions of peaceful coexistence. The substance of what the President said boiled down to the notion that a sort of dam should be erected to stem the movement of the peoples towards establishing in their countries political systems that go against the grain of Western ruling circles.... [This] would mean that if a people in some country wished to alter the socio-political system, this should not be allowed to happen.

Khrushchev believed that a social and economic revolutionary process was working its way out all over the world and that it had to be accepted by the Western powers as inevitable. Wars fought by a people to 'liberate' itself were part of this process, and were therefore both just and justifiable. They did not come into the same category as wars fought over national boundaries between two or more states, which the policy of coexistence sought to restrain because of the danger of their escalation into world-wide nuclear conflict. The belief that the world was changing in the direction prophesied by Marx was absolutely central to Khrushchev's way of thinking. After a long meeting with him in 1958, Walter Lippmann wrote: 'Mr Khrushchev has for the most part a pragmatic and earthy temperament, and he is not much given to Utopian speculation. But he has in him also the basic revolutionary faith that a new history has begun, and that a communist man is a new kind of man.' Khrushchev found it hard to understand why so many Western leaders could not see what was so plain to him. He himself could not appreciate Western fears that changes in Africa and Asia, let alone Latin America, would dangerously alter the balance of power on which the agreement to coexist was based. For Western leaders to complain of this process was as pointless in his eyes as would, for a medieval Christian, have been the protests of unbelievers when they found themselves condemned to hell. There is no evidence that either the Soviet conflict with China or the growing difficulty of fitting developments in Africa and Asia into a Marxist pattern ever shook this belief of Khrushchev that the world was moving in a direction which could in the long run only benefit both communism and the Soviet Union.

It is tempting to see in Khrushchev's own attitude to America a synthesis of all that revolutionary Russia had come to feel about the most powerful of the capitalist states. First and foremost Khrushchev was always absolutely on his dignity wherever America was concerned. Although he had done much to destroy the stupid Stalinist silence about American achievements and spoke out against Russian '*kvasnoi patriotizm*',* both as a Russian and as a communist he was deeply convinced of his own country's superiority. There is an old Russian story about how once the Tsar of Russia was presented with a silver flea made by some English craftsmen. Everyone was amazed at their skill until Levsha, a left-handed smith from the town of Tula, went even further by making shoes for the tiny insect. It is a story which reflects the old Russian amazement, mixed with resentment, at

* 'Coca-cola patriotism' would be the equivalent American phrase.

the foreigners who made so many wonderful things and were seemingly always needed to teach the Russians, and at the same time the deep national self-confidence that a Russian craftsman could always be found to achieve even greater wonders. Khrushchev once used this story to rub home to a Russian audience what the Soviet Union was trying to do in her competition with the West.

> In the circumstances of poverty-ridden, backward Russia a craftsman was found from among the people who put shoes on a flea. But now it's not a case of us being able to shoe a flea, we have set ourselves the task of catching up with and overtaking the most developed capitalist country – the USA. We are certain that we shall accomplish this task and so 'put shoes' on capitalism.

The demand that the Soviet Union be recognized as an absolute equal of America explained much of Khrushchev's bragging about Soviet strength. He was ready to boast at times quite shamelessly about anything that seemed to prove that backward Russia, the 'lapotnaya' (bast-shoe) peasant Russia of his childhood, could beat America at its own game, and this gave the competition between the two countries in space exploration a particular importance for him. The first sputniks, the moon shots, Gagarin and Titov, were all welcomed as a repetition on a national scale of the left-handed smith's legendary feat. In the world of diplomacy this meant that Khrushchev would never be able to accept any solution to a problem that did not absolutely respect Soviet dignity – a fact that President Eisenhower and his advisers seemed to forget during the U2 affair, but which President Kennedy luckily remembered during the Cuban crisis. Khrushchev always made it clear that this was a condition for improving East-West relations. He told the American journalist James Reston as early as 1957 that Russia wanted to reach agreement with the USA, 'but only on a footing of equality, without diktat or discrimination'. This was one of the major themes he tried to put across when he came face to face with the American people in 1959.

If it was the Russian, quite as much as the communist, in Khrushchev that made him so careful of his dignity in dealing with the West, it was his communist training that gave him a deep and lasting suspicion of Western politicians. The two worlds see each other through distorting mirrors. In Moscow mention of a 'Western capitalist' generally touches off more or less the same instinctively unfavourable reactions as talk of a 'Soviet communist' does generally in London or New York. If disarmament negotiations break down, it is a matter of course to blame the West, and, whether it be misguided or not, the sense of indignation is more genuine than anything that could be created just by propaganda, active though that is. Khrushchev's first experience of the Western world came in the shape of his various Donbas employers before the Revolution. For all that he saw of the world in later years, and despite his appreciation of the way in which capitalism had come to make its workers prosperous, those experiences as a young man in his early twenties still often seemed very much in his mind when he spoke of modern capitalism. During the Civil War he saw the great powers of the Western world, including the United States, invade his country apparently with the intention of restoring a system of government that any American democrat would have been quick to revolt against. Khrushchev never forgot the 'offence' of intervention. And Soviet ideology made it easy for him to concentrate all his admiration for a country like America on 'the people', while reserving his suspicion for the groups which he believed manipulated the system. In one of the most substantial interviews he ever gave an American journalist (in the summer of 1957), Khrushchev said, in answer to the question whether he believed that America and her allies were preparing aggression against the Soviet Union:

> I consider that to be an indisputable fact.... There is no doubt that the American people do not want war, but the United States of America is a highly developed centralized capitalist state, the Government of which represents big banks and monopolies.... Among American leaders there are irresponsible people who for the sake of egoistic aims pursue an adventurist policy which they call... 'balancing on the brink of war', a policy of strength.... Unfortunately the American people have practically no influence on the policies of the USA. They are cleverly tricked during election campaigns and virtually do not even know for what they are voting.

Khrushchev was too good a politician not to make debating points whenever he could about Western elections. 'Do you suppose we consider it a free election when the voters of New York State have a choice only between a Harriman and a Rockefeller?' he once asked Averell Harriman. But it was a subject he was not altogether easy about. On the other hand there is no doubt that he genuinely considered power in the United States to be in the hands of a few groups whose intentions towards the Soviet Union were far from friendly. In this mood he was apt to describe American statesmen as 'representatives of the Duponts, Rockefellers and Harrimans'. John Foster Dulles, he said, before he became Secretary of State, 'had a law practice and was in effect in the pay of the Rockefellers. Then Dulles was made Secretary of State. Dulles took a Rockefeller as his "adviser". Who served whom? ... It was Dulles who served Rockefeller.' The pronouncements of the wilder military men of the West, the propaganda of extreme right-wing groups, let alone such an authoritative warning as President Eisenhower's against the growing power of the military-industrial machine in American politics, reinforced the prejudices of Khrushchev and his colleagues. Ironically in many ways Khrushchev approached first Eisenhower and then Kennedy as he was in turn approached by them – as a man who had to be encouraged for fear that more hostile and irresponsible forces would take power instead.

Given Khrushchev's reservations about the nature of Western politics and politicians, it would perhaps not have been surprising if he had preferred to pursue the necessary East-West *détente* through impersonal and diplomatic channels. The argument in favour of such an approach was strengthened by increasing Chinese hostility to the whole course of Soviet policy and considerable criticism by the Molotov group at home of Khrushchev's personal diplomacy. There is no doubt, however, that Khrushchev's heart was set on a personal meeting with Western leaders, and above all with the American president, from the moment that Malenkov was replaced by the far more pliable Bulganin as Soviet Premier in 1955. There were two reasons for this. First Khrushchev's incorrigible lifelong habit of seeing things, and speaking to people, for himself still guided him as a statesman. His 'summitry' was to this extent a projection of a domestic technique into foreign affairs. Second, paradoxically the mutual suspicion between East and West – for Khrushchev particularly the fear that the American establishment would always work against any true *détente* – made the creation of a sort of personal confidence between the leaders of the blocs seem overwhelmingly important. Khrushchev had to convince the Western leaders of his intention to abandon nuclear warfare as a means of achieving Soviet aims: and in return he had to convince himself that they were genuine in their protestations that they did not plan to remove the Soviet threat once and for all by a sudden nuclear attack.

The visit he made with Bulganin to Britain at the start of 1956 was clearly regarded by Khrushchev as a necessary first step towards an American visit and long consultations with President Eisenhower. Khrushchev was at first thwarted in this by a series of crises, beginning with the Hungarian revolt and the Anglo-French Suez operation at the end of 1956. The Middle Eastern crisis in the summer of 1958, which resulted in the Eisenhower doctrine justifying American intervention in the area, was a further setback to hopes of the summit that Soviet diplomats had been suggesting in one form or another since 1957. It was against this background that Khrushchev launched his most famous personal diplomatic ploy. On 27 November 1958 he called foreign correspondents in Moscow to the Kremlin and declared that it was time to 'perform a surgical operation' to remove the 'cancerous tumour' of West Berlin. Whatever the merits of Khrushchev's case that the time had come to change the occupation status conferred on the city at the end of the war, there can be no doubt that it was remarkably successful as a tactical move to embarrass the West, and by it Khrushchev showed that he was as clever at seizing the initiative in foreign affairs as he was in domestic politics. Khrushchev created the Berlin crisis. He was able to increase and decrease its gravity at will, and he could end it as suddenly as he had begun it. Above all he put the West on the defensive, and over the issue of Berlin the Western allies never recovered their balance during the rest of his period of office. Again and again he was to use it to conjure up visions of a world war which in fact he had no intention of starting. Not surprisingly in this way he managed to create division among the Western powers and to set up considerable tensions between the Western governments and their electors. Although there were good reasons why the Soviet Union should want to end the existing state of affairs in Berlin, there is little doubt that Khrushchev wanted above all to provoke a crisis which would allow him to make all the running and so lead the Americans into accepting the need for a summit. Within weeks the six-month time limit that Khrushchev had attached to his Berlin ultimatum was extended, and in March of the following year he himself told another Moscow press conference that the best way 'to clear away the vast accumulations that have piled up in international relations' would be a summit meeting. By then Khrushchev had stirred things up still further by issuing a draft peace treaty that he said he proposed to sign, unilaterally if need be, with East Germany. Western proposals for a Foreign Ministers' conference were followed in February by the arrival in Moscow of the British Prime Minister, Mr Macmillan, bent on smoothing ruffled feathers in a way that suited Khrushchev very well. The next month Khrushchev agreed that the Foreign Ministers should meet, but the actual conference was quite overshadowed by the arrival of another eminent Western visitor in Moscow, the American vice-president, Richard Nixon. Even this disastrous visit, during which Nixon and Khrushchev managed to provoke each other into crude public wrangles on the level of an untalented high-school debating society, was not allowed to get in the way of the longed-for summit. In early August a relieved world heard that the American and Soviet leaders had agreed to exchange visits and that Khrushchev was to start with a trip to the United States the following month.

To many people in the West the solid little man who landed in Washington on that sunny September day was a figure of inscrutable and menacing power. Had he not told the American people, in an interview recorded with an American television company in 1957, that their grandchildren would live under communism? And had he not offhandedly announced that the Soviet Union would 'bury' the United States? No wonder the Roman Catholic Cardinal Cushing had urged the American people 'to pray in the street, pray any place' while this man was in their country. Perhaps largely out of fear, perhaps inevitably, the West overestimated Khrushchev's strength. It was an overestimate that was to lead almost to disaster when the U2 storm suddenly broke and too few people outside Moscow realized that Khrushchev needed a helping hand as much as any other casualties of the crisis. In fact the American visit was a considerable gamble for

Khrushchev. He was not initiating any policy of his own by going there, but he was rushing to identify himself with a process of reconciliation between the two great world blocs that was bound to be slow and exceedingly tricky. His greatest weakness was his own insistence on speed. Those boasts about overtaking America had been written into the seven-year plan begun in 1959. All the Soviet Union's resources would be strained to accomplish the goals set down in that plan. Any world crisis that forced an increase in Soviet military spending would mean the diversion of essential resources from the seven-year plan's projects and make those boasts look dangerously stupid for their author. On the other hand, if the American trip succeeded, Khrushchev had definite ideas on how to reshape Soviet defence to achieve what he believed to be adequate security for the minimum cost. Khrushchev knew that the men in the Soviet Union who thought like Molotov would be watching carefully for his mistakes. More ominous, he was by this time well aware that the whole course of Soviet policy was causing considerable disapproval in Peking. Only a few days before Khrushchev left for America, the Soviet government had issued a statement declaring that 'it would be wrong not to express regret' that the recent border incidents between China and India had taken place. This refusal of the Soviet Union to support Peking was to be cited later by the Chinese as a crucial moment in the development of the Sino-Soviet conflict.

Khrushchev had two main aims in going to America: one was to convince the American people in general that the Soviet Union was a country with which the United States could live at peace; the other was to lay the foundations of a relationship with President Eisenhower that was essential if he himself was to believe that the long-term prospects for coexistence were good. Perhaps Khrushchev's greatest achievement was simply to leave the American people with a lasting impression of his vivid and at times prickly personality. It is most unlikely that Khrushchev himself believed that he could 'seduce' the Americans. Indeed his basic demand of the Americans – that they accept the Soviet Union as a great country and pay it due respect – meant that he was bound to be touchy about anything that he considered a slight on his country's or his own dignity. This was made plain when he attended a lunch given by the National Press Club in Washington the day after his arrival. Khrushchev made a prepared speech after the meal, but traditionally the main interest at such gatherings lay in the impromptu questions and answers that followed. The first question repeated a story of how Khrushchev had been sent an anonymous note after his secret speech at the 20th Party Congress asking why he had never spoken out against Stalin during the latter's lifetime. Khrushchev was supposed to have asked the writer of the note to identify himself, and when no one had moved, had replied, 'There's my answer.' A more disastrous question could scarcely be imagined. When it had been translated to him Khrushchev, according to one eye-witness, 'went red. His mouth contracted and his little eyes almost completely disappeared. One felt the mounting fury.' Soviet officials and journalists at the lunch were clearly appalled. The explosion that followed was cunningly softened by the Soviet interpreter, but not before Khrushchev had given a display of that blacker side which many successful politicians possess but few reveal in public. It was an unforgettable sight, and not all his later joviality nor his wife's conquest of the American press by her gentleness and good humour could make an anxious world forget it. But it was also, when goaded by a hostile audience, that Khrushchev made what was perhaps his most convincing plea to the American people. Angered by the Mayor of Los Angeles' tendentious interpretation of his unfortunate 'We shall bury you' remark (which Khrushchev on several occasions in America had insisted he had not meant literally), and still annoyed that he had been prevented from visiting, of all places, Disneyland, he launched into a passionate demand that the Americans take him and his message seriously.

You know that I have come here with good intentions, but it appears that some of you would like to reduce matters to a joke. I repeat that it is a question of extremely serious things – a question of peace and war, of the life and death of people. We offer you the hand of friendship. If you don't want it, say so.... Make your choice: shall we advance together to peace, or shall we continue the 'cold war' and the arms race? I have not come to plead with you. We are no less strong than you. I have already made many speeches in the United States but have not once resorted to the word 'arms', let alone 'missiles'. And if I have spoken about it today, you must understand that I had no choice.'*

The row in Los Angeles somehow cleared the air, and Khrushchev's trip from then on went considerably better. Even a monumental row with leading American trades unionists (reminiscent of his flare-up with the British Labour Party leaders during his visit to Britain in 1956) was not allowed to spoil things for long. The day after the row Khrushchev was in his best humour with American businessmen at a visit to IBM's Californian factory, declaring, 'When I meet businessmen we find a common language in our conversations. Being men of action we are quick to understand one another.' Even the persistent presence at his side throughout the trip of Henry Cabot Lodge, deputed by President Eisenhower to defend the American way of life, failed to rouse him. 'Every snipe praises his own bog,' remarked Khrushchev calmly after one of Lodge's speeches on capitalism.

The climax of the tour came on 26 and 27 September in two days of talks with President Eisenhower at his Pennsylvania retreat of Camp David. It did not produce concrete results beyond an agreement that Eisenhower should postpone his Soviet visit, planned for October, until the spring, so that his grandchildren could accompany him. But this in itself apparently innocent decision was to have very important consequences. Khrushchev certainly did not hope for anything more definite than he got. He persuaded Eisenhower that a Great Power summit was desirable. He himself made it clear that he would not press the Berlin question, which was easy to concede in return for Eisenhower's apparent willingness that the whole question of Berlin and East Germany should be thoroughly examined. What was most important for Khrush-

* It was after this that Khrushchev scared his hosts by hinting that he might end the trip suddenly and fly back to Moscow. Considering Khrushchev's extremely volatile behaviour during the first part of the visit, it is odd that many people in the West continued to regard him as a shrewdly calculating man who lost his temper according to design. Khrushchev certainly was something of an actor and loved performing in front of people, whether Russian, American or anything else, but he was extremely impulsive. In the opinion of Averell Harriman, as expert an observer of Khrushchev as any, he was definitely 'less calculating and careful' than Stalin. Perhaps it was the mystery that still seemed to envelop the Kremlin together with the Western superstition that Soviet politicians must be as foresightful as Soviet chess-players that helped Khrushchev keep a reputation for calculation that he did not deserve.

chev was to see for himself if Eisenhower could be relied on to work towards more ordered relations between the two countries, in spite of the anti-Soviet pressures to which he believed the American president would be subjected. It seems likely that Khrushchev found the American as troubled as he was himself by the responsibility placed on both of them by their countries' possession of a vast nuclear arsenal. And it is easy to believe that Eisenhower managed by his startling simplicity to persuade Khrushchev of his sincerity. It is hard to gather what Khrushchev really thought of Eisenhower. In his public statements before and during his American trip he naturally praised the American's courage and statesmanship. After the U2 incident and the collapse of the Paris summit, he subjected him to a torrent of coarse, personal ridicule. But it is very probable that although Eisenhower convinced Khrushchev of his sincerity at Camp David, Khrushchev's opinion of his ability as a leader was more cautious. He once recalled (admittedly after the Paris summit failure) how dependent Eisenhower had been on Dulles's advice at the 1955 Geneva Conference, and that he had used notes passed him by the Secretary of State whenever he spoke. 'Such a President can take God knows what kind of decisions, and his is a vast, great and powerful nation,' Khrushchev commented. 'One shuddered at the thought that such great force was in such hands.' Khrushchev, like all Soviet leaders, went into any conference fully briefed and seldom referred to his advisers. It was out of the question for him to ask substantial advice in public from his long-suffering Foreign Minister, Andrei Gromyko. He may well have calculated that, once alone with Eisenhower, his superior experience and skill would count for much, and he may have been right.

The link between Khrushchev's visit to the United States and his concern for the development of his own country's economy was made clear at a meeting of the Supreme Soviet in January 1960. Khrushchev announced that he proposed to cut the Soviet armed forces by 1,200,000 men over the next eighteen months. This, together with reductions made between 1955 and 1958 of just over two million, would bring the number of men under arms to just below two and a half million, compared with over five and a half million at the start of 1955. Without the improvement in the international atmosphere that he could claim to discern after the Camp David talks, Khrushchev would scarcely have been able to get enough support for this measure. Even so he felt obliged to answer directly the question whether such a cut would decrease Soviet defence capacity. It was also significant that the problem of reintegrating into civilian life the quarter of a million officers scheduled for demobilization was treated as a matter of considerable urgency. Criticism of the new cuts was inevitable among the military, and Khrushchev clearly wanted to keep it to a minimum. Behind the reduction lay a typically bold – some would, and did later, say rash – decision to concentrate Soviet defence efforts on the creation of a missile force. Khrushchev claimed that the cuts would mean a saving of as much as 17,000 million roubles. He pooh-poohed the idea that the heavy capital needs of the seven-year plan had anything to do with this, but nevertheless went on to say that the government was considering the reorganization of all its armed forces on a territorial basis, regardless of whether agreement was reached with the West on disarmament. This, Khrushchev explained, would mean that the bulk of Soviet soldiers would get their military training outside their ordinary working hours. Khrushchev cited Lenin's authority for the scheme (often a sign that he was set on a controversial policy), and articles in the Soviet press made it quite clear that the main attraction of the scheme was its low financial cost and its saving in manpower which would not have to be deflected from productive work. Khrushchev clearly calculated that with America unlikely to start a war, it would be safe for the Soviet Union to rely on the ultimate deterrent of an all-out missile strike against the United States. And despite all the damage done by the U2 crisis to his plans for diverting much of the conventional military manpower into civilian production, Khrushchev did not abandon his fundamental idea.* While he was in power there was no public discussion of the possibility that the great powers might fight a conventional war or a graduated nuclear war including conventional troops. The American suggestion made in 1962 that both sides should agree to direct missiles only at military targets was dismissed for similar reasons. Khrushchev's strategic choice finally reduced itself to saying that any war with America would

* The demobilization scheme was abandoned in the summer of 1960, and the idea of a territorial-type army was never raised again.

have to be a nuclear one, even if the Western powers themselves were prepared to see if it could be limited to conventional troops. It was a decision which made much sense for a man whose growing concern was the Soviet economy. But, as we shall see, it led to dangerous discontent among more careful military men.

Khrushchev's plans were shattered when early in the morning of 1 May a Soviet anti-aircraft unit managed at last to bring down an American U2 reconnaissance plane. The whole unfortunate affair began with appropriate drama. Khrushchev, who had been woken early that morning with the news that the American plane had crossed the Soviet frontier, received word that it had been brought down and its pilot captured while he was reviewing the troops at Moscow's traditional May Day parade in Red Square. Perhaps Khrushchev wished that Major Voronov and his anti-aircraft missile unit had not done their job so well, because he can have had no doubt that his own reputation was likely to be as badly damaged by the affair as Gary Francis Power's plane. Khrushchev had already pushed the Soviet rapprochement with America to the point of open clash with China over communist world strategy. He had personally vouched for President Eisenhower's good faith. The U2 wreckage now put in question the reliability of that judgement, and could be used, by his Soviet critics, as indisputable evidence of the need to strengthen Soviet military might. Khrushchev, always acutely aware of his personal political position, could be counted on to lead the chorus of Soviet attacks on America, but his indignation was by no means contrived. He was eventually patently angered by the affair. He was never the sort of man to offer the other cheek. 'Mine is a different principle,' he once said. 'If anyone hits me on the left cheek, I would hit him on the right one, and so hard that it would knock his head off.' The remarkable thing about Khrushchev's performance in May 1960 was not the extent of his rage, but of his restraint. In the course of two speeches at a meeting of the Supreme Soviet a few days after 1 May, he stressed that it was very likely that Eisenhower had known nothing of the plane's flight. The speeches were otherwise full of much rough invective against America, and he made considerable fun out of Powers's emergency equipment: the French gold francs 'nicely wrapped in cellophane in the American style' and the two gold watches and seven gold rings – 'Perhaps the pilot should have flown higher – to Mars, and was preparing to seduce Martian women?' But the important thing was that he did not blame Eisenhower. And when Eisenhower, in spite of all these hints from Khrushchev, admitted responsibility for the flight, even then Khrushchev refused to give up hope. After visiting the exhibition of the U2's wreckage in Moscow's Gorky Park, he still told foreign journalists that he was 'an incorrigible optimist'.

On 14 May Khrushchev left for Paris, accompanied by his Minister of Defence, Marshal Malinovsky. There can be no doubt that he still hoped that the summit conference might be saved, although he must also have realized that the price he had to ask now from Eisenhower – an apology – was almost certainly too high. It has often been said that Khrushchev wanted to wreck the Paris summit, but this is to ignore the extent to which he had linked an East-West *détente* with his domestic plans and his attitude to the world communist movement. In particular the Soviet dispute with China, which reached a climacteric in 1960, made it politic for Khrushchev to show through a summit that his his policy of peaceful coexistence could work, although at the same time it meant that he could in no way allow himself to look as if he was begging favours from the West. His own position forced him to demand a high price from the American President. But by the time Eisenhower reached Paris the demands of American and Soviet dignity had grown so great, and the atmosphere so tense, that it was inevitable Eisenhower should refuse to apologize. Eisenhower did announce that further U2 flights had been cancelled, but to Western suggestions that this should satisfy Moscow Khrushchev replied, 'That's a lackey's way. When a gentleman slaps a lackey's face and then gives him a sixpence, the lackey at once says thank you ... But we know who we are and whom we represent.' The last hope of a meeting disappeared in a wrangle over procedure on 17 May. Khrushchev left Paris after a stormy press conference, still publicly hoping that a summit might meet within six to eight months. Curiously, on his return to Moscow Khrushchev still maintained that Eisenhower had known nothing of the flights but had found it impossible to admit this. Khrushchev joked about the President's preoccupation with golf and later offered him a job as a Soviet orphanage director ('I'm sure he will not hurt the state') when he left the White House. He was ready to ridicule Eisenhower and made it clear that he would abandon personal diplomacy until the next president was elected. But significantly he took trouble to make it plain that he had not been deceived or tricked by the American.

The summit failure seemed to herald terrifying events, and Khrushchev himself at the Paris press conference appeared to many like a Soviet Samson set on pulling the temple down about his ears. But in fact the direction of Soviet policy was not to be deflected by such things as Khrushchev's temper, or even an American reconnaissance plane. Although it took many people in the West a considerable time to realize this, the Soviet leadership was irrevocably set on those policies which had made Khrushchev's journey to America possible. And in fact it was towards Peking, and not towards Washington or any other Western capital, that Khrushchev's greatest fury was directed in 1960.

Chapter 17
China

China was the third in the great trinity of problems that confronted Khrushchev and the Soviet leadership after 1953. To a very large extent the Chinese problem derived from the decisions taken in Moscow about the other two – the course of Soviet internal development and the pattern of Soviet relations with the Western world – and this explains why it was almost five years after Stalin's death before Khrushchev began to realize fully how very difficult relations with Peking were going to be. The Sino-Soviet quarrel, which cast such a blight on Khrushchev's last years of rule, was above all the result of a conflict of interests between two great and neighbouring states. At the root of this conflict of interests was the simple fact that China was a poor country, and Russia, by world standards, a rich one. By 1953, thanks to the years of construction under Stalin's ruthless guidance, the Soviet Union could hold her own with the West in many areas of defence and heavy industry and in much of its technology, while China, for all her ancient greatness, was still a backward country. The strategy evolved by the Soviet leadership in the years after 1953 was based on the relatively advanced state of Soviet defence potential and of the Soviet economy: the possession of nuclear weapons ultimately led to the doctrine of peaceful coexistence with the other world nuclear bloc; and the achievements of the Soviet economy made it possible to propose prosperity at home as the new weapon for defeating the West in peaceful competition. For China, rich only in human resources and revolutionary spirit, the implications of these Soviet policy decisions were unpleasant. China was to serve the communist cause by cultivating her own garden (with not too much help from the Soviet Union, either) and not by encouraging revolution among her small neighbours. The Soviet Union, on the other hand, would dazzle the poor, ex-colonial and coloured nations by the wonders of her economic progress and so draw them away from the Western world. Of course it took some years before the consequences of Soviet policy for China, summed up here in an excessively simplified form, became plain for all to see, and indeed one of the strangest aspects of the Sino-Soviet quarrel was the slowness of both sides to realize what was happening to them. As far as it is possible to tell, Khrushchev was as unaware of the storm ahead as everyone else. True, he and the other Soviet leaders must have known that even under Stalin Soviet relations with China had had their difficult moments. Stalin's advice to Mao Tse-tung in the years of struggle before the Chinese Revolution in October 1949 had at times proved disastrous. And after the Revolution there had been unmistakable signs of tension between the two leaders when Mao appeared to be setting himself up as a Marxist sage quite independent of Moscow. A sensitive consideration for the feelings of her allies had seldom been a Soviet strong point, but after Stalin's death there was a genuine attempt by Moscow to create healthier and somewhat more equitable relations with the other communist countries. It was in this spirit that Khrushchev had flown to Peking with Bulganin and Mikoyan in October 1954 to sign a treaty which gave China long-term credits and also promised substantial deliveries of capital goods. Khrushchev is quite likely to have supposed that this would be enough to wipe out any old Chinese grievances. It is also possible that Khrushchev used this trip to inform the Chinese of the campaign against Malenkov which was then reaching its peak. He could with some justification put himself forward as China's friend because the treaty he signed in Peking, which obviously put considerable demands on Soviet heavy industry, could be seen as running counter to Malenkov's emphasis on the production of consumer goods. If this was the case, it would go some way to explaining why the Chinese were slow to understand what was really in Khrushchev's mind.

Much of the confusion over the origins of the quarrel was caused by China's acceptance, at the time, of the decisions of the Soviet 20th Party Congress. True, Khrushchev's attack on Stalin in the secret speech (about which he had not conferred in advance with Peking) struck the Chinese as unwise, but they gave him no reason to suppose that they objected to the rest of the Congress and in particular to the new ideas contained in his main report. In fact it was these ideas (peaceful coexistence; the non-inevitability of war; and the tolerance of different, and even peaceful, roads to socialism) which formed the core of the Soviet strategy and which the Chinese were eventually to reject. There are two main reasons why the Chinese did not find these objectionable at the time. First, it was not until the autumn of 1957, when the Chinese leadership in obscure circumstances adopted a far more 'left', revolutionary attitude to both home and foreign affairs, that the latent differences between the two countries began to be accurately mirrored in different political attitudes. And secondly, it needed Khrushchev to display in actions just how the Soviet leadership interpreted the decisions taken at the Party Congress before the Chinese could properly appreciate their full significance. It so happened that Khrushchev's handling of foreign affairs provided the necessary demonstration only a very few months after the all-important swing to the left had occurred in Peking. Before this, however, there was another (it turned out to be the last) convincing display of Sino-Soviet unity. In 1957 Khrushchev was extremely concerned with the problems of the world communist movement. Although he had just managed to save the situation in Poland and Hungary and had come through the biggest personal crisis in his own career, he still needed to restore stability and a sense of direction to world communism. He aimed to do this by getting a reaffirmation of Moscow's right to leadership but without completely abandoning the new deal for communist parties implicit in the decisions of the 20th Party Congress. An appropriate occasion was at hand – the 40th Anniversary of the Russian Revolution – and after the world's communist leaders had gathered in Moscow for the celebrations, Khrushchev stage-managed a conference which duly produced a Declaration in the required spirit. Or rather this was how it seemed at the time to the outside world: in reality it was not nearly so simple a matter. Khrushchev's attack on Stalin had begun a process of rethinking among communists which he had completely failed to foresee and which he never properly understood once it had begun. In countries like Poland and Italy, communists had started to reconsider such fundamental questions as the role of a communist party and the relationship of the Soviet Party to other communist parties. Ideas had developed like 'polycentrism', according to which there should be no central authority for the communist movement, ideas that Khrushchev could never at any time have tolerated. It is a comment on Khrushchev's failure to grasp the nature of the forces he had released by the secret speech that he believed the Moscow Declaration of 1957 could restore the old stability which Stalin had only achieved by the use of force. He certainly never realized that the extension of communism into Europe, for which Stalin ironically was responsible, had to lead one day to a revision of Marxism-Leninism in the light of the European political tradition.

In the event, the Moscow Declaration was no more than a tactical defeat for those principally championing the rights of individual communist parties to independence – the Yugoslavs (who refused to sign it), the Poles and the Italians. And that Khrushchev achieved this much was very largely thanks to Chinese support. Although China had advised him to accept the Gomulka régime in Poland during the crisis of October 1956, a year later Mao Tse-tung wanted a disciplined communist movement under the acknowledged leadership of Moscow. This was clearly in keeping with the revolutionary mood that had gripped Peking since the autumn. Moscow was the traditional centre of such authority, hallowed by Lenin and Stalin and the blood of the first successful communist revolutionaries. Mao moreover was anxious to admit that the Soviet Union should lead by virtue of its strength. He expressed China's deference to Moscow when he told the assembled communist leaders 'The Soviet Union has two sputniks, while China has not even a quarter sputnik.'

It was this Chinese confidence in the Soviet strength so brilliantly demonstrated only weeks before by the two sputnik launchings that was to be the start of the trouble. Khrushchev was happy enough for Mao to make such a comparison between the Soviet Union and China, but Mao did not stop there. While in Moscow in November he made an even more significant comparison between the relative strengths of East and West, largely based on his assessment of the military significance of Soviet space achievements. The international situation, Mao said, had reached 'a new turning point', because 'the socialist forces are overwhelmingly superior to the imperialist forces'. This was the meaning behind his pretty allegory about the east wind prevailing over the west wind. A certain amount of the 'Peking spirit', indeed, found its way into the Moscow Declaration, which adopted a far tougher stance towards the non-communist world than the 20th Party Congress, although without going back on any of the principles that Khrushchev had introduced then. What mattered to Khrushchev in November 1957 was to get an acknowledgement of Moscow's right to lead. His anxiety to achieve this, and his ignorance of what was happening to the communist movement, may have led him to accept the Chinese endorsement (in fact the Chinese were co-sponsors with the Soviet Union of the Moscow Declaration) and even some toughening of attitude at their suggestion, without bothering too much about where the Chinese were heading.

If this is something like the truth, one can only comment that another Soviet leader, with a more speculative cast of mind and a better understanding of ideology than Khrushchev had, might perhaps have spotted the danger in Mao's remarks, because they implied no less than a new definition of a key concept in Marxist-Leninist thinking – the so-called character of the epoch. Only when this has been defined, it is held, can the correct course of action for communist parties at any given time be determined. The Mao-ist definition given in Moscow reflected the new revolutionary mood in China and her optimism about the military implications of the sputniks. It was the source of the new-found Chinese belief that the time had come to push hard against the imperialists. The Chinese now accepted that local wars would be started by the Americans in defence of their eroding position, and on the other hand that communists should encourage wherever possible 'wars of liberation'. The complete shift in the balance of power to the East would nevertheless prevent the imperialists from starting a world war. Admittedly all this had not been spelled out by Chinese actions and statements in November 1957. Yet Khrushchev and his colleagues must have realized that Mao's boasts about strength went much farther than anything they had ever said. The Soviet position was, and remained, far more cautious: that the balance of forces in the world had simply changed in favour of the socialist bloc. Neither Khrushchev nor any other Soviet leader ever made any claim so outspoken as Mao's that socialism was now 'overwhelmingly superior' to imperialism.

It is quite easy, with the advantage of hindsight, to see how Khrushchev and Mao would extract very different meanings from the Moscow Declaration, but what mattered at the time was that a Declaration had been made which seemed to restore unity to the communist movement. Khrushchev seems to have believed that Mao's recognition of Soviet authority also implied approval of the Soviet line for the world communist movement. Mao in turn apparently believed that Khrushchev would use the leadership conferred on the Soviet Union to further world communism in the Chinese style. It did not occur to Khrushchev that the Chinese or anyone else could justly accuse the Soviet Union of pursuing her own interests at the expense of other communist countries. Khrushchev failed to see how, as the communist world grew more diversified, unity of interest would become more difficult to achieve. In particular Khrushchev seems not to have realized that the days had passed when the Soviet Union was virtually world communism. At one time the pursuit of the Soviet national interest may well have been the best way of helping the communist cause. Stalin in his later years had artificially preserved this state of affairs even to the extent of murdering, when necessary, recalcitrant foreign communist leaders. Matters were confused further for Khrushchev, and indeed for everyone else, by the Marxist dogma about the impossibility of any real contradiction existing between communist states – a dogma which in turn delayed recognition of the nature of the Sino-Soviet conflict and then made efforts for its resolution all the more feverish.*

Within a year of signing the Moscow Declaration, Khrushchev and Mao had plenty of disturbing evidence to show how very different their interpretations of that document were. Neither side seems to have made a calculated challenge to the other's interests; events seemed to be pushing them that way. China, faced with a substantial cutback in Soviet aid because Khrushchev had had to pour money into Eastern Europe after the 1956 crisis, adopted the policies of the Great Leap Forward and the communes, a sort of poor man's do-it-yourself industrialization. Khrushchev, acting in the spirit of peaceful coexistence, authorized discussions with America on the possibilities of a nuclear test ban; almost went to

* It remains an important point of theory on the part of both the Soviet Union and China that the conflict is not between the Soviet and Chinese peoples (whose interests, according to Marxism-Leninism, must be one) but is caused only by the deviation of the other side's leadership from correct principles.

a summit meeting to settle the Middle East crisis which blew up in the summer; and gave the Chinese no more than political support in the Formosa crisis which they had provoked by their bombardment of the offshore islands of Quemoy and Matsu. In short Khrushchev disappointed every Chinese hope for revolutionary progress in his handling of foreign affairs, while the Chinese with their communes seemed to be charting a completely new course for socialist construction in the underdeveloped world.*

By the end of 1958 all the main ingredients of the Sino-Soviet quarrel were present. The Soviet Union had no doubt about the threat presented by Chinese policy at home and abroad. Not only were the Chinese unconcerned with damaging the difficult Soviet rapprochement with the West, but they were now putting themselves forward as the model for the whole underdeveloped world. The communes were represented by Peking as a short cut to communism for countries which like China had a mainly peasant population (at last the significance of the fact that the revolution in China had been peasant, and not proletarian, in origin was beginning to tell). Any Soviet leader must have seen in this a threat to the authority of his country in the communist movement and, equally important, in those areas of the world which were supposed to be particularly susceptible to communist influence. But the Chinese had also annoyed Khrushchev personally by opposing certain of his strongest convictions and prejudices. First, the communes made absolutely no sense to Khrushchev. They were for him the brainchild of people 'only with a vague idea of communism'. Enthusiasts had tried them in Russia after the Civil War, but they simply 'fell to pieces'. Any system which ignored material incentives, as the communes purposely did, was ludicrous in Khrushchev's eyes. After all, he had been associated

* The Chinese communes were designed to make the best possible use of the only reserve in which the country was rich – human labour. They were meant to organize labour both for agriculture and industry so as to compensate for the lack of machinery. The communes also had certain features – such as, originally, absence of payment in cash – which communists have usually associated with an advanced stage in any socialist society's development. They were therefore clearly of interest to other countries rich only in population and at the same time suggested that the Soviet Union might soon not be the most advanced socialist country in the world.

with the policy of incentives in Soviet agriculture since before the war. Khrushchev believed that his years of experience as an administrator had given him proof that egalitarianism without incentives simply did not make economic sense. But worse still, from his point of view, was the Chinese inability to understand what communism itself was about. The ideals of communism without prosperity did not interest Khrushchev. The whole point of his working life, particularly as he had come to regard it in later years, was to give the Soviet people the houses, food and clothes that they lacked. The idea of communism as a sort of puritan brotherhood was completely foreign to him, perhaps largely because his approach to communism from the earliest days had been quite unintellectual. And now that he had begun to travel round the world, he believed that he saw further proof for his argument that communism could not hope to win over people unless it offered them as much as, and even more than, any other system did. Back in 1954 he had said, 'Communists want to raise the living standard of their people to a great height, and then it will be difficult for capitalists to hold their peoples in obedience.' It was as though he saw himself conducting a vast electoral campaign over the whole world, in which the people would be called on to vote when the Soviet Union had achieved communism and greater prosperity than anyone else. In this context the new Chinese ideas were as much an annoyance to him as those of left-wing extremists often are to a West European Labour Party leader who is trying his hardest to win an election. At the same time Chinese foreign policy in 1958, with its goading of America over Formosa and eagerness to exploit the troubled situation in the Middle East, touched Khrushchev on another of his most sensitive spots – his idea of his responsibilities as the leader of a nuclear power. Khrushchev not only differed from the Chinese in his estimate of how far America would tolerate communist pressure. At some stage after Stalin's death he had undergone the shock of realizing the terrible destructive power possessed by his country and America (a process familiar to all American presidents in the nuclear age), and from that moment on he could not accept large-scale war as an instrument of Soviet policy. Although in fact the Chinese never argued in favour of nuclear war, their actions, based on a different assessment of the United States, seemed in

Soviet eyes to suggest that they did. (It should be remembered that, by this time, any idea of the Soviet Union helping China to develop nuclear arms was out of the question. This Soviet decision was one of the crucial moments in the conflict.) Accordingly, as the Sino-Soviet dispute developed, Khrushchev played more and more on two themes which seemed both particularly important to him personally and which also, in his calculation, would have most effect on the people he wished to prevent from going over to the Chinese side. He said bluntly that 'communism in our understanding – is abundance' (a very Khrushchevian gloss on Marxism-Leninism). And he consistently held up to ridicule a caricature of the Chinese idea of communism: 'One must not imagine communism', he said in 1962, 'in the shape of a table with empty plates at which are sitting "highly politically conscious" and "completely equal" people.' At the same time he filled his speeches with remarks on the horror of any future world war. The days when he had attacked Malenkov for saying the same thing were forgotten. By 1963 Khrushchev was estimating in public that the first strike alone in a nuclear war would kill up to eight hundred million people and destroy all the world's great cities, including those of China. Marxists-Leninists, he told the East German Party Congress in January 1963, 'cannot propose to establish a communist civilization on the ruins of the centres of world culture.' Only a few years before Khrushchev had insisted that, although a world war would do terrible damage, communism would survive it while capitalism would perish. But as the quarrel with China grew more intense, he even abandoned this token bow in the direction of the Marxist belief in the inevitability of communist victory.

On 31 July 1958 Khrushchev flew suddenly to Peking. He had been caught off balance by the revolution in Iraq and the quick military aid provided by America and Britain to an apprehensive Lebanon and Jordan. Chinese disapproval of Khrushchev's handling of the crisis and particularly of his willingness to attend a summit meeting in the United Nations Security Council (which, of course, precluded the attendance of China) added to his confusion. But the importance of Khrushchev's talks in Peking went beyond a basic difference in foreign policy; they were very likely the origin of that personal quarrel with Mao Tse-tung which was to play such an important part in the Sino-Soviet dispute. It is difficult to see how two such different men as Mao and Khrushchev could in the best of circumstances have been close, but now they seemed to personify to a startling degree the very different policies which their countries had begun to pursue. If Khrushchev is to be believed, Mao lectured him at length on the theory behind the communes. This may well have taken Khrushchev by surprise because the experiment, although well under way, had not yet been much publicized. Mao, according to Khrushchev, did not ask for Khrushchev's advice on the subject, but 'expounded the truth, so to speak, and I, as a guest, listened to him'. The experience clearly rankled with Khrushchev, and well it might. Here was the leader of an admittedly vast but still backward communist country in effect telling the Soviet leader that he had discovered an important Marxist-Leninist truth which Khrushchev believed had been disproved by Soviet experience years ago. Khrushchev's telling Mao about the failure of the Soviet communes was so much wasted breath, and by the time he left Peking he must have realized the unpleasant truth that the Chinese saw in the communes not just their own quick way to communism (possibly quicker, the Chinese implied, than the Soviet Union's) but also a way that could be followed by any other Afro-Asian country. The meeting at Peking in August 1958 thus brought Khrushchev face to face for the first time with Mao in his threatening role as the Asian heir to the line of Marx, Lenin and Stalin. Khrushchev was later inclined to ridicule such pretensions. Shortly before his fall he remarked meaningfully that he did not 'in the least pretend to the role of a prophet who solemnly hands down the truth, as some people do'. He does not seem to have realized that this was perhaps not such a very good thing to confess. What Khrushchev failed to see was that with the death of Stalin world communism, as well as the Soviet Union, had lost its philosopher-king. Stalin, who took over the role from Lenin, appreciated its importance only too well: he made it an essential part of his system of personal tyranny. He understood that in a society governed by an absolute philosophy, an absolute ruler must claim for himself exclusive access to that philosophy's truths. Khrushchev, by reason of his training and talent, was quite unsuited to the role of philosopher-king, and in the limited world of post-Stalin Soviet politics this was actually to his advantage. The last thing that the Soviet leaders then wanted was another philosopher-king in the Kremlin, and their tolerance of Khrushchev, in spite of faults that must have been quite clear to them, can partly be explained by the fact that he provided no threat of this sort whatsoever. But once the quarrel with China had started, and Khrushchev had to stand comparison with Mao Tse-tung, his inability and disinclination to take the part of a philosopher-king was a disadvantage. The man who 'expounded the truth' about the communes to Khrushchev at Peking in August 1958 was not only prepared but eminently well qualified to be a philosopher-king. Of all the world communist leaders he was the only one genuinely in the Lenin-Stalin tradition. His contribution to Marxist thought made Khrushchev's greatest literary achievement – eight volumes of his speeches on agricultural practice – look like a bad joke. Mao was quite ready to accept Moscow's senior status as the capital of Marxist truth, even if there was no great sage resident there any more, as long as its policies were in accordance with the Chinese interpretation of the communist movement's interests. But once he had decided that Khrushchev and his colleagues were set on a mistaken course, his forbidding intellectual talents instantly conferred an authority on the Chinese case which Khrushchev was – in many communist eyes – quite unable to give to Soviet arguments. Had theory not mattered so much in the communist world, Khrushchev's pragmatism and the personal qualities which helped him fascinate the Western world might have been enough. But, as it was, the unfavourable comparison that the Chinese were able to make between the two leaders as Marxist wise men made it far easier for them to challenge Khrushchev, even in areas of special Soviet interest such as Eastern Europe and indeed even within the Soviet Union itself.

From 1958 onwards Khrushchev took no important step without calculating its likely effect on Peking. The 21st Party Congress in early 1959 was largely a defence of the course of development chosen by the Soviet Union in the face of the completely different Chinese approach, although Khrushchev's main speech at the Congress contained a lengthy denial of Yugoslav suggestions about Sino-Soviet differences. But undoubtedly the move that completely destroyed Chinese trust in Khrushchev was his

American visit in the following September. Khrushchev's performance in the United States was totally distasteful to the Chinese, who could see nothing but a betrayal of communism in the spectacle of a Soviet leader praising the qualities of an American president. Immediately after the American trip Khrushchev flew to Peking for the tenth anniversary celebrations of the Chinese Revolution. It cannot have been a pleasant experience, because Khrushchev did not offer the Chinese any satisfactory explanation of what he was up to with America. On the contrary, it is clear from the speeches he made in Peking that he argued vigorously the case for relaxing international tension and avoiding war. He insisted that President Eisenhower was genuinely committed to similar policies. Above all, he warned against any plan to test the strength of the West by force. And it was shortly after the Peking visit, in a report on his American trip to the Supreme Soviet, that Khrushchev gave perhaps his most detailed account ever of his understanding of peaceful coexistence, an account which he by then knew ran counter to everything that Peking believed. He told the Supreme Soviet that sober counsels were beginning to prevail in the West and hinted that this meant that any plans to use force against the communist bloc would be scrapped. 'The point at issue now', he went on, 'is not whether or not there should be peaceful coexistence, for peaceful coexistence there is, and will be if we want to avoid the lunacy of world nuclear and rocket war. The point is to coexist on a reasonable basis.' Such a basis, he suggested 'presupposes reciprocal concessions in the interests of peace.' Khrushchev knew that the phrase 'mutual concessions' would enrage the Chinese, who argued on the contrary that the overwhelming superiority of communist bloc strength over the West demanded a quite opposite policy. The Chinese, however, had miscalculated if they thought that they could press Khrushchev into abandoning or even modifying his policies. In fact, the reverse occurred. Chinese hostility, combined with his optimistic assessment of the results of his American trip, made Khrushchev define the implications of Soviet policy in more detail than he had ever done before. If the U2 incident the following May, together with Eisenhower's handling of it, had not put Khrushchev on the defensive, he would almost certainly have challenged China further by matching that definition with actions.

For Khrushchev himself, the Sino-Soviet dispute became irrevocable in 1960. This early recognition that there could be no reconciliation between the two countries short of surrender was from now on his main personal contribution to the quarrel. Khrushchev came to this conclusion partly because of his impatience, but also partly because of his simple approach to complicated problems. He had already shown this tendency to carry his thinking farther and faster than his colleagues did in other key areas of policy. In foreign affairs he was ready to accept that the Soviet Union had to do some sort of a deal with America. In home affairs it seemed obvious to him that all attention must be concentrated on economic production. And by the end of 1960 he was quite ready to accept that the Soviet Union was now locked in battle with China, not only for the control of the world communist movement but for influence over the Afro-Asian countries which hovered in a third world between the East and West power blocs. While events (as of 1966) seem to have proved Khrushchev right in his analysis, his actual handling of the dispute in 1960 was by no means so apt. In two stormy communist gatherings – the first at the Rumanian Party Congress in June, the second at Moscow in the following November – the full extent of the quarrel between the two greatest communist powers was revealed to the other parties. The Chinese in the end provided Khrushchev with his justification when at the Moscow meeting the General Secretary of the Chinese Party in effect claimed the right to split the movement, just as Lenin had split the Russian Social Democrats at the beginning of the century to form the Bolsheviks. Khrushchev miscalculated because he underestimated the world communist movement's fear of a split. A split threatened not only long sacrosanct communist convictions but also communist prospects of keeping, or extending, their power. The movement badly wanted the Declaration that the Moscow meeting eventually produced, patched up though it was out of the opposing views of the Chinese and the Russians. Khrushchev's tactics in the second half of 1960 paid little attention to this feeling. In Bucarest he amazed the delegates by making a personal attack on Mao and by pouring scorn on everything Chinese, for all the world as though he was making one of his anti-American tirades. In August he withdrew the Soviet technicians and specialists in China, the first serious reflection on the level of inter-state relations of a dispute that many communists still hoped was just a matter for learned Marxist discussion between fraternal parties.

If one takes Khrushchev's own criteria for success in the contest with China – influence over the 'third world' of uncommitted countries and control over the world communist movement – then his performance cannot be rated higher than satisfactory. From 1959 onwards Khrushchev's personal diplomacy in the third world was aimed as much against the Chinese as against the West. In early 1960 he travelled again to Asia. In autumn of the same year his curious visit to the United Nations, conducted with as much rumpus and fuss as he knew how, was also largely aimed at impressing the neutral countries. Even the most startling achievement of the East-West *détente*, the 1963 nuclear test ban treaty, was substantially a manoeuvre to isolate China on what Khrushchev all along had calculated to be her weakest point – her seeming indifference to the perils of a nuclear war. But considering the opportunities that the Soviet Union had by comparison with China – particularly her far greater opportunity both to scare and to reward – his success was only limited. His impulsiveness and brashness sometimes brought rapid results, such as the firm friendship with India, but there was usually a price to be paid: in this case, leaving Pakistan a certain prey to Chinese overtures and so indirectly helping to establish Peking's influence on the Indian sub-continent.* But perhaps Khrushchev's greatest disadvantage in dealing both with the neutral world and other communist countries was that he was to such a large extent the prisoner of his own experience. The greater part of his life had been spent in helping turn Russia into a powerful modern state and he was genuinely impressed by what he and others like him had achieved. He found it very hard to believe (very much like a certain sort of American) that anyone who visited the Soviet Union in a truly objective spirit would not be as impressed as he was by the contemplation of its wonders. This was a dominant theme in his

* It is very hard to imagine Khrushchev playing the role of a patient and self-effacing mediator between Pakistan and India as his successor as premier, Aleksei Kosygin, did at Tashkent in January 1966. Kosygin's success was arguably far more profitable for the Soviet Union than any of Khrushchev's more flamboyant ventures into the Indian sub-continent.

dialogue with the third world. On his second Indian trip in early 1960 he told a meeting in Calcutta:

> Everywhere I speak with my own voice, expound my own convictions. But that doesn't oblige those to whom I speak to agree with my convictions. I say – this is what we have achieved in forty years of Soviet power. I say – this is what we were and what we have become. Look – this is the capitalist world, and here is our socialist world. I do not boast. Figuratively speaking – the goods are their own recommendation.

The shortcomings of this approach were displayed most clearly in Khrushchev's dealings with Cuba. After the Cuban crisis, Fidel Castro paid two visits to the Soviet Union. The second, in the winter of 1964, took him on a long trip round some of the most famous Soviet industrial centres and was clearly meant to impress him with the successes of the Soviet method of building a communist society. Castro certainly was impressed at the time, and when he left, Khrushchev was able to glow with all the pride of an old man confirmed in the rightness of his ways by the acknowledgement of a promising youngster. But once Castro had returned to Cuba, the Soviet experience seemed rather less relevant for his country, and in the long run Soviet-Cuban relations were not to be all that different from those of any pair of rich and poor states.

The trouble was that Khrushchev's pride in Soviet achievements and belief in their general relevance ran counter to a resurgence of nationalism throughout the world. The dispute with China, in which Khrushchev himself genuinely often could not disentangle his motives as a Russian from his motives as a communist, in fact ended by pointing up the national character of Soviet policies. In Eastern Europe Khrushchev's insensitivity on this score led to the emergence of Rumania, a hitherto apparently obedient satellite, as the defender of a national communism which made nonsense of Khrushchev's belief that there should be no conflict of interests between fellow communist states. The Rumanian trouble had its immediate origins in Khrushchev's anxiety to find a way to bind the Soviet bloc more closely together without resorting to the obvious forms of pressure which he himself had in principle renounced. In 1962, fearful of the disruptive effects of Chinese influence, alarmed by the apparently sturdy growth of the European Common Market, and faced with serious domestic economic difficulties, Khrushchev decided to transform the Council for Mutual Economic Aid (Comecon), a hitherto not very lively economic organization of European communist states, into something like a communist Common Market. The aim was to introduce a far greater division of labour among the member countries, and there was clearly much to recommend it on economic grounds – with one exception, that the least developed East European countries, such as Rumania, would be required to forgo the development of all-round modern industry which would duplicate established plant in more advanced countries like Poland and Czechoslovakia, and concentrate instead on producing food and raw materials. Shortly after the outline of the scheme was published, Khrushchev, once again in too much of a hurry, suggested that Comecon would very soon have to have an overall authority, with power to take decisions affecting basic economic matters in the member countries. The upshot was a solid Rumanian refusal to abandon her industrialization plans or to countenance any outside control over her economic life, and in less than a year the core of Khrushchev's scheme was destroyed. There is little sign that Khrushchev ever learned the main lesson of this unhappy affair: that the Soviet interest, in a world where cultural, regional and even racial differences seemed quite as likely to divide men as Marx had once supposed the banner of one economic class would unite them, could no longer convincingly be equated with the interest of world communism in general. Khrushchev himself unknowingly demonstrated the truth of this as he pushed the dispute with China further away from the comparative decorum of an interminable theoretical debate to a slanging match in which he did not scruple to exploit the most basic Russian fears about the 'yellow peril'. In the last two years of his rule, when the quarrel could no longer be hidden from public view, he allowed the Soviet press to write about such matters as frontier incidents and the Chinese sterilization programme, and to give accounts of gross misbehaviour by Chinese citizens in the Soviet Union. He personally went so far as to accuse Mao of harbouring a Hitler-style 'lebensraum' theory. The communist world, already appalled at the seriousness of the quarrel, found these revelations of its origins in national rivalry extremely distasteful. The crude, often very funny remarks which had been acceptable when aimed at

Albania, China's only ally in communist Europe, ceased to amuse when applied to China, whatever legitimate criticism there might be of her current policies. Anxious communists could be excused for their growing uneasiness that behind this increasing stridency, Khrushchev the Russian was beginning to gain the upper hand over Khrushchev the communist.

Although his handling of the dispute with China was finally to count against him (this last stage in the quarrel is described in the next chapter), in one important respect Khrushchev gained much from it. Nothing could have been better calculated to prove his commitment to the main Soviet domestic and foreign policies than the Chinese attack on them. Another Soviet leader might in his place have at first tried to stress the similarities of the Chinese and Soviet positions. Khrushchev could not have done this. In the first place he was too easily angered. But above all his grasp of the fundamental issues in the Soviet position was too firm. Peace abroad, prosperity at home: these were the practical tasks that Khrushchev set himself. True, on the final goal – the global triumph of communism – Khrushchev still agreed with China. Khrushchev himself had explained that the aim behind peaceful coexistence and the repeated Soviet disarmament moves was ultimately to soften up the West and destroy its unity. But Khrushchev was nothing if not concerned with what could and should be done here and now, and nothing shook his conviction that the first things to be done were those contained in that dual and simple slogan. Many thinking people in the Soviet Union realized that Khrushchev's willingness to quarrel with China was the strongest possible pledge of his commitment to that slogan. Unfortunately, it was a deduction that people in the West were much slower to make.

Chapter 18
Fall

The single most important factor in the events which led to Khrushchev's fall in the autumn of 1964 was the failure of the Soviet economy to sustain its remarkable performance of the mid-1950s. Khrushchev was particularly vulnerable in the face of economic disappointments because, partly from natural impatience, partly to further his own political ends, he had stressed above all the speed with which the Soviet Union would satisfy the needs of her citizens and at the same time match the performance of her American rival. At the 21st Party Congress in January 1959 he had announced that the country would outproduce the United States in gross and *per capita* production by 1970. Just over two years later, when the downturn in the economy was starting to be perceptible, Khrushchev enshrined his optimistic forecasts in the sacred pages of the new Party programme which he introduced to the 22nd Party Congress. The programme ended with the triumphant announcement that 'The present generation of Soviet people will live under Communism', and Khrushchev did not hesitate to give a date for the millennium. 'We base ourselves,' he told the Congress, 'on strictly scientific estimates, which indicate that we shall, in the main, have built a communist society within twenty years.' The new programme spelled out what communism meant in terms that the ordinary person could readily understand. By 1980 all public utilities would be free; every family would have its own flat; *per capita* real income would be 250 per cent higher than in 1960; there would be an abundance of all sorts of food. Khrushchev had not only staked his reputation on an extremely optimistic assessment of the Soviet economy's potential: he had also assumed personal responsibility for the performance of its agriculture, on which the achievement of the ambitious overall targets fatally depended. Yet even while he was describing the material delights of communism to the 22nd Party Congress, his outrageous boasts that Soviet livestock farming would overtake America by 1960 were already being discreetly forgotten, and in the event the abandoned boast proved to be a truer augury of the future than the new promises.

The failure of the Soviet economy to meet the targets planned for it weakened Khrushchev's position towards both the West and China. He, more than anyone else, had dramatized the struggle between East and West in terms of economic competition, and – admittedly not through his own choice – the Soviet dispute with China had come also to turn very largely on the question of whose method of 'building communism' was best. In these circumstances it is not surprising that the Soviet leaders, faced by greater economic problems than they had anticipated and less capital resources to solve them with, were obliged to make increasingly difficult decisions about priorities. It was here that Khrushchev's obsession with speed, his increasingly personal vendetta with China, and his deep commitment to a *détente* with America which would allow the Soviet Union to concentrate her inadequate resources on domestic development, all combined to alienate his more cautious colleagues. The size of the problem confronting Khrushchev can best be summed up in a few figures. The growth rate of Soviet industrial production fell from an annual eleven per cent in 1959 to seven and a half per cent in the last full half year of Khrushchev's rule, and this latter composite figure disguised the fact that heavy industry was maintaining a yearly expansion of over ten per cent while the Soviet consumer goods industry, which was of special importance to Khrushchev, fell from ten per cent in 1959 to two per cent in Khrushchev's last months. Equally threatening to Khrushchev was the complete failure to meet the housing programme of the seven-year plan. Khrushchev knew as well as, if not better than, any other Soviet politician that housing was far and away the chief concern of the ordinary citizen. In a memorandum to the Presidium written in March 1961 after one of his regular tours round the country, he noted: 'Everywhere I received hundreds, in some towns even thousands of letters, largely asking to be given housing, and about increasing the network of children's institutions (i.e. kindergartens and creches), schools, hospitals. . . .' But for all his awareness of popular discontent about housing (paradoxically increased by the vastly greater attention paid to it by the Soviet leaders after Stalin's death), Khrushchev was not able to prevent a more or less steady decrease in the amount of new housing built. The agricultural problem was even worse: the seven-year plan had demanded a seventy per cent increase in farm production by 1965, but all that Soviet farmers managed to achieve by 1964 was an annual increase of about 1·7 per cent, which did not even keep pace with the growth of population.

Khrushchev's realization that the plan was failing in just those areas that were of prime concern to him came at the worst possible moment. The collapse of the *détente* with America after the U2 affair and the Paris summit put an end to his radical schemes for cutting defence costs. The first budget of the newly elected President Kennedy in March 1961, with its vast allocations for increasing American missile and conventional military strength, could certainly not be ignored by the Soviet defence chiefs, and after the June meeting of the Soviet and American leaders in Vienna the Soviet military budget was also increased, to be followed by the Soviet resumption of nuclear tests in August of the same year. These moves were reflected at the 22nd Party Congress in October 1961, when Khrushchev announced that the seven-year plan's targets for heavy industry (and notably those branches which included arms production) were to be raised. This from the Khrushchev who at the beginning of the year had laughed at 'some comrades' whose one-sided vision, 'like a plaice with eyes only on the top of its head', persuaded them that always more and more metal should be produced. Significantly Khrushchev hinted to the Congress that he had nevertheless managed to restrain 'some people', who had wanted to increase the steel target still more, by reminding them that 'along with steel production we must think of housing construction, children's institutions, the production of footwear and clothing and so on'. The first clear sign of the damage that might be done to Khrushchev's schemes came at a meeting of the Central Committee in March 1962. In his opening speech at the plenum Khrushchev elaborated on agriculture's need for supplies and machinery. He wanted the production of agricultural machines to be doubled, and it was quite obvious that he hoped the necessary capital would be found for this. But it was not to be. At the end of the meeting Khrushchev was obliged to say that he had never had any intention of boosting agriculture at the expense of heavy industry and defence, and all he could produce to help the farms was an administrative reorganization (described in Chapter 15). This was probably the most painful rebuff that Khrushchev had had to suffer from his colleagues since he had taken over the Soviet leadership. He knew that more money had to be found for agriculture, and there was now only one way left – to raise the prices of agricultural products. On 1 June *Pravda* announced to a displeased nation that meat prices were to go up by thirty per cent, and butter by twenty-five per cent. No one knew better than Khrushchev how much this would be resented, and indeed in Moscow it was common to hear unfavourable comparisons even with the last years of Stalin's rule, when as a matter of policy many retail prices had been reduced each year. The speeches that Khrushchev made in the weeks after the announcement included passages unprecedentedly apologetic in tone, which is scarcely surprising, remembering all that he had promised in the far from distant past. On one occasion he explained bluntly that the alternative to the price rise was to cut military spending, and remarked wryly that he knew 'people buying meat would not cry hurrah!' He even admitted that Party members had criticized the price rise, quoting them as saying '. . . At the 22nd Party Congress we adopted a programme for building communism. And then meat prices went up. Where are we moving, forward or backward?' That summer there were rumours that popular indignation was turning into public demonstrations and even riots. It was against this threatening background that Khrushchev took two fateful decisions: to produce at one stroke a missile balance by sending Soviet strategic missiles to Cuba; and to alter the whole basis of the Soviet Communist Party by splitting it into two and entrusting one half with the supervision of industry and the other with agriculture.

The Cuban decision was Khrushchev's most dangerous miscalculation in the nearly ten years that he dominated the conduct of Soviet foreign policy. It was a miscalculation made under pressure: Khrushchev knew that to make good the Soviet missile lag by conventional methods would mean an intolerable postponement of his ambitious plans for the Soviet economy. He was already deeply worried by the unsatisfactory performance of the Soviet economy, which even without new defence expenditures seemed incapable of the tasks that had been set it. And he knew probably better than anyone else that his own area of responsibility, agriculture, had to have more money if serious, perhaps fatal, damage to his own reputation was to be avoided. Yet at the March plenum he had been forced to accept that there was simply no money available. The unpopular price rise in June was followed in September by the announcement that the promised tax cuts (promised in May 1960, when Khrushchev still, in spite of the U2 incident, had great hopes for an East-West *détente*) would have to be 'temporarily postponed'. Khrushchev had already decided to concentrate the military energies of the Soviet Union on a missiles force, which he seemed to regard as a short cut to defence parity with the United States, by-passing the need to maintain also large and expensive conventional forces. But if he could place Soviet medium-range missiles in Cuba, the main Soviet deficiency – in long-range ICBMs – would to a considerable extent be overcome. The heavy pressure on him to concentrate all available resources on the defence industries would be largely relieved, and Khrushchev would be able to argue more convincingly that the Soviet defence potential was satisfactory enough to allow the diversion of more funds to civilian purposes. Although these must surely have been Khrushchev's main considerations, the current state of Soviet–American relations provided the necessary setting for such a move. Khrushchev had greeted the new American president with a new Berlin crisis, and the first encounters between the two men created a mutual mistrust and lack of understanding that forced both into increasingly tough attitudes, whereas in happier circumstances they might have been able to grasp that they could work together far better than Khrushchev and Eisenhower. Kennedy's immediate attention to strengthening the American military machine seems to have aroused all Khrushchev's old suspicion of the United States; but at the same time Kennedy's behaviour in the Bay of Pigs affair suggested to Khrushchev that he did after all lack self-assurance. When the two leaders met at Vienna in June 1961, Khrushchev certainly wanted to test Kennedy. We know that Kennedy himself found it an unpleasant experience, and Khrushchev seems to have left Vienna convinced that he could get away with some daring moves. The American acquiescence in the Berlin wall, which the Russians allowed East Germany to build the following August and so provide a *de facto* solution to the pressing German problem of losing refugees to the West, was probably taken by Khrushchev as confirming his estimate of the American president. The truth was that Khrushchev found it hard to understand Kennedy. He was to tell an American businessman during the Cuban crisis that American handling of the affair would have been more 'mature' had Eisenhower still been in the White House, and that one of the difficulties was that Kennedy was so much younger than he. On another occasion he spoke regretfully of the passing of Dulles, implying that in his day there had been at least no doubt about where America stood. Much of the trouble lay in Kennedy's sophistication. When Khrushchev and Dulles had faced each other, it was like two huge primitive animals glaring and snarling from their mutually respected lairs. Kennedy's more flexible approach confused Khrushchev. The intricate thinking that went on in Washington about escalation, graduated responses, and all the other academic concepts of the Cold War were unlikely to be studied with similar intellectual inquisitiveness and dispassion by Khrushchev (although it was thinking of this sort which provided Kennedy with the formula for Khrushchev's escape from the Cuban crisis).

Khrushchev almost certainly broached the Cuban project with Raoul Castro, the Cuban leader's brother and Defence Minister, during the latter's long and unpublicized visit to Moscow in July. Khrushchev argued that Cuba should accept the missiles in order to 'strengthen world socialism' – and this indeed was an accurate enough description of his general intention. The missiles were to be manned by Soviet troops and under the complete control of Moscow. Khrushchev considered the Cubans a 'volatile' people and never meant them to get at the missiles, whatever some people in the West may have thought in the heat of the crisis. The first Soviet ships carrying the weapons left for Cuba at the end of the same month. Khrushchev then carried out various diversionary tactics: in September it was announced that Russia had no need of a military base, but that she would help Cuba to construct a fishing port. He apparently hoped to smuggle the missiles on to the island secretly, but this was another miscalculation, and by 19 October the American intelligence services had collected sufficient evidence of Soviet missile sites on Cuba to persuade President Kennedy to break off his election campaign.

The crisis was on, and the size of Khrushchev's mistake very soon became apparent. He had clearly not foreseen the confusion caused by the discovery of the missiles and the wild assumptions that gripped the West, such as that the missiles were to be used for a surprise attack on America or at least to strengthen Khrushchev's hand over Berlin and his proposed German Peace Treaty. Most important, he had not bargained for the strength of Kennedy's response. Khrushchev's own behaviour during the crisis makes perfect sense once his purpose in sending the missiles to Cuba in the first place is grasped. Although he was obliged to have the armed forces put at combat readiness on 23 October, he was careful not to create a crisis atmosphere in Moscow. He made pointed public appearances throughout the crisis week, and significantly gave an interview to an important American businessman and chatted with an American singer appearing in the title role of Boris Godunov at the Bolshoi Theatre. There can be no doubt that Khrushchev personally had no intention of letting the crisis deteriorate to a point where a nuclear war became even likely, let alone inevitable. Important to him though the Cuban missile scheme was, he can have had no qualms about sacrificing it once he was convinced that Kennedy would not tolerate the weapons on the island. Already by 24 October he had ordered the Soviet ships bearing the latest load of missiles to stop before they reached the American warships lying in their path, although he had attacked the American quarantine both in public and in two private letters to Kennedy as 'piracy'. On 26th, in another rambling private letter to the American president, he indirectly implied a solution to the crisis: he would withdraw the missiles if the United States agreed not to attack Cuba. Khrushchev badly needed that American undertaking, because it alone would allow him to argue that, far from being defeated, he had got what he had all along wanted. In other words he was now at the mercy of the young American whom he had tried to bully in Vienna; and luckily for him Kennedy proved to be far more able than Khrushchev had then supposed. The president grasped what Eisenhower had failed to see during the U2 crisis – that Khrushchev had always to be offered a dignified way out of his difficulties – and the undertaking was given.

The Cuban crisis was a less terrifying experience for Khrushchev than for Kennedy, because it was lack of knowledge about the former's motives that had mainly caused such alarm in Washington. For Khrushchev, who had never meant to go to war, the main problem once he had realized his basic miscalculation was to prevent any damage to his own and Soviet standing. The Cuban crisis did not materially affect the Sino-Soviet conflict, which for Khrushchev had already passed the point of no return, although it did give the Chinese propagandists a perfect example of alleged Soviet inability to handle America. For the world at large, the difficulty that so many people had in realizing just how impatient and impulsive Khrushchev could be, luckily prevented many from drawing as damaging conclusions from the crisis as they might otherwise have done. It is impossible to tell with certainty how much Khrushchev suffered inside the Soviet Union from the affair, because so little is known about the part of the other Soviet leaders in planning the Cuban operation. Although Khrushchev was becoming increasingly wilful in his leadership, it is inconceivable that the Presidium should not have been informed of the plan from the start. It was certainly possible for Khrushchev to get Presidium acquiescence in radical schemes for which the majority had no enthusiasm – the splitting of the Party was soon to prove this. But would it really have been possible for Khrushchev to send missiles to Cuba in the face of vigorous opposition from his senior colleagues? It seems very unlikely. Nonetheless the whole venture had the unmistakable Khrushchev mark about it. It was typical of a man who all through his life had made daring and even dangerous moves to extricate himself from difficult situations. It seems most probable that he carried the Presidium with him by force of argument – and Khrushchev's view of Kennedy would have seemed plausible enough in the Kremlin before Cuba – but that there was disagreement on how the crisis should be handled once Kennedy had shown his strength. There were signs, at the end of the crisis, that Khrushchev was under pressure to adopt a tougher line. The day after his private letter of 26 October to Kennedy, a public letter demanded the removal of American missiles from Turkey, as an exchange, which suggests that some people in the Kremlin thought that Khrushchev was retreating too fast under American pressure.

The Cuban crisis, in the event, was only a further irritant in an already threatening political situation. Over a month before the world knew anything about Soviet missiles in Cuba, Khrushchev had sent a memorandum to his Presidium colleagues outlining his ideas for splitting the Party into industrial and agricultural sections. Khrushchev wrote that, after a Presidium meeting in August which had discussed the state of Soviet industry, he had given much thought to improving the structure of the Party and State apparatus, 'having in view finding a way to raise sharply the level of Party control over the country's economy'. Part of the trouble with the present system was the 'campaign character' of Party leadership. When a Central Committee plenum directed people's attention to industry, everyone forgot about agriculture, and *vice versa*. The new scheme would put an end to this. Khrushchev clearly expected his proposals to be adopted at the forthcoming Central Committee meeting in November: in other words he expected a scheme which altered entirely the traditional principles on which the Party worked to be formulated and accepted within two months. He was apparently now convinced that only if the Party could be turned into a sensitive instrument to control all aspects of the country's economic life could the expensive mismanagement of which there was increasing evidence be halted. Vast sums of money, for instance, were frozen in unfinished construction projects: although it was essential, given the scarcity of investment funds, that every kopek should be fully utilized, over 26 billion roubles had been made useless like this in 1962, compared with 17·5 billion in 1958. Khrushchev himself provided in almost every speech that he made on agriculture staggering examples of waste and bad management which cost the country dear. It is difficult to believe that he would have produced this scheme, indeed, had it not been for increasing evidence of the damage being done to the economy in this way. True, it did contain the essence of his political 'thinking', but he had never been a man to indulge in speculation for its own sake, and had always produced his ideas in response to a given state of affairs. Only heavy pressure would have made him embark on a scheme that was bound to upset extremely powerful interests in the country. Certainly, he had to use all his powers of persuasion to get his colleagues on the Presidium to accept the plan. Almost their first act when they removed him two years later would be to revoke it.

Perhaps even more important, the plan was bound to upset just those Party officials on whom Khrushchev had to a large extent built his own power. In particular it threatened the interests of the regional Party bosses by splitting their domains in two and so reducing their influence and status.

The scheme to split the Party according to the 'production principle', as Khrushchev put it, was the first significant sign that he was moving away from the traditional power bases and entrusting his fortunes to little more than a group of skilled publicists and personal assistants. It was this shift that was ultimately to make his removal possible when to all outward appearances his power was as firmly rooted as ever. Doubtless an increasing tendency towards autocratic methods was also to blame. The way he sprang his new plan for the Party on the Presidium is itself evidence of his wilfulness. Another example was provided by the tour of Central Asia which Khrushchev made only just before the Cuban storm. In memoranda sent to the Presidium from Central Asia, Khrushchev proposed a reorganization for the area that was clearly an idea of his own as yet undiscussed with his colleagues. He suggested that the Central Asian republics be turned into one administrative unit for economic purposes and that a single overall Party bureau for the area be established. And he forced the hand of his colleagues by saying in successive memoranda that wherever he had mentioned the plan there had been enthusiasm. In his speeches to the Soviet Asians he had in turn implied that the proposals were already accepted by Moscow.

Khrushchev nevertheless knew that more than this sort of cunning was needed to back up his proposals for the Party reorganization. On 28 September *Pravda* published a hitherto unknown Lenin document in which the master conveniently expressed the opinion that the Party should concentrate on economic, rather than political, tasks. (This incident illustrates one of the most telling differences between Stalin and Khrushchev. If Stalin needed theoretical justification for any move, at least in later years, he provided it himself and in his own name. Khrushchev, on the other hand, always had to fall back on Lenin.) The document was an excellent all-purpose weapon for Khrushchev. It provided the text for the speech at the November plenum in which he announced the Party reorganization, and it was also an invaluable theoretical justification for the Soviet Union (victory through economic achievement) against China (victory through propaganda and revolution). There was also a hint that Khrushchev was preparing to deal with any obstinate opponents of his plans by whipping up a new campaign against 'Stalinists'. On the eve of the Cuban crisis *Pravda* published a poem by the young writer Yevtushenko called 'Stalin's Heirs' which hinted broadly that the followers of the old dictator were only waiting for the right moment to get up to their old tricks again. The poem had been doing the Moscow literary rounds in manuscript form for some time, and the decision to publish it at that moment was certainly a political one – and Khrushchev's. Khrushchev continued this tactic at the plenum itself, when he gave his blessing to one of the most sensational literary works to be published since Stalin's death, Solzhenitsyn's prison-camp story *One Day in the Life of Ivan Denisovich.* The signs were that he was encouraging a wave of anti-Stalinist feeling in the hope that it would carry him over any political opposition – which would, in fact, by no means necessarily be Stalinist – to his revolutionary plan for the Party.

Khrushchev's tactics succeeded up to the November plenum. As so often before, he had worked up such a momentum that the first signs of discontent appeared only after he had got his way (the same had been true of his reorganization of industry in 1957). The trouble began in a uniquely Soviet fashion – with a visit to an art exhibition. On 1 December, a week after the plenum had ended, Khrushchev and other Presidium members paid a surprise visit to a retrospective exhibition of work by Moscow painters and sculptors. The next day the papers carried a Tass report that Khrushchev had been horrified by certain examples of 'formalistic' art that he had seen there. But his special wrath was reserved for a selection of semi-abstract pictures by young painters that had been specially gathered for him to see in a side-room and which were not part of the public exhibition. Khrushchev denounced these in language which would have won him the vote of critics of modern art the world over. He declared that they looked like daubs made by a donkey's tail. The newspapers left no doubt that Khrushchev had been very angry indeed. But what was it all about? The officials of the Artists Union, who were notorious for their neo-Stalinist views on culture, certainly had something to do with it. But it is impossible not to believe that some politicians also had a hand in it. The campaign against 'liberal' trends in all areas of Soviet culture that developed out of this visit was to be turned into an implicit attack on Khrushchev for allowing his concern with economic matters to get out of hand to the detriment of ideology and politics (the very same charge that had been made against his rule in the Ukraine and Moscow before Stalin's death). Khrushchev in turn, sensing what was in the air, apparently decided that any attack on himself could be deflected by blowing up a full-scale campaign first against the wretched painters and then against all the 'liberals' in the Soviet cultural establishment. It is most unlikely that, at this juncture, he would otherwise have chosen of his own free will to turn the Party's energies to ideology when he had just carried out a radical reorganization aimed at enabling it to concentrate better on the direction of agriculture and industry. It was not even clear, from what he said at the plenum, just how the officials charged with ideological matters would fit into his new scheme of things. And yet in April it was announced that the next Central Committee plenum would deal with ideology, and before that he attended long meetings with members of the cultural intelligentsia at which he bullied and cajoled them and – most significant of all – spoke positively of Stalin, when only eighteen months before he had had his body removed from its place of honour beside Lenin in the mausoleum on Red Square.

The ideological campaign was only one aspect of the pressure now on Khrushchev. Important changes were made in February and March to the government economic apparatus which again ran completely counter to Khrushchev's own reforms of the previous November. A new state economic overlord authority was set up (the Supreme Council of National Economy) under the chairmanship of the former defence industry chief. The powers of the state planning authorities were increased (Khrushchev had singled them out for criticism in a memorandum to the Presidium in October), and the State Committees were also given increased power so that they began to resemble the old Ministries which they had been set up to replace by Khrushchev in his 1957 reorganization. The effect of these changes was clearly to increase government control over the direction of the economy and was not compatible with Khrushchev's November reforms. (Inevitably once Khrushchev had weathered the crisis, these changes were whittled away, and the Supreme Council in particular fell into virtual abeyance.) There were other unmistakable signs of a conflict at the top. In April, the traditional slogans for May Day somehow forgot to give Yugoslavia its correct title as a 'Socialist' country. This was amended a few days later, but the impression had already been created that Khrushchev's pro-Yugoslav policy, with all its liberal implications, was now also under attack. Most significant of all, Khrushchev began to talk about his own possible retirement. At the end of April, in a speech to an industrial conference, after using his age – he was then sixty-nine – as justification for his outspokenness, he said

> After all, everyone understands that I cannot hold the post I now occupy in the Party and Government for ever.... The leader who restricts the concept of the role of the individual in society to his own personal interests ... is a poor leader.... I am at what you might call pensionable age.

Exactly a year earlier Khrushchev had spoken of the 'strength and energy welling up' inside him, and had pledged that he would not 'take it to the grave' with him but use it up in the service of socialism. If there was now a suggestion that Khrushchev might 'retire' from one if not both of his main posts, it was certainly not Khrushchev's. Exactly whose suggestion was it, then? The May Day celebrations in Moscow, traditionally attended by all the Soviet leaders who had no special obligations in one of the republics, were marked by the absence of Frol Kozlov, Khrushchev's generally acknowledged second-in-command. Three days later *Pravda* published an odd announcement 'in response to queries received' that Kozlov had been prevented from attending by illness. It was odd because no announcements were usually made about the health of this or that leader. The next day Khrushchev's son-in-law Aleksei Adzhubei remarked in the presence of foreign journalists that Kozlov had had a stroke that would prevent him from ever returning to political life. And from that moment Khrushchev's fortunes began unmistakably to revive.

Frol Kozlov had been Khrushchev's heir-apparent since the

previous holder of that dangerous title, Aleksei Kirichenko, had fallen from grace in obscure circumstances in 1960. Kozlov was born a peasant and eventually based his power on the Leningrad Party. He was fourteen years younger than Khrushchev and had the distinction of being unquestionably the most handsome member of the Presidium. Very little was known about where he stood politically except that he had had possibly unpleasant connexions with Stalin's plans for his final purge. But it was noticeable that when the great ideological campaign was launched in December 1962, Kozlov was given increasing prominence in Soviet press accounts of the various meetings between the politicians and the intelligentsia. Also, as Khrushchev's second-in-command, Kozlov's responsibilities included the day-to-day running of the Party and the supervision of the armed forces. Khrushchev's November reorganization almost certainly was not to his taste. His contacts with the military may also have made him their chief spokesman in the Presidium's difficult debates over priorities. It is possible that Khrushchev, anticipating Kozlov's reaction to his reorganization of the Party, had him, among others, in mind when he encouraged the literary campaign against neo-Stalinists. There was a curious reference in Yevtushenko's poem 'Stalin's Heirs' to politicians who had suffered heart attacks, and this could well have been aimed at Kozlov, who had certainly suffered in this way.

Much of this is necessarily conjecture; but if it is true, it would explain why, apart from the failure of his health at a crucial moment, Kozlov was unable to defeat Khrushchev. The most important fact about the overthrow of Khrushchev in the following year was that it was aimed at the man and not at the core of his policies, which had been accepted by the post-Stalinist leadership. Khrushchev was removed and what has been called 'Khrushchevism' largely abandoned, but otherwise the Soviet Union did not in any essential way alter course. If Kozlov, on the other hand, represented a more conservative attitude, the majority of Presidium members, much as they may have been worried by Khrushchev's schemes for the Party and perhaps too by his conduct in the Cuban affair, would scarcely have wanted him to replace Khrushchev. Part of the muddle surrounding the 'ideological crisis' in the winter of 1962–3 was caused by Khrushchev's cunning in persuading the world at large that his only threat came from 'Stalinists', when in fact an opposition of quite a different sort was building up against him.

In the event Kozlov's disappearance meant only a respite for Khrushchev. In the year and a half until his fall Khrushchev continued to take decisions which alienated influential people in every important Soviet power group. Inevitably the economy lay at the heart of the trouble, and just as inevitably, the performance of Soviet agriculture above all. Quite undeterred by past failures, Khrushchev was already spinning ambitious new schemes for Soviet farming by July 1963. His main idea was that agricultural production could now only be increased significantly by the large-scale application of the chemical products that had so long been denied it – fertilizers, pesticides, herbicides, artificial feed stuffs. Khrushchev was in other words asking for what he had failed to get in 1962 – large allocations of capital for basically agricultural purposes through investment in the much-neglected Soviet chemical industry. At the same time it must immediately have been clear to his colleagues, who received a memorandum on the subject in mid-July, that Khrushchev had completely altered the direction of his agricultural policy. In the past he had argued for agricultural growth by an extension of the area under cultivation. The virgin lands programme and his later campaign to have grassland put under the plough were both aspects of this. But now he was proposing more intensified agriculture (which Malenkov had favoured in the old days). Two important developments lay behind this. Relations with the West appeared to be developing satisfactorily towards a new *détente* which promised a possible return to his old paring away of military expenditure (the military budget was, in fact, cut by 4·3 per cent the next December). In June Khrushchev had agreed with President Kennedy to set up the so-called 'Hot Line' between the White House and the Kremlin, a decision which accurately reflected Khrushchev's thinking on the peculiar responsibilities of the leaders of the chief nuclear states. Also, ten days before he sent his new memorandum to the Presidium, he had announced Soviet willingness to sign a limited nuclear test ban treaty that excluded the vexed question of underground tests and so was almost certain of success. (The treaty was of course also a trap for the Chinese, with Khrushchev calculating correctly that they would attack it.) The other development was less encouraging, but probably even more important. By July Khrushchev must have received a good deal of extremely depressing information about the forthcoming harvest, even if he did not yet realize that it was going to be so disastrous as to force him to buy millions of tons of grain from the West. The memorandum to the Presidium said nothing about this, but Khrushchev was quite possibly preparing his position for the trouble he feared might come.

The memorandum once again showed the vast importance that Khrushchev attached to Soviet economic success:

A rapid increase in the production of grain and the complete satisfaction of demand for agricultural products would have not only a great economic but also a huge political significance both inside our country and also abroad. We shall then show the advantages of our Soviet system in the agricultural sphere as well, and take the American imperialists down a peg or two.

The American successes, he went on, were not due to any special 'wisdom' on their part. 'We simply did not have the chance to assign the necessary amount of capital investments to the production of mineral fertilizers and machinery. . . .' But 'Now that we have that chance, we must use it.' Khrushchev's obsession with the need for rapid results was now pushing him a dangerous distance from his colleagues. He more or less got what he wanted over the expansion of the chemical industry, although his ambitious target for fertilizer production was cut. But his insistence that this time he really did hold the key to agricultural abundance began to sound grotesque as the results of the 1963 harvest were made known, and were followed by bread and flour rationing throughout the country. Any other man might have been discouraged, but not Khrushchev. It was clear by the autumn of 1964 that he had now set his heart on making the production of consumer goods and services the top priority in the next Five-Year plan, due to start in 1966. Khrushchev outlined his proposals at a meeting of political and industrial leaders in September and then tried to rush his colleagues by having a summary of his speech printed in *Pravda*, so implying that there was general agreement for his idea.

The decision to remove him had almost certainly already been taken by the core of anti-Khrushchev plotters, but the September proposals provided them with excellent ammunition. Khrushchev had now declared war on heavy industry, the sacred cow of the Soviet economy, and made it clear that he would give short shrift to military demands for money, at the very time when arguments for an increase in conventional military strength had been made more strongly and more publicly than ever before. By the autumn of 1964 Khrushchev had alienated by his policies, implemented or proposed, the Party bureaucrats, who never liked his Party reorganization of November 1962; the state officials and industrialists who believed that both political and economic considerations demanded that heavy industry continue to take priority; and the military men who were increasingly dismayed by the implications of Khrushchev's schemes to get defence at the lowest possible cost. He had also failed to win over the more experimentally minded members of the establishment, who were by no means without support among the leaders. Khrushchev had not tried to stop the debate on reforming the Soviet economy which had come largely to centre round proposals made in 1962 by the Kharkov economist, Professor Liberman. At the root of Liberman's suggestions was the idea that economic factors - such as a form of profit - should be allowed, rather than nagging control by the centre, to force factories into efficiency. But at the same time as these and other ideas were being cautiously discussed in the Soviet press, Khrushchev was falling back on extended control by the Party as his remedy for all economic ills. The two were hardly reconcilable, and the new ideas were to receive far greater encouragement under Khrushchev's successors.

Khrushchev might perhaps have still avoided trouble had he not so angered his closest colleagues by the growing wilfulness of his leadership. The way in which he publicized his new economic plans was just one example of this. Even more alarming was his readiness to pursue his vendetta against Mao Tse-tung even when it obviously meant ignoring world communist opinion. Khrushchev had now set his heart on a meeting of communist parties to excommunicate China, whereas his colleagues were by no means ready for this irrevocable step. Furthermore, Khrushchev's growing habit of bypassing opposition in the Soviet establishment by using his personal apparatus reached a new peak when he sent his son-in-law Aleksei Adzhubei to West Germany in the summer of 1964 to prepare the way for a later visit by himself, even though his colleagues clearly distrusted his flirtation with West Germany and were prepared to sabotage it. There were also rumours that Khrushchev had plans to promote Adzhubei to an important government post (another sign that he was getting careless about the base of his power because Adzhubei, though certainly able, had no political standing independent of his relationship with Khrushchev). There can be little doubt that Khrushchev was now a very difficult man to work with. He knew he was pressed for time and so was unwilling to accept any frustration of his schemes. Colleagues who crossed him could expect short shrift, and very possibly there was some fear that he might try to remove his most persistent opponents. He had after all somehow managed to get rid of Kozlov in 1963.

By the autumn of 1964, while Khrushchev's power still looked from the outside as secure as ever, it was in reality as near collapse as a building that has had its structural supports removed. The final proof of this was provided by the complete success of the plot against him. In theory Khrushchev still had control over every important power group in the country, either by virtue of the positions he held or through men whom he had appointed and who were personally linked to him. The majority of the Presidium could even have been called with some justification 'Khrushchev men'. Yet Khrushchev did not hear one single whisper about the conspiracy against him. And no one was more active in the plotting than some of the young 'Khrushchev men'. The final preparations for the coup were made when Khrushchev went on holiday in October to his villa on the Georgian coast of the Black Sea. The first hint of trouble came in an urgent summons to Khrushchev on 13 October to attend a Presidium meeting in Moscow. He went, and walked straight into the trap. The secret police seem to have been completely under the plotters' control and are believed to have taken precautions to see that Khrushchev would be isolated from any possible outside help. The Presidium meeting turned out to be his trial, with the prosecution led by the Party's ideological expert, Mikhail Suslov, and Dmitri Polyansky, one of Khrushchev's protégés. Khrushchev defended himself. He may possibly have had passive support from one or two Presidium members such as Nikolai Podgorny, the ex-Ukrainian Party chief who had shown more enthusiasm than the rest for Khrushchev's reorganization schemes. But the final blow was delivered by the Central Committee. Khrushchev demanded that his case be put to the vote there, doubtless remembering how he had defeated Molotov and Malenkov's attempt to remove him in 1957. This time his opponents were more far-sighted. They had anticipated Khrushchev's request and already summoned – and prepared – the Central Committee. The vote there went against Khrushchev, although there was probably some measure of support for him. In a way it was his finest hour: ten years earlier no one would ever have imagined that Stalin's successor would be removed by so simple and gentle a process as a vote.

Conclusion

Khrushchev's rule was marked by the emergence of three dilemmas, affecting the most important aspects of Soviet policy, which he never fully understood, let alone was able to resolve. Within the Soviet Union itself there was a conflict between the Party's claim to total authority, which was the essence of the Soviet political system, and the growing need for freedom of initiative as the economy and social structure became more sophisticated. While Khrushchev at times recognized the need for the latter, and was even ready to allow more scope to the country's writers and artists in the same spirit, he always turned back to the weapon of Party control when faced with any frustration or trouble. His difficulty should not be underestimated. The Party had been created to wield totalitarian power. It claimed the right to dictate to everyone about everything. A renunciation of its right to control even the smallest area of Soviet life threatened its claims over the rest. This partly explains Khrushchev's quite inconsistent approach to the cultural world, where every relaxation he allowed seemed to develop into an attack on the authority of the Party which he then had to step in to restore. Khrushchev realized that the scientists and technocrats who, as in any other advanced country, were increasingly its chief creators of wealth could not be subjected to ideological control and political terror. And yet he would on no account accept that the advanced industries, any more than the army, or the farms, or the universities, should ultimately be outside Party control. Khrushchev was not to blame for the dilemma. He merely worked the political system in which he had been brought up, and which he clearly could not imagine changing in any significant way. In all his reflections on what the communist future might bring he never suggested that the Party's role should diminish; in fact, quite the reverse. The resolution of this dilemma, on which the future of the Soviet Union very largely depends, he left to his successors without realizing the nature of his bequest.

Another conflict lay at the heart of the relations between the

Soviet Union and the rest of the communist world. Khrushchev had been brought up in a world where communism was the Soviet Union, and even after there had been other successful communist revolutions, the unity of the communist movement meant no less than the acceptance by all of Moscow's word. Again Khrushchev tried to do something about this. He realized that Stalin's empire was no way to run a communist commonwealth, and he eventually came to rejoice in countries like Poland and Hungary which appeared to him to combine deference to Moscow with certain specifically national policies. But he did not grasp the paradox that as communism spread, the influence of the Soviet Union must necessarily decline. Nor did he see that in this situation what the Soviet Union defined as a policy for world communism would be seen by others as a policy designed specifically for the Soviet Union. Khrushchev cannot be blamed for this: Marxism-Leninism provided him with no guidance because it did not consider that such a problem could arise.

Khrushchev's third dilemma was the conflict between his policy of peaceful coexistence with the West and his long-term conviction that communism would defeat capitalism. He genuinely believed that nuclear war had to be avoided. But at the same time he thought that the American position would gradually be weakened as the neutral countries turned towards communism and were followed by America's allies. And he had been brought up to believe that faced with such a situation, 'Imperialism' would strike out. Khrushchev had to keep his belief in the inevitability of communist victory. More practically, he had to announce his support for wars of liberation and the like which were a necessary part of that victory. Thus Khrushchev's understanding of the *status quo*, which both East and West would preserve by abandoning nuclear war as a weapon of policy, was quite different from the West's. The *status quo* for Khrushchev was in fact changing all the time, and changing in his favour. He did not discover how a really stable relationship with the West could be worked out on such a basis. He probably did not even realize the incompatibility of his aims. Once again, the main problem of Soviet foreign relations was handed on to his successors.

Khrushchev's rule was a transition period from something he clearly wished to abandon to something he could not properly imagine. He understood the need for change, but not the implications of that change. And yet the recognition of the need for change, and his realization that this depended on the development of the Soviet economy, was an enormous contribution. Khrushchev was not the only man to realize these things: they became the common policy of the Soviet leadership. But it was a policy that gave meaning to the whole of Khrushchev's life work in particular and which he, in his rough but powerful way, was able to project better than anyone else. Some of Khrushchev's worst qualities – rashness, lack of foresight, a tendency to bully – were at first invaluable here. They helped him to lead the attack on the walls of Stalinism, which none of his colleagues, eager though some were to follow him, seemed ready to do on their own. Time after time Khrushchev confronted an issue fraught with danger and announced his intention of coping with it. Immediately after Stalin's death he was ready to reveal the critical state of agriculture and to assume personal responsibility for it. He had the boldness to visit America and so make credible the Soviet commitment to peaceful coexistence although the visit could have badly damaged himself. His motives were obviously mixed; most of his moves included a careful calculation of their effect on his own political position. This was never more true than in his most famous feat of daring – the attack on Stalin in the secret speech. But in spite of the motives behind the speech, its half-truths and worse, something like that speech had to be made, and Khrushchev was the only Soviet leader who was then capable of making it. His successors have argued that Khrushchev's leadership in the last years became too impetuous and impatient, and they were probably right that Khrushchev's talents were increasingly unfitted to the problems facing the Soviet Union by the end of 1964. Above all Khrushchev's obsession with speed threatened to prevent careful consideration of the radical reforms so badly needed by the Soviet economy. Nonetheless the proper epitaph for his rule remains more impressive than that deserved by many politicians: that he left his country a better place than he found it, both in the eyes of the majority of his own people, and of the world.

Index